ISBN 978-1-331-51459-6
PIBN 10200384

1 MONTH OF
FREE
READING

at
www.ForgottenBooks.com

By purchasing this book you are
eligible for one month membership to
ForgottenBooks.com, giving you
unlimited access to our entire
collection of over 1,000,000 titles via
our web site and mobile apps.

To claim your free month visit:
www.forgottenbooks.com/free200384

English
Français
Deutsche
Italiano
Español
Português

www.forgottenbooks.com

Mythology Photography **Fiction**
Fishing Christianity **Art** Cooking
Essays Buddhism Freemasonry
Medicine **Biology** Music **Ancient
Egypt** Evolution Carpentry Physics
Dance Geology **Mathematics** Fitness
Shakespeare **Folklore** Yoga Marketing
Confidence Immortality Biographies
Poetry **Psychology** Witchcraft
Electronics Chemistry History **Law**
Accounting **Philosophy** Anthropology
Alchemy Drama Quantum Mechanics
Atheism Sexual Health **Ancient History**
Entrepreneurship Languages Sport
Paleontology Needlework Islam
Metaphysics Investment Archaeology
Parenting Statistics Criminology
Motivational

SIDE-LIGHTS ON
MERICAN LITERATURE

BY

FRED LEWIS PATTEE

NEW YORK
THE ·CENTURY CO.
1922

TO

WILLIAM WEBSTER ELLSWORTH
Lover of good books, loyal friend, and
generous Maecenas to many struggling authors,
this book is affectionately dedicated

CONTENTS

SIDE-LIGHTS ON AMERICAN LITERATURE

SIDE-LIGHTS ON AMERICAN LITERATURE

THE AGE OF O. HENRY

The apparition of O. Henry is the most extraordinary literary phenomenon of the new century. He and Jack London emerged almost at the same moment, unheralded, full-grown, sudden: few arrivals in all literature have been so startling. Hardly had we learned his real name before he was filling the whole sky. He was William Sydney Porter, we were told, a native of North Carolina who had had wild experiences as a cow-boy on the ranches of the Southwest. He had been adventurer, we gathered, tramp, knight-errant of the chaparral in the roughest areas of that wildest West so swiftly passing into tradition, and now he had sent East stirring tales of adventure: another Bret Harte, up to date, breezy, original. And his earliest specimens in the magazines seemed to bear out the report. Then quickly had come a new sensation: this Western cow-boy had lived in New Orleans, had vagabonded through Honduras and South America, and he was bringing what no one had brought be-

3

fore, wild exotic atmospheres and exciting adventure from uncharted realms to the west and the south of the Caribbean.　At once he was hailed as Harte had been hailed and as Kipling, and as quickly Jack London was to be hailed, as a new sensation in a jaded age.

That was in 1902.　Then had come a sensation as startling as the first apparition: suddenly we heard that this cow-boy, this vagabond from South America, had become—amazing metamorphosis!—the interpreter of New York City; the Scheherazade of "Bagdad on the Hudson"; total stranger in New York, yet vouched for as doing for that world of a city what had been done for London by Dickens, who had spent his life there and who knew nothing else.　"McClure's Magazine" had discovered him; a dozen other periodicals fought for his wares and secured them with loud trumpetings; the New York "World" named a figure that mortgaged for months his whole future product: a story a week, for its Sunday supplement, just as a generation before "The Atlantic Monthly" had purchased for a year the pen of Bret Harte.　Then at the height of his powers suddenly he vanished: dead at forty-eight. He had come like a comet; he had filled the whole sky; he had disappeared like a comet.

That was in 1910.　But the paradox of O. Henry had hardly begun.　Stories written for the Sunday supplement are as ephemeral as the comic section which they neighbor, but these ephemeræ were to outlast even the classics of the "Atlantic." Some volumes of them were collected even during the headlong six years of his productiveness, but with his unexpected death there came a scramble to secure every scrap of his product for a subscription set. He had been enormously creative. During the two years following "Cabbages and Kings" he had produced 115 stories, and his total product, almost all of it the work of six years, was 250 pieces, not counting the scraps in a thirteenth volume of his set.

And now came the second stage of O. Henry, O. Henry as a subscription set advertised with all the latest enginery of the art like a soap or a breakfast-food, guaranteed creations of a genuine "Yankee Maupassant," books with "stories that will live as long as speech": "England has her Dickens, France her Hugo, and America her O. Henry." When the sales began to slacken a set of Kipling was thrown in free, and later still, after another lull, a set of E. Phillips Oppenheim, seven quivering volumes, with an offer of $500 in prizes for the buyers writing the best letters descriptive of the thrills in a "collection of thrills unparalleled in literature." And the public responded—is even yet responding—to a degree that staggers the imagina-

tion.   In 1919 his publishers announced that "Up
to the present time about four millions, one hundred thousand of O. Henry's books have gone to
the public," or about one to every twenty-five of our
population.   Since then the market has been more
difficult to follow and the publishers will venture
no figures, but the sale, they declare, has gone steadily
on as from the first.   The conclusion is inevitable:
the people would not have bought these volumes
had they not wanted them, had they not craved just
those things the advertising sheets so vividly promised; the reading public of America undeniably
wants O. Henry.   With such figures and facts before us, is it too much to say that the last two
decades in America have been the age of O. Henry,
and that we are still befogged within it and with
little promise of emergence?

O. Henry is paradox; at every point you touch
him, paradox.   Four years after his death the city
of Raleigh, North Carolina, erected a memorial
to him—to this columnist of a Sunday supplement
—and the orator of the day was the Poe professor
of English at the University of Virginia, a scholar
of distinction.   Then with an acclaim that was national and international came the O. Henry Hotel
dedication in a Southern city and another burst of
superlatives.   Then just as calm was settling again
and it seemed to the conservative that Time was

preparing her inevitable verdict, there came the Smith biography. Amazing paradox! The man never had been a cow-boy at all, at least not a rider of horses. During his eleven years in Texas he had been for the most of the time a newspaper reporter and a clerk, his last clerkship in a bank. Accused of too great freedom with the bank funds, he had made a plunge into South America by way of New Orleans. For months he had vagabonded "with Momus beneath the tropic stars where Melpomene once stalked austere," but returning at last to Texas he had been arrested, convicted of embezzlement, and condemned to prison, where he had spent four years. It was in prison that he had taken to writing, and from his cell, with an assumed name necessarily (for was he not a convict?), had actually marketed those stories which first had brought him into notice. When "Whistling Dick's Christmas Stocking" appeared in "McClure's," its author had two and a half more years to serve on his prison sentence. Sensational, surely! The author of the biography was stormed with abuse because he had refused to conceal the truth. Delicious irony! The public should not know too much about its idols. The South is chivalrous: *de mortuis nil nisi bonum;* the good fellows who had helped shorten his days were chivalrous; he was a good fellow; he was dead, therefore he should be canonized. Concerning the quality of his work, all this made no difference either way, but it is interesting.

That was in 1916. Could these fastidious critics North and South, have seen 1921 and its "Through the Shadows with O. Henry" with its prison cover-design, its jacket puff of "an amazing revelation, with a thrill in every chapter," and its author, Al Jennings, reformed desperado and convict described by O. Henry himself as "pickpocket, supper man, second-story man, yeggman, box man, all-round burglar, card-sharp and slickest con man west of the Twenty-third Street ferry landing," and, he might have added, murderer and gun-man and thug and boon companion during the South American experience, and general model for the desperadoes and bad men of most of his picaresque stories of the Southwest and of South America—had this revelation appeared in 1916 what would have been the sensation? American literature of late is becoming picturesque in its personalities.

So much for the paradox of O. Henry himself: what of the 250 tales in the twelve volumes of his literary remains?

Conservative criticism has been inclined to withhold its verdict and wait. A comet, be it ever so brilliant, fades if you give it time, but in the case of O. Henry the critic has not been allowed to wait. He has been forced to render judgment. It has become impossible to ignore the voices that have poured upon him from barber-shop and university, from home and public library, from club and pulpit, from reviews in popular journals and critiques in quarterlies and solemn volumes. And the volume of praise seems to be increasing. Editors of college texts have admitted him among the time-tried classics. A recent book of selections from "the world's greatest short story writers," made by a sober critic, includes five Americans: Irving, Hawthorne, Poe, Bunner, O. Henry. Dr. C. Alphonso Smith, the breadth of whose scholarship no one questions, sent forth his biography with the dictum: "O. Henry's work remains the most solid fact to be reckoned with in the history of twentieth century literature." This same critic at the dedication of the Raleigh memorial had added the man to the great American four: Irving, Hawthorne, Poe, and Harte. "O. Henry," he declared, "has given the American short story a new reach and a widened social content . . . he has socialized the short story." The Canadian humorist and critic, Stephen Leacock, has published an essay entitled "The Amazing Genius of O. Henry," and in it he has dared to use words like these: "The time is coming, let us hope, when the whole English-speaking world will recognize in him one of the great masters of modern literature." Some of the most discriminating of scholars both in America and abroad have found joy in him: the late William James, we are told, had read his every story. University men everywhere, and conservative critics even, have turned to him for relaxation and have praised him in superlatives. Few authors, indeed, have ever so completely captured the high and the low of their generation.

In view, then, of this no uncertain verdict of his era, his work becomes important. To study it is to study an epoch, for a people and a generation are to be judged by what they read and enjoy, by what they teach in their schools and crown in their academies. A success like O. Henry's means imitators, a literary school, a standard of values. And what are these values to be? What of the age of O. Henry?

II

Before one may crown O. Henry or dismiss O. Henry one must read him, all of him, thirteen volumes: it goes without saying. But let the reader keep his balance: the mixture is intoxicating; it blunts after a time all the critical faculties. One emerges from the thirteenth volume of this strange harlequin epic completely upset, unable for a time rightly to evaluate anything, condemning, yet at

the same time inclined to praise—one hardly knows
why or what. Surely one has been diverted. Where
else in all literature is there such a mélange—
stories bedeviled and poured into bombshells; traves-
ties of all things holy and unholy; sermons in
motley and the ten commandments of yeggdom;
pure fun and again barbarous farce as vulgarly
primitive as the comic supplement; short stories vio-
lating every canon of the text-books, yet so brilliant
as to set one forming a new canon of the art;
sketches ending in cart-wheel capers, philosophiz-
ings through a horse-collar, burlesques hilarious.
Everywhere everything too much. What spirits!
what abandon! what zest in life! what curiosity!
what boyish delight in the human show! One must
go back to the adolescent Dickens to match it—the
Dickens of the "Sketches by Boz" and "Pickwick."
Not a dull page, not a paragraph that does not re-
bound upon you like a peal of laughter, or startle
you, or challenge you, or prod you unawares, and
roar at your surprise. No repose in these books:
they are peppered and deviled meat for jaded palates.
One goes not to these for delicate flavors, or subtle
spiceries, or refined and exaggerated nuances of
style. The tones are loud, the humor is grotesque
and boisterous, the situations are extremes, the characters are as artificial and as exaggerated as those
of Dickens. It is pitched, all of it, for men, for

healthy elemental men: men of the bar-room and the club foyer and the barracks. In no writings since Dickens does liquor flow so freely: "drink shall swell the theme and be set forth in abundance," shrills "The Rubaiyat of a Scotch Highball." "The Fourth In Salvador" is the most besotted tale in all literature. And yet for all that, and notwithstanding the fact that the stories many of them record life on isolated masculine ranches, in vice-reeking tropic towns, and in unspeakable areas of New York City, at every point that touches the feminine—paradox again!—the work is as chaste as Emerson.

Before one has spent an hour with the books one is aware of a strange duality about them, one that must have had its origin in the man himself. It is as if a Hawthorne had sold his pen to Momus. There are pages where the style attains a distinction that is rare indeed. One might cull extracts that would imply marvelous wholes. We realize before we have finished a single tale that we are dealing with no uncouth ranchman who has literary aspirations, who writes in slang because slang is the only language he knows. We are in the hands, we feel, of one who has read widely and well; his quotations and allusions cover an area that is surprising. His vocabulary also is extraordinary, and I do not refer to the amazing nature of his slang.　He is as accurate in his choice of words and as rich in his variants as a professional stylist like James.　His biographer records that for years the dictionary was his favorite reading, that he pored over it as one pores over romance; and the reader of his stories may well believe it.　One professor of literature has confessed that he is drawn to O. Henry simply because of his vocabulary, because of the exquisite ability* he has to capture the one fleeting word of all fleeting words for his purpose. Take a paragraph like this, a paragraph as piquant and as uniquely individual in style as if it were penned by Charles Lamb:

In the restaurant of El Refugio are served compounds delightful to the palate of the man from Capricorn or Cancer.　Altruism must halt the story thus long.　Oh, diner, weary of the culinary subterfuges of the Gallic chef, hie thee to El Refugio!　There only will you find a fish—bluefish, shad or pompano from the Gulf—baked after the Spanish method. Tomatoes give it color, individuality and soul; chili colorado bestows upon it zest, originality and fervor; unknown herbs furnish piquancy and mystery, and— but its crowning glory deserves a new sentence. Around it, above it, beneath it, in its vicinity—but never in it—hovers an ethereal aura, an effluvium so rarefied and delicate that only the Society for Psychical Research could note its origin.　Do not say that garlic is in the fish at El Refugio.　It is not otherwise than as if the spirit of Garlic, flitting past, has wafted one kiss that lingers in the parsley-crowned dish as haunting as those kisses in life, "by hopeless fancy feigned on lips that are for others." And then, when Conchito, the waiter, brings you a plate of brown frijoles and a carafe of wine that has never stood still between Oporto and El Refugio—ah, Dios!

And here is a tropical sunset:

The day died in the lagoons and in the shadowed banana groves and in the mangrove swamps, where the great blue crabs were beginning to crawl to land for their nightly ramble. And it died, at last, upon the highest peaks. Then the brief twilight, ephemeral as the flight of a moth, came and went; the Southern Cross peeped with its topmost eye above a row of palms, and the fireflies heralded with their torches the approach of soft-footed night.

At times in his earlier South American sketches he caught the very soul of the tropics, "the fetterless, idyllic round of enchanted days; the life among this indolent romantic people—a life full of music, flowers, and low laughter; the influence of the immanent sea and mountains, and the many shapes of love and magic and beauty that bloom in the white tropic nights." Note a sentence like this describing the head-hunters of Mindanao:

Those grim, flinty, relentless little men, never seen,

but chilling the warmest noonday by the subtle terror of their concealed presence, parallelling the trail of their prey through unmapped forests, across perilous mountain-tops, adown bottomless chasms, into uninhabitable jungles, always near with the invisible hand of death uplifted, betraying their pursuit only by such signs as a beast or a bird or a gliding serpent might make—a twig crackling in the awful sweat-soaked night, a drench of dew showering from the screening foliage of a giant tree, a whisper at even from the rushes of a water-level—a hint of death for every mile and every hour—they amused me greatly, those little fellows of one idea.

But one catches only fitful glimpses of this more serious O. Henry. The Momus who ruled his pen nodded seldom more than a moment at a time. The sentence or the paragraph that starts in serious tone ends most often with a sudden pigeonwing. Note for instance the Emersonian opening and the harlequin close of this paragraph from "Squaring the Circle":

Nature moves in circles; Art in straight lines. The natural is rounded; the artificial is made up of angles. A man lost in the snow wanders, in spite of himself, in perfect circles; the city man's feet, denaturalized by rectangular streets and floors, carry him ever away from himself. The round eyes of childhood typify innocence; the narrowed line of the flirt's optic proves the invasion of art. The horizontal mouth is the mark

of determined cunning; who has not read Nature's
most spontaneous lyric in lips rounded for the candid
kiss? Beauty is Nature in perfection; circularity is
its chief attribute. Behold the full moon, the enchant-
ing golf ball, the domes of splendid temples, the
huckleberry pie, the wedding ring, the circus ring, the
ring for the waiter, and the "round" of drinks.

Never can we trust him. His tale of Southern
life, "The Guardian of the Accolade," beguiles us.
It rings true; it is exquisitely told. Uncle Bushrod
is as feelingly and convincingly drawn as any before-
the-war negro in recent literature. The feeling
grows as we read that we have discovered a classic:
at last from O. Henry a work of serious art with
no harlequin tricks and no vaudeville capers. Then
comes the final sentence. Ah! it is all a trick:
the master was not absconding with the bank
funds after all; the faithful old negro had not,
as he so proudly supposed, rescued the family from
the gulf of dishonor: all he had done had been
to prevent his master from taking with him on a fishing trip his favorite satchel, and that satchel of stolen
bonds, as the negro supposed when he had returned
it with such care to the bank—"there was two quarts
of the finest old silk-velvet Bourbon in that satchel
you ever wet your lips with." We have been trifled
with. We no longer think of the piece as an exquisite tale of the old South: the author has prostituted

his art, he has been watching the reader and grinning in his sleeve all the while. He has deliberately fabricated the whole story for no other purpose than to serve as an ambush for this single vulgar moment of surprise. One begins the next piece, however fine its opening, with little of enjoyment. We have been trifled with: this is not a maker of literature, it is a boy with a bean-shooter who is waiting for you to get into range; it is an impish practical joker, who is never really serious. Everywhere the cap and bells. In "The Door of Unrest" we have a central idea worthy of Hawthorne, but it is embroidered with cheapness. It is pure linen edged with bunting.

III

Before one has finished even the first volume of the set, and no matter which volume one has chosen, one has discovered that primarily and almost solely O. Henry was a humorist, a professional harlequin, an inheritor of the tradition of John Phœnix and Artemus Ward. To consider him seriously from any other point of view is to be confronted swiftly with a non sequitur. He had been trained precisely as Phœnix had been trained and Artemus Ward and Mark Twain and all the others of the distinctively American group of literary comedians.

To create such a writer there must be schooling on the frontier, in some remote area of America where individualism is religion and where men are living under primitive conditions in the rush and excitement of some moving enterprise. Before he was twenty-one O. Henry had observed for some months, never, however, as an active participator, the rough life of a sheep ranch in the heart of the Southwest, and he had learned among other things how the primitive man laughs. Then for twelve years he had lived in Texas cities—Austin, Houston—surrounded by men who had been a part of the early lawless days of the State. Western breeziness there was in these little cities, boundless spirits, hilarious optimism, sentiment in abundance. To the young O. Henry, by nature as sensitive to the incongruous as was even Artemus Ward, it was school and college.

He was a comedian born; as a boy he was considered a wag and a practical joker; during all of his Western period his companions were on the broad grin at the very sight of him: he was a mimic, a caricaturist, a punster; he moved always in a gale of laughter. It pointed the way he was to go. As early as 1887 he was contributing his regular budget of jokes to the "Detroit Free Press," and by 1895 he was editor and proprietor of a humorous journal of his own, "The Rolling Stone," "out for the moss," one dollar and fifty cents a year, with the special inducement to new subscribers that during one month all who would bring two dollars would be given on the spot a premium of fifty cents, a brand of humor that a generation before had been made familiar to all Americans by Artemus Ward. A year it was before "The Rolling Stone" ceased to roll, and then its editor transferred himself to the "Houston Daily Post," where, as a variant to his work as bank teller, he filled a Eugene-Field-like column entitled "Tales of the Town." There he might have remained until he died, pouring his newspaper-column comedy into the bottomless pit of a Texan daily, had not sudden good fortune in the form of seemingly annihilating disgrace overtaken him and sent him flying from an environment that had all but swallowed him. Until he was thirty-five O. Henry was a professional newspaper columnist of the later American type with Texas extravagance, and so far as literature is concerned he was nothing else.

It was the humor of O. Henry that gave him his first readers. The entire body of his work may be classed as humor. It is significant that when in 1903 the Harpers accepted his genrè story "The Whirligig of Time," a story written unquestionably for the body of the magazine, they printed it in "The Editor's Drawer." And his humor is all of it uniquely American humor, as indigenous to the American soil as the early Mark Twain. His point of view, his materials, his methods, his characters, and the language they used are American or they are nothing. His comparisons and allusions and figures of speech are so ingrained with American life and expression that translation into other languages must be difficult, if not impossible. For examples one may open literally at random:

They're as full of apathy as a territorial delegate during the chaplain's prayer.

They became inebriated with attention, like an Atlanta Colonel listening to "Marching through Georgia."

The common people walked around in barefooted bunches, puffing stogies that a Pittsburgh millionaire would n't have chewed for a dry smoke on Ladies' Day at his club.

He first saw the light of day in New York at three years of age. He was born in Pittsburgh, but his parents moved East the third summer afterward.

Every trust bears in its own bosom the seeds of its destruction like a rooster that crows near a Georgia colored Methodist camp meeting, or a Republican announcing himself a candidate for governor of Texas.

Original as he was, however, he added few devices to those already associated with distinctively American humor. He used exaggeration as out-

rageously as did John Phœnix or Mark Twain.
No one, indeed, has ever pressed this device to
deeper abysses of absurdity. After a political
gathering many cigar-stubs undoubtedly may be
found scattered in the vicinity, but when O. Henry
tells the story the cigar-stubs are knee-deep for
a quarter of a mile about. A man has chills and
fever: "He had n't smiled in eight years. His
face was three feet long, and it never moved except
to take in quinine." A man with the rheumatism,
asked if he had ever rubbed the affected part with
rattlesnake-oil, replies: "If all the snakes I have
used the oil of was strung out in a row they would
reach eight times as far as Saturn and the rattles
could be heard at Valparaiso, Indiana, and back.
And of a casual doctor in one of his tales:

If Doc Millikin had your case, he made the terrors
of death seem like an invitation to a donkey party.
He had the bedside manners of a Piute medicine-man
and the soothing presence of a dray loaded with iron
bridge-girders. He was built like a shad, and his
eyebrows was black, and his white whiskers trickled
down from his chin like milk coming out of a sprin-
kling pot. He had a nigger boy along carrying an old
tomato-can full of calomel, and a saw.

In the originality of his exaggerations no humorist has ever excelled him. His comparisons are

unique. There is not a hackneyed expression in all his volumes. One might quote indefinitely:

She had hair the color of the back of a twenty-dollar gold certificate, blue eyes, and a system of beauty that would make the girl on the cover of a July magazine look like the cook on a Monongahela coal barge.

He was the red-hottest Southerner that ever smelled mint. He made Stonewall Jackson and R. E. Lee look like abolitionists.

Her eyes were as big and startling as bunions.

He had a voice like a coyote with bronchitis.

Ten minutes afterward the Captain arrived at the rendezvous, windy and thunderous as a dog-day in Kansas.

He loosened up like a Marcel wave in the surf of Coney.

Fate tosses you about like cork crumbs in wine opened by an unfeed waiter.

The mark of O. Henry is upon such work as peculiarly and exclusively as is the mark of Artemus Ward on the speeches of the genial showman. He has, too, the American fondness for aphorism, and at times is as pregnant with quaint philosophy as Josh Billings. It is an O. Henry philosophy, however.

A story with a moral appended is like the bill of a mosquito: it bores you, and then injects a stinging drop to irritate your conscience.

A straw vote only shows which way the hot air blows.

What a woman wants is what you 're out of.

The lover smiles when he thinks he has won; the woman who loves ceases to smile with victory. He ends a battle; she begins hers.

There ain't a sorrow in the chorus that a lobster cannot heal.

Words are as wax in his hands:

Annette Fletcherized large numbers of romantic novels.

The stage curtain, blushing pink at the name "Asbestos" inscribed upon it, came down with a slow midsummer movement. The audience trickled leisurely down the elevator and stairs.

We laugh often at the very freshness and newness of his phrases. He hits at times the nail on the head precisely. One feels the glow that only the perfect can give when one comes upon felicities like these:

She was as tidy as a cherry blossom.

At length he reached the flimsy, fluttering little soul of the shop-girl. Tremblingly, awfully her moth wings closed and she seemed about to settle on the flower of love.

Her uplifted happy eyes, as bright and clear as the water in trout pools.

Something mushy and heavily soft like raised dough leaned against Jim's leg and chewed his trousers with a yeasty growl. [This of a pug dog.]

No device for raising a laugh but he has used it to the utmost, and for the most part with a zest that is primitive in its emphasis. Open him anywhere, at random: outrageous non sequiturs, most hideous coinages, malaproprieties, deliberate misquotations, slang exaggerated to the limit of endurance—nowhere outside of the comic supplement can you find a wilder hodgepodge of incongruity. Not even John Phœnix has made such startling use of irreverence. To him nothing is sacred: "Be considerable moanin' of the bars when I put out to sea," soliloquizes the Toledo man while he is dying of consumption; "I've patronized 'em pretty freely." He delights in biblical exegesis. This is his version of the Samson story:

She gave her old man a hair cut, and everybody knows what a man's head looks like after a woman cuts his hair. And then when the Pharisees came round to guy him, he was so ashamed he went to work and kicked the whole house down on top of the whole outfit.

But the most prominent humorous mannerism of O. Henry, the one that runs like a falsetto motif through all his work, is a variety of euphemism, the translating of simple words and phrases into resounding and inflated circumlocutions. So completely did this trick take possession of him that one may denominate it a literary cliché, the trademark of O. Henry. All his characters make use of it as a dialect. Sometimes it is even funny. A waiter is not a waiter but "a friendly devil in a cabbage-scented hell"; a tramp becomes a "knight on a restless tour of the cities"; a remark about the weather becomes "a pleasant reference to meteorological conditions." Mr. Brunelli does not fall in love with Katy: "Mr. Brunelli, being impressionable and a Latin, fell to conjugating the verb *amare* with Katy in the objective case." John Hopkins buys not a cheap cigar but a "bunch of spinach, car-fare grade." A reasonable amount of this, when at its best, is tolerable, perhaps, but O. Henry wears the device threadbare. Constantly he seems straining for bizarre effect, for outrageous circumlocutions, for unheard-of methods of not calling a spade a spade. A plain statement like "the woman looked at him, hoping he would invite her to a champagne supper," becomes with O. Henry "She turned languishing eyes upon him as a hopeful source of lobsters and the delectable, ascendant globules of effervescence." It is too much.

And at this point lies O. Henry's chief failure as a humorist. Mark Twain was laughable even when he was trying to be serious. He was born with a drawl both in his voice and his pen. Humor with him was a spontaneous thing. It was so with Artemus Ward. But the humor of O. Henry is a manufactured humor, the humor of a man who is brilliant rather than droll. The artificiality of it at times is painfully obvious. One of his mannerisms, for instance, is the use of incongruous mixtures, of a series of threes for the last unexpected and outrageous ingredient of which the reader feels he must have strained hard. Such compounds as these are deliberately concocted, and the laugh that follows is of the variety that follows a pun:

He seems to me to be a sort of mixture of Maltese kitten, sensitive plant, and a member of a stranded "Two Orphans" company.

He was dressed somewhere between a Kansas City detective, Buffalo Bill, and the town dog-catcher of Baton Rouge.

Another of his overworked devices, laughable at first but distressingly artificial and tiresome after one reads long in his books, is incongruous association.

His hair was opalescent and his conversation fragmentary.

She possessed two false teeth and a sympathetic· heart.

He had gout very bad in one foot, a house near Gramercy Park, half a million dollars, and a daughter.

They took me by surprise and my horse by the bridle.

O. Henry is a humorist, a John Phœnix up to date and beyond, an entertainer of the journalistic school, a wood-pulp comedian whose sketches should be illustrated by the creator of Mutt and Jeff and, if dramatized, should be acted by Charlie Chaplin. That his work has in it oases of beauty, that he has moments when he shows himself possessed of surprising powers, that he is original even to a startling degree, only emphasizes the tragedy of his literary career. His undoubted powers he surrendered deliberately to Momus; instead of making himself, as undoubtedly he might, the Cervantes or the Mark Twain of his generation, he expended himself in impish capers and jocosities for "the groundlings, who, for the most part, are capable of nothing but inexplicable dumb-shows and noise."

IV

If his admirers would but accept him simply as a humorist, a literary comedian, the latest member of the John Phœnix, Artemus Ward, Josh Billings,

Bill Nye school, one might go with them at times even to superlatives, but to label him simply as a humorist is not enough: he must be classified with Poe and Hawthorne and Maupassant; he must be added to the great short story writers of the world; he must be credited with having given to the form a new social content. And the voices that demand this are voices not to be disregarded. What of O. Henry as a writer of fiction?

With the recent biography has come a document of peculiar value for our study: the author's own list of his first twelve stories in the order he wrote them during the years 1898-1901 while he was in the Ohio State prison. "Whistling Dick's Christmas Stocking," it would seem, was his first attempt at the short story, and as we read it we feel that it was by no accident that it was accepted and published by the first standard magazine to reduce its subscription price and popularize deliberately its literary content.

Beginning with the closing years of the century had come a demand for the unusual, for realistic and exciting fiction made by writers who had been a part of what they told. Jack London with his vivid tales of the Alaska winter was coming into focus; Richard Harding Davis, reporter extraordinary, who had been everywhere and had seen the feet of clay of all idols, was in the center of the literary stage. The epoch of historical romance was passing. A story writer to be read now must have had an experience,

> Quaeque ipsi miserrima vidi,
> Et quorum pars magna fui.

The new tale with the strange signature "O. Henry" gained at once a hearing from the clientele of "McClure's" because of the strangeness and freshness of its content. It dealt with the winter exodus of tramps from the North toward New Orleans, and it was told apparently by one who had himself been a tramp, who knew all the ritual and all the argot of the order, and who spoke with authority.

This initial story, as we study it now, knowing its origin, reveals much. The transition from Sydney Porter, the Texan newspaper columnist, to O. Henry, the short story writer, came through Bret Harte. It is a story of sentiment, theatric rather than realistic, theatric indeed to the point of melodrama and falseness to life. The central incident is clearly impossible: *one* stocking from a newly-puchased pair—are not new stockings fastened together or at least rolled together?—works out of the bundle of Christmas goods lying at the bottom of the wagon and falls at the feet of a tramp who is trudging wearily along the highway. A little later this same stocking with a stone and a note in it is hurled at least a quarter of a mile—as the story is told it cannot be less—straight through a window to fall exactly at the feet of its owner. The central character is clearly manufactured and not true. As with so much of the work of Harte, the tale is a dramatized paradox with lay figures: a besotted tramp, after years of vagrancy, becomes a man again because a little girl by a happy impulse wishes him "Merry Christmas"; then—second paradox—when a permanent home is offered him as a reward for saving the house, he awakes and flees in utter terror into his old life of vagrancy. Even the style reveals the influence of Harte. "Ther bloomin' little skeezicks!" says *Whistling Dick* reminiscently, as he looks at the stocking; "The d—d little cuss!" says *Kentuck,* as he looks at the thumb the baby had grasped.

Precisely the same attitude toward life and material we find in "An Afternoon Miracle," "The Sphynx Apple," "Christmas by Injunction," and indeed in all his stories of the Southwest. All were molded by Harte, as Harte was molded by Dickens. The West is used as startling and picturesque background; the characters are the conventional types of Western melodrama: desperadoes, cow-boys, train-robbers, sheep-men, miners—all of them redolent of the paint-box and resplendent from the costume-room. Like Harte, the writer had no real love for the West, and like Harte again, he never worked with conviction and with sympathy to show the real soul of it. A few times the glow of insight and sympathy hovers over the fifteen studies he made of his native South—by all means the best part of his fiction—but rarely does one find it in the rest of his work; certainly not at all in the fifty-seven tales that deal with the Southwest. There is nothing about them *fundamentally* Western. By a change of two hundred words or so any one of them could be transferred to the East, and even to New York City, and lose not at all by the transfer. Simply by changing half a dozen proper names, "The Indian Summer of Dry Valley Johnson" could be laid in Hoboken, New Jersey, and gain thereby. Johnson could just as well be a milk-man from Geneva, New York. Try it. Yet it is for its wild Western setting that most readers find it attractive.

The external manner of Harte he outgrew, but never did he free himself from the less obvious faults that make the work of both men inferior when compared with those absolute standards that time has decreed a work of art must have if it is at all to endure: neither of the men had a philosophy of life, and neither of them presented humanity as humanity actually is or as sane idealists dream that humanity should be. Neither of them told the truth. Of the two Harte is by far the greater, for Harte's work is single—never does he give us the serious mixed with buffoonery—and Harte once or twice in all his work did succeed in making us feel an individual human soul.

In the second group of O. Henry's stories fall the South American sketches and "The Gentle Grafter" studies that fill up two entire volumes and overflow into other volumes of the set. Despite much splendid description and here and there marvelous skill in reproducing the atmosphere and the spirit of the tropics, they are literature at its worst. Without a doubt the *Gentle Grafter* had an actual prototype. The stories may have had their basis in actual happenings as related by a voluble convict in the Ohio prison; all his material for his tales of bank-robbers and train-robbers and fugitives from justice probably was from evidence gathered at first hand. Al Jennings's amazing book throws much light here, but, for all that, the tales are false. This is not life: it is opera bouffe. The characters are no more flesh and blood than *Punch* and *Judy*. They talk a dialect unknown outside the comic theater. Sophomores at dinner sometimes use circumlocution in the excess of high spirits, and "drive up the cow" takes the place of "pass the milk": but here everybody is sophomoric and super-sophomoric; here the veriest yokel converses in vocables sesquipedalian.

Just a common Indiana hotel-keeper is asked casually concerning the ownership of a house:

"That," says he, "is the domicile and the arboreal, terrestrial, and horticultural accessories of Farmer Ezra Plunkett."

Andy Tucker and *Jeff Peters,* the confidence men, talk always in this amazing strain:

It does seem kind of hard on one's professional pride to lope off with a bearded pard's competency, especially after he has nominated you custodian of his bundle in the sappy insouciance of his urban indiscrimination.

An Irishman in the wilderness bids a stranger to dismount in terms like these:

Segregate yourself from your pseudo-equine quadruped.

The sheep-herder *Paisley Fish* and his companion talk always at this astounding altitude:

"I reckon you understand," says Paisley, "that I 've made up my mind to accrue that widow woman as part and parcel in and to my hereditaments forever, both domestic, sociable, legal, and otherwise, until death us do part. The smiles of woman," goes on Paisley, "is the whirlpool of Squills and Chalybeates, into which vortex the good ship Friendship is often drawn and dismembered."

This is not an occasional pleasantry for humorous

effect: it is the every-day speech of all the characters. They talk nothing else from the beginning of "The Gentle Grafter" volume to the end of "The Heart of the West" collection, and not one of the characters in the other volumes is entirely free from it. George Ade wrote in slang; but this is not slang, for slang is the actual words of actual men; and since the world began no human being, even in Texas, ever used language like this, save as he manufactured it deliberately for the burlesque stage.

Art is truth, truth to facts, truth to actual human nature; and art also is truth to the presumption, fundamental at least in civilized lands, that truth is superior to falsehood, that right is superior to wrong, and that actual crime is never to be condoned. Despite the freedom of his pages from salacious stain, O. Henry must be classed as an immoral writer; not immoral because he used vulgarly picaresque material or because he recorded the success of villainy, or dealt with areas of life "where there are n't no ten commandments," but because he sided with his law-breakers, laughed at their crimes, and condoned their schemes for duping the unwary. It does not excuse *Jeff Peters* to explain that he fleeces only those who have fleece to spare, or those rich ones who enjoy an occasional fleecing because it affords them a new sensation.

One needs not be a Puritan or a blue-law maker to assert with all emphasis that where honesty ceases to be fundamental there civilization lapses and the jungle begins to enter. "The Gentle Grafter" stories are cloth of the same loom that wove "Raffles" and "Get-Rich-Quick Wallingford," and all the others on that shelf of books which are the shame of American literature.

VI

The last period in O. Henry's life began in 1904 when the New York "World" engaged him to furnish a story a week for its Sunday supplement. He had been in the city two years, and had supported himself by writing for the magazines his stories of life in the Southwest and in South America. He had studied the demands of the time from the New York point of view. Moreover he had discovered Maupassant. His biographer records that during his later years he kept the work of the great *conte*-writer always within reach; we should have known it had he not told us. His style began to change: he was gaining in ease, in structural art, in brilliancy of diction. He had discovered the possibilities of finesse, of carefully balanced climaxes, and of unexpected dénouement. Now it was, at the opening of his "World" supplement period, that there was

born what many of his readers consider the real
O. Henry. Seldom now did he attempt regular plot
stories of the type of "A Black Jack Bargainer" and
"Georgia's Ruling." The greater number of his
137 or more New York "World" pieces cannot be
called short stories at all. They are familiar narrative sketches, expanded anecdotes told by a raconteur who expects an explosion of laughter at
the proper moment: they are humorous "stories".
in the newspaper sense of the word.

The "newspaper": the word brings illumination.
When asked his profession in the Ohio prison, he
replied "newspaper reporter." With the exception
of a single story in "Harper's Magazine" and one in
"The Century"—"The Missing Chord," June, 1904
—all his work was first of all published on wood-
pulp paper—in the daily press or in the ten-cent
magazine. His "World" stories make up more than
one third of his entire product. What the paper
really did was to engage him as a reporter—a highly
privileged reporter at large, told to roam the city
for material and to bring in one entertaining "story"
each week.

The requirements of the newspaper "story" are
exacting. It must be vivid, unusual, unhackneyed,
and it must have in it the modern quality of "go."
It is usually an improvisation by one who through
long practice has gained the mastery of his pen,

and by one, moreover, who has been living in contact with that which he would portray. It is written in heat, excitedly, to be read with excitement and thrown away. There must be no waste material —no "lumber," no "blue-pencil stuff," and there must be a "punch in every line," a constant bidding for attention. After the Devil's Island explosion in New York, a friend sent me the "story" of the tragedy that one of the city dailies published not many minutes after the event, and demanded where in classic literature I could find a more vivid piece of composition. Yet it had been dashed off in headlong haste to be read in headlong haste and then thrown away. It was a brilliant tour de force called forth by the demand of the time for sensation, for utter newness, for fresh new devices to gain, if only for an instant, the jaded attention of a public supersaturated with sensation.

The complaint has come that one does not remember the stories of O. Henry. Neither does one remember the newspaper "stories" he reads from morning to morning, brilliant though they may be. The difficulty comes from the fact that the writer is concerned solely with his reader. The dominating canon of his art is, Anything to catch the reader. He is catering, he knows, to the blasé, he is mixing condiments for palates gross with sensation. If the "story" is to be printed as fiction, wider latitude

is allowable.   Humor is the surest device with which
to catch Americans, but it must be American humor,
grossly strong, stingingly piquant, sensationally new.
The soul of the Sunday supplement is the unexpected; its style is an exploitation of the startling.
Everywhere paradox, incongruity, electric flash-
lights, "go"—New York City, jazz bands, Coney
Island, the Follies, Charlie Chaplin, the colored
monstrosities of Boob McNut, twentieth century
America in maddest career.

O. Henry lacks repose, and art is serene.   He does
not lift us.   He moves us tremendously at times,
but so does a narcotic.   Even in his brief moments
of seriousness we cannot take him seriously.   How
can we approach in the spirit of art, serious art that
is worth living with, a story with the title "Psyche
and the Pskyscraper," or one that opens like
this:

The poet Longfellow—or was it Confucius, the in-
ventor of Wisdom?—remarked:

"Life is real, life is earnest;
And things are not what they seem."

As mathematics are—or is: thanks, old subscriber!—
the only just rule by which the questions of life can
be measured, let us, by all means, adjust our theme to
the straight edge and the balanced column of the great
goddess Two-and-Two-Makes-Four.

If readers would only be content to use O. Henry as a condiment, exhilarating at times and highly stimulating, but never to be used as a food, if they would place him where he belongs as vaudeville— brilliant, humorous, stimulatingly original—for the beguiling of an empty hour, even the most old-fashioned of critics would have no complaint, but to rate him as the army of copy-readers and reviewers, even professors of literature, have rated him, as a maker of classics, as the great master of modern literature, as the creator who has socialized the short story, as the equal of Poe and Hawthorne and Harte on their own ground, is deplorable. To make him the recommended reading of the rising generation, to teach him in the schools, to give him to the new rising group of young authors as a model until the O. Henry manner and methods have become a dominating force in the fiction of the day, is to teach that literature is frivolity, that it is not necessarily to be based on truth or on the fundamentals that underlie human life, and that it is to be created for no other purpose than to give a momentary titillation, a beguiling thing to be taken up with the pipe and the cigar in moments of relaxation and to be brushed out with the ashes. If this be the ideal, then the civilization of our day is written on wood-pulp fiber with water.

O. Henry is not a writer of literature in the sense

that the word literature has been used by all the generations up to our own; he is not a model to be studied by any writer save the professional newspaper humorist. The daily columnist may give his days and nights to O. Henry and profit thereby, but not the writer who is writing for publication on really durable material. Always is he in altitudissimo; the music is always at full orchestra with the traps in furious action. It is keyed to the jazz note, to hilarious familiarity, to end-man high spirits. The author slaps his reader on the back and laughs loudly as if he were in a bar-room. Never the finer subtleties of suggested effect, never the unsuspected though real and moving moral background; seldom the softer tones that touch the deeper life and move the soul, rare indeed the moments when the reader feels a sudden tightening of the throat and a quickening of the pulse. It is the humor—again I say it—of the comic journalist, an enormously clever and original journalist to be sure, rather than the insight of a serious portrayer of human life; it is the day's work of an experienced special reporter eager that his "stories" shall please his unpleasable chief and his capricious readers long ago outwearied with being pleased.

VI

On the mechanical side of short story construction O. Henry was skilful indeed. He had the unusual power of gripping his reader's attention and compelling him to go on and on to the end. Moreover, he was possessed of an extraordinary originality, finesse, brilliancy of style and diction, and that sense of form which can turn every element of the seemingly careless narrative to a single startling focus. It is this architectonic quality of the work of O. Henry that has endeared him to the makers of handbooks and correspondence courses. It was this in addition to the freshness and originality of his humor and his diction that has given him as his most enthusiastic admirers that most difficult of all groups to please, the manuscript readers for publishing houses and the professional reviewers of books. Amid the dead mass of material that constituted their day's work O. Henry shone like a star. His technique is peculiar. \He began at the end of his story always and worked backward. With him it was primarily an intellectual problem: the reader and his psychological processes were constantly before him. A typical O. Henry tale begins with seemingly random remarks of a facetiously philosophical nature illustrated at length with an example seemingly taken on the impulse of the moment. The example widens into a rather unusual situation. The reader becomes interested as to the solution of the increasingly complex problem, finds that materials have been given in abundance, sees clearly at length how it is going to end, is about to throw the tale aside as not worth pursuing further—then suddenly is given an absolutely other solution that comes like a jet of water in the face. Study the mechanism of such tales as "Girl," "The Pendulum," "The Marry Month of May," and the like. One may detect instantly the germ of the story, the sole cause why it was written. A whole narrative is built up carefully to bring this sentence into startling focus at the end: "At last I have found something that will not bag at the knees," or this " 'Oh, Andy,' she sighed, 'this is great! Sure I 'll marry wid ye. But why did n't ye tell me ye was the cook? I was near turnin' ye down for bein' one of thim foreign counts.' "

Intellectually brilliant as all this may be, however, one must not forget that it concerns only the externals of short story art. The failures were at vital points. A short story must have characterization, and O. Henry's pen turned automatically to caricature. We seldom see his characters: we see only the externals of costumes, masks and make-ups, and exaggerated physical peculiarity. He gives us types, not individuals, and often he describes them in terms of types. Here is the wife of one of his heroes:

Mrs. Hopkins was like a thousand others. The auriferous tooth, the sedentary disposition, the Sunday afternoon wanderlust, the draught upon the delicatessen store for home-made comforts, the furor for department store marked-down sales, the feeling of superiority to the lady in the third-floor front who wore genuine ostrich tips and had two names over her bell, the mucilaginous hours during which she remained glued to the window sill, the vigilant avoidance of the instalment man, the tireless patronage of the acoustics of the dumb-waiter shaft—all the attributes of the Gotham flat-dweller were hers.

One never sees in his stories *a* shop-girl; it is always *the* shop-girl, described in generalities like this:

She was a wonder. Small and half-way pretty, and as much at her ease in that cheap café as though she were only in the Palmer House, Chicago, with a souvenir spoon already hidden in her shirt waist. She was natural. Two things I noticed about her especially. Her belt buckle was exactly in the middle of her back, and she didn't tell us that a large man with a ruby stick-pin had followed her up all the way from Fourteenth Street.

Or this:

Masie was beautiful. She was a deep-tinted blonde,

with the calm poise of a lady who cooks butter cakes in a window. She stood behind her counter in the Biggest Store; and as you closed your hand over the tape-line for your glove measure you thought of Hebe; and as you looked again you wondered how she had come by Minerva's eyes.

But generally he is not so specific even as this. How shall one visualize a character described in these terms:

She was looking like a bulbul, a gazelle, and a tea rose, and her eyes were as soft and bright as two quarts of cream skimmed off the Milky Way.

Or a hero like this:

He had a face like a picture of a knight—like one of that Round Table bunch—and a voice like a 'cello solo. And his manners! Lynn, if you'd take John Drew in his best drawing-room scene and compare the two, you'd have John arrested for disturbing the peace.

Again, to speak only of fundamentals, a short story should have dialogue that is natural and inevitable. The characters should talk as such people in life would actually talk. In his sketch "The World and the Door," O. Henry makes this pertinent remark: "I read in a purely fictional story the other day the line: 'Be it so, said the policeman.' Nothing so strange has yet cropped out in Truth,"

and yet in the same volume he makes a college professor talk like this: "You wind-jammers who
apply bandy-legged theories to concrete categorical
syllogisms send logical conclusions skallybootin' into
the infinitesimal ragbag."

And I wonder if there ever was a man in the
world who, chosen at random at night from the
bread-line in New York and given a dinner by a
whimsical millionaire who has sent a servant out to
secure some one to dine with him, would greet his
host whom he has never seen with these preliminary
words:

Good! Going to be in courses, is it? All right,
my jovial ruler of Bagdad. I'm your Scheherazade
all the way to the toothpicks. You're the first Caliph
with a general Oriental flavor I've struck since frost.
What luck! And I was forty-third in line.

Again, a short story should be true, and exaggeration is not truth. A short story should leave sharp
and indelible the impress of a vital moment in the
history of a human soul. It should, as O. Henry
himself has expressed it, "take you by the throat like
a quinsy," and not because of a situation and not
because of a skilfully prepared moment of surprise,
but because of a glimpse into the depths of a human
heart. To deal with types—the shop-girl, the
grafter, the border desperado—or with the stock

figures of comedy—the mother-in-law, the fat man, the maiden lady—is to work with abstractions and not with an individual soul, and the short story by its very nature is restricted to the individual. To treat of types is the province of exposition.

But his shop-girls—are they not individuals? O. Henry himself confesses that they are not. In describing Nancy he realizes that he is giving only the characteristics peculiar to the clan, and tries to shift the responsibility upon the reader.

Nancy you would call a shop-girl—because you have the habit. There is no type, but a perverse generation is always seeking a type; so this is what the type should be. She has the high-ratted pompadour, and the exaggerated straight front. Her skirt is shoddy, but has the correct flare. No furs protect her against the bitter spring air, but she wears her short broadcloth jacket as jauntily as though it were Persian lamb! On her face and in her eyes, remorseless type-seeker, is the typical shop-girl expression. It is a look of silent but contemptuous revolt against cheated womanhood; of sad prophecy of the vengeance to come. When she laughs her loudest the look is still there. The same look can be seen in the eyes of Russian peasants; and those of us left will see it some day on Gabriel's face when he comes to blow us up. It is a look that should wither and abash a man; but he has been known to smirk at it and offer flowers— with a string tied to them.

Had he wished to avoid "the remorseless type-seeker," why did he not take an individual and seek for differences rather than for similarities? Maupassant looked at things which were seemingly alike until he saw startling unlikenesses. That was his art. O. Henry writes expositions upon typical wrongs done the shop-girl class in American cities, and it is exposition by means of a single test case. The problem is worked out with *a* and *b* which are fixed constants. Maupassant avoids the type and shows the unique soul. O. Henry in a sermon like "An Unfinished Story," dealing with the pernicious system that creates the type, or in "Elsie in New York," a jibe at reformers and nothing else, may succeed in moving his reader to anger against an evil, but he leaves no single person for us to love or hate or pity. "A Harlem Tragedy" is not at all a study of New York tenement life: it is a clever exercise in paradox, and it is not true. His atmosphere is too artificial for real emotion; the construction over-balances the material. "A Lickpenny Lover" is brilliant technique, but it is not fundamentally the story of *a* shop-girl, and it is based upon an untruth. The form of the lover's proposal had to be managed with care to make possible that final sentence which is the cause of the tale, and no intelligent lover as ardent in his love as here represented would have failed to make himself perfectly clear. It smells of the footlights; it was deliberately manufactured to cause a moment of laughter at the end.

Much of his later work impresses us as stories from the lips of a skilful raconteur in a hotel lobby or a club room. One feels almost the physical presence of the man as one reads an opening like this: "Suppose you should be walking down Broadway after dinner, with ten minutes allotted to the consummation of your cigar while you are choosing between a diverting tragedy and something serious in the way of vaudeville. Suddenly a hand is laid on your arm," or this: "I don't suppose it will knock any of you people off your perch to read a contribution from an animal. Mr. Kipling and a good many others have demonstrated the fact that animals can express themselves in remunerative English." One has the impression of a man blinking over his cigar in after-dinner reminiscence and story-telling hilarity. The tales are brief—2500 words the later ones average—and they follow each other in rapid-fire order like a round of good ones at a commercial travelers' convention. He is familiar with his reader, asks his advice on points of diction and grammar, winks jovially, slaps him on the back, and laughs aloud: "There now! it's over. Hardly had time to yawn, did you?" "Young lady, you would have liked that grocer's young man yourself"; "It began way up in Sullivan County, where so many rivers and so much trouble begins—or begin; how would you say that?" And how he rambles:

Ileen was a strictly vegetable compound, guaranteed under the Pure Ambrosia and Balm of Gilead Act of the Year of the Fall of Adam. She was a fruit-stand blonde—strawberries, peaches, cherries, etc. Her eyes were wide apart, and she possessed the calm of the storm that never comes. But it seems to me that words (at any rate per) are wasted in an effort to describe the beautiful. Like fancy it is engendered in the eyes. There are three kinds of beauties—I was foreordained to be homiletic; I can never stick to a story. The first is the freckled faced, snub-nosed girl whom you like. The second is Maude Adams. The third is, or are, the ladies in Bouguereau's paintings. Ileen Hinkle was the fourth.

He opens a story like a responder to a toast at a banquet, with a theory or an attitude toward a phase of life; then he illustrates it with a special case, holding the "point" carefully to the end, to bring it out with dramatic suddenness as he takes his seat amid applause.

Never a writer so whimsical. Who else would dare to write a short story with these rules: "Let the story wreck itself on the spreading rails of the *Non Sequitur* Limited, if it will; first, you must take your seat in the observation car 'Raison d'être' for one moment. . . . It is for no longer than to consider a brief essay on the subject—let us call it: 'What's Around the Corner.'" "Cabbages and Kings," to use his own words, is "tropical vaudeville," and the book is not widely different from all he wrote. A few times he tried to break away from the method that made him and that ruined him, as in "Roads of Destiny" with its Hawthorne suggestion, and the delightful "The Church with the Overshot Wheel," but it was not often. "The Enchanted Kiss," an absinthe dream with parts as lurid and as brilliant as De Quincey, shows what he might have done had he given himself completely to such effort, but the ephemeral press had laid its hands upon him and he rendered it its full demands.

VII

The influence of O. Henry upon the short story of the decade after his death has been alarming. He more than any one else helped to turn the tide of this popular form toward the present all-tyrannizing demand for manner. The ghost of O. Henry flits now over even the standard magazines, and it all but dominates some of the more popular journals like "The Saturday Evening Post." It has been remarked many times that it is hard to remember

O. Henry titles and to locate quotations from his stories. Let the O. Henry specialist try his skill at these typical passages:

He was unhappy. As he consumed his sensitive luncheon of roast beef, Yorkshire pudding, French fried potatoes and deep-dish apple pie, he occasionally roared at his wife, who had limousine upholstery on a fliver chassis. "What is it, dear? Do you feel the sadness of things?" inquired Mrs. J. Bolivar Whipple.

He slipped from the expression of a man who wants that check to that of a man presented with a cocktail at a dinner he had expected to be dry.

Sylvester Lehigh Pennyworth Tibble landed in New York City in the dark of the moon, with the left hind foot of a graveyard rabbit dangling from his watch chain, and starting at the foot of Liberty Street, where he stepped off the ferry-boat, began his assault upon the Fortress of Fortune, an attack of which the harrowing details shall form the warp and woof of this chronicle.

The neck-torturing office buildings of the lower city did not catch up the vibrations of S. L. P. Tibble's firm tread upon the cobblestones of West Street. Little old N'York did not noticeably notice Sylvester.

I went on to the Eagle Bird, to get something for the nerve strain I'd been suffering from, owing to me having got a necktie that was made by a lady who had lost her husband a few years back and didn't think she'd ever get used to not having a man round the house. Having got about three fingers of relief I went over to the faro table and sat down, and pretty soon Simmy come in and we got to talking about church socials. I allowed that they was a low form of recreation, with all the dangers to an unmarried man that there was at a dance and none of the fun, etc.

"I'm commonly known as 'Aps,'" says the little man. "I'm a darling and a daisy and a killaloo bird," he says, mighty boastful. "Luck's my pup and follows me around," he says. "Any man that does me a favor wears diamonds in the near future, and the man who bucks my game is a prey to bitter and unavailing regrets shortly subsequent. I'm cold pizen with no known anecdote, or I'm milk and honey blest —according as you want to take me. I've jumped your coal claim."

If there were a hundred men in a crowd and Chester K. Pilkins was there he would be the hundredth man. I like that introduction, etc.

The city of Anneburg, situate some distance south of Mason and Dixon's line at the point where the Tobacco Belt and the Cotton Belt, fusing imperceptibly together, mingle the nitrogenous weed and the bolled staple in the same patchwork strip of fertile loam lands, was large enough to enjoy a Carnegie Library, a municipal graft scandal, and a reunion of the Confederate Veterans' Association.

These were picked almost at random from the first

miscellaneous collection of copies of "The Saturday Evening Post"—some twelve numbers there happened to be altogether—that I could lay my hands upon. The quotations are from Sinclair Lewis, Henry Pason Dowst, Kennett Harris, and Irvin Cobb.

The Society of Arts and Sciences at a dinner in honor of the genius of William Sydney Porter in April, 1918, voted to award a prize of $250 a year for the best short story published the following year. Two O. Henry Memorial Award volumes, containing the crowned short stories of 1919 and 1920, have been given to the public. Instead of characterizing the general content of the latest of these volumes myself, let me quote a very recent review of the book by Vera Gordon:

On the whole it is manner and not matter, treatment and not theme that counts. Realistic handling and a vivid, semi-slangy, pseudo-epigrammatic style will excuse any theme, however slight. . . . There is everything in this remarkable book: slap-stick farce, sob stuff, melodrama, coincidence, and Grand Guignol horrors. There are also three or four good stories. The collection has only one thing in common—good craftsmanship.

This is the legacy, then, which O. Henry has left to the short story.

VIII

He admitted his failure. In the last weeks of his life, the power of wizard expression gone forever, the physical sinking into collapse when it should have borne him through thirty years more of creative effort, came his pathetic cry: "I want to get at something bigger. What I have done is child's play to what I can do, to what I know it is in me to do." And again in connection with "The Dream," that last story of his, never finished: "I want to show the public I can write something new —new for me, I mean—a story without slang, a straightforward dramatic plot treated in a way that will come nearer my ideal of real story-writing." He was planning a novel, "The story of a man— an individual, not a type," as he expressed it. It was too late. What he had written he had written.

We may explain him best perhaps in the terms of his story "The Lost Blend": a flask of Western humor—John Phœnix, Artemus Ward; a full measure of Bret Harte—sentiment, theatricality, melodrama; a drop of Maupassant—constructive art, brilliancy of diction, finesse; a dash of journalistic flashiness and after-dinner anecdote; and then—insipid indeed all the blend without this—two bottles of the Apollinaris of O. Henry's peculiar soul, and lo! the exhilarating blend that is intoxicating a generation—"elixir of battle, money, and high life."

Exhilarating indeed, but a dangerous beverage for steady consumption. Sadly does it distort the perspective and befuddle the heart and the soul. It begets dislike of mental effort, and dependence solely upon thrill and picturesque movement. It is akin to the moving pictures which, seen too often, do to death all thought and all imagination. A college president complained to me recently of the difficulty of finding chapel speakers who would hold the attention of the students. "There must be nothing abstract," he said; "everything must be in the concrete. The preacher must be hot from some battle where he has grappled with stirring problems at first hand, and he must present graphic pictures in breathless succession."

We need not complete the connection. Are we arriving at a period when all literary art is ephemeral, a shallow period without philosophy of life or moral background, a period where manner shall rule and not matter, and brilliancy is all in all, a period, in short, where O. Henry is the crowned literary classic?

A CRITIC IN C MAJOR

To live in the age of O. Henry is to be aware
sooner or later of the *enfant terrible* of its latest
phase, the author of "Prejudices." Opinions of
this phenomenon run as widely asunder as men
ever drift. To some he is a diabolical boy with a
bean-shooter, amazingly accurate of aim; to others
he is Demogorgon straight from hell with Orcus
and Ades whose name is Nathan; to still others
he is a smart Aleck mouthing the argot of the tribe
—shall not the editor of "The Smart Set" be smart?
But there is a minority very respectable to whom
he is a genuine critic, the voice of his era. A recent London "Athenæum" reviewer has him "rapidly
becoming the most important critic in America."
That the "literati of New York" and beyond are
fearfully aware of this high-vocabularied new censor
of art and morals, ducking nervously at his very
shadow, is ludicrously evident. The New York
"Literary Review," for instance, with a critic of
distinction for editor, has mentioned him or al-
luded to him on its editorial pages more often than

any other contemporary. Is <u>Mencken</u> the typical
critic of the O. Henry age, the type of critic that
journalism is evolving—the critic of the future?

The man is so recent an arrival that few can
honestly say they have read him, save in fragments.
My own experience, perhaps, has been typical.
There was a time not so long ago when the name
Mencken called up for me only certain smashing
reviews, O. Henry-like in their general effect. I
smiled over them as work keyed to "The Smart
Set"—smart.   But the man was not to be dismissed.
I found myself one day with "Prefaces" in my
hand, and opening by chance my eye fell on this:
"Huneker comes out of Philadelphia, that depressing intellectual slum." I opened again: *"O Doctor admirabilis, acutus et illuminatissimus!* Need-
less to say the universities have not overlooked this
geyser of buttermilk: he is an honourary A. M. of
Yale"—this concerning one Krehbiel. Who would
lay down a book as piquant as that promised to be?
I finished it with gusto, though its ram's-horn
roared against every wall I had ever stood upon. I
am of the Puritans for six generations, I am a
Methodist, I am a college professor: imagine the
massacre of this book in a future number of "The
Smart Set"! At the end of a furious charge upon
a woolly little lamb of a publication this reviewer
once worked himself up to this thunderous climax:

the United States "is the Billy Sunday among the nations." I was inclined after "Prefaces" to say, "Yes, and H. L. Mencken is the Billy Sunday among her critics." He defends the negative thunderously; he can out-Billy Billy himself. His vocabulary is richer. Consider such tremendous pulpit-thrashings as these:

The American people, taking them by and large, are the most timorous, sniveling, poltroonish, ignominious mob of serfs and goose-steppers ever gathered under one flag in christendom since the fall of the Eastern Empire.

In the presence of the Methodist clergy, it is difficult to avoid giving away to the weakness of indignation. What one observes is a horde of uneducated and inflammatory dunderheads, eager for power, intolerant of opposition and full of a childish vanity—a mob of holy clerks but little raised, in intelligence and dignity, above the forlorn half wits whose souls they chronically rack. In the whole United States there is scarcely one among them who stands forth as a man of sense and information. Illiterate in all save the elementals, untouched by the larger currents of thought, drunk with their power over dolts, crazed by their immunity to challenge by their betters, they carry over into the professional class of the country the spirit of the most stupid peasantry, and degrade religion to the estate of an idiotic phobia. There is not a village in America in which some such preposterous jackass is not in irruption.

The man puzzled me. Was he not perhaps a phenomenon of the war period? I thought so once; his most destructive eruptions have been since 1914. A world conflict waged long without quarter drives every man to extremes of speech, very often to phobia. Here was a young man undoubtedly running amuck. He attacked indiscriminately, it seemed to me, like a typhoon in a jungle. He did nothing but destroy. After me the deluge! Every cherished ideal, every hero, every idol, every sweet delusion, our whole America, "a nation of third-class men"—he damned with a crackle of superlatives. Note the range and execution of his guns: This of Virginia, the mother of Southern States:

Her education has sunk to the Baptist seminary level; not a single contribution to human knowledge has come out of her colleges in twenty-five years; she spends less than half upon her common schools, *per capita*, than any northern state spends. In brief, an intellectual Gobi or Lapland. Urbanity, *politesse,* chivalry? Go to! It was in Virginia that they invented the device of searching for contraband whisky in women's underwear.

This of Roosevelt, and written in the period of laudation just following his death:

A glorified longshoreman engaged eternally in cleaning out bar-rooms—and not too proud to gouge when the inspiration came to him, or to bite in the clinches, or to oppose the relatively fragile brass knuckles of the code with chair-legs, bung-starters, cuspidors, demijohns, and ice-picks.

Are you a Puritan? Read this:

The Puritan, for all his pretensions, is the worst of materialists. Passed though his sordid and unimaginative mind, even the stupendous romance of sex is reduced to a disgusting transaction in physiology. As artist he is thus hopeless; as well expect an auctioneer to qualify for the Sistine Chapel choir. All he ever achieves, taking pen or brush in hand, is a feeble burlesque of his betters, all of whom, by his hog's theology, are doomed to hell.

And did you ever review a book, or enjoy a book review? Behold yourself:

Consider the solemn ponderosities of the pious old maids, male and female, who write book reviews for the newspapers. Here we have a heavy pretension to culture, a campus cocksureness, a laborious righteousness—but of sound æsthetic understanding, of alertness and hospitality to ideas, not a trace. The normal American book reviewer, indeed, is an elderly virgin, a superstitious bluestocking, an apostle of Vassar *Kultur;* and her customary attitude of mind is one of fascinated horror. (The Hamilton Wright Mabie complex! The "white list" of novels!)

Let us turn to a more universal theme, the poet's dream of romantic love:

The business of poetry, remember, is to set up a sweet denial of the harsh facts that confront all of us—to soothe us in our agonies with emollient words —in brief, to lie sonorously and reassuringly. Well, what is the worst curse of life? Answer; the abominable magnetism that draws unlikes and incompatibles into delirious and intolerable conjunction—the kinetic over-stimulation called love.

And again:

The lover sees with an eye that is both opaque and out of focus. Thus he begins the familiar process of editing and improving his girl. Features and characteristics that, observed in cold blood, might have quickly aroused his most active disgust are now seen through a rose-tinted fog, like drabs in a musical comedy. The lover ends by being almost anæsthetic to disgust. While the spell lasts his lady could shave her head or take to rubbing snuff, or scratch her leg at a communion service, or smear her hair with bear's grease, and yet not disgust him. Here the paralysis of the faculties is again chiefly physical—a matter of obscure secretions, of shifting pressure, of metabolism. Nature is at her tricks. The fever of love is upon its victim. His guard down, he is little more than a pathetic automaton.

And when it comes to marriage:

A man, when his marriage enters upon the stage of regularity and safety, gets used to his wife as he might get used to a tannery next door, and *vice versa.* . . . Who are happy in marriage? Those with so little imagination that they cannot picture a better state, and those so shrewd that they prefer quiet slavery to hopeless rebellion.

Even the Ten Commandments are not immune:

They [Shaw's platitudes] are as bullet-proof in essence as the multiplication table, and vastly more bullet-proof than the Ten Commandments or the Constitution of the United States.   .

But it is the condition of American art and literature that especially infuriates him. This at random:

Find me a second-rate American in any of the arts and I'll find you his master and prototype among third, fourth, or fifth-rate Englishmen.

America is for him a land cursed with third-rateness, with morals, with sentimentalism, with uplift mania, with Pollyannaism. Of Henry Sydnor Harrison, "merchant of mush":

He is touched by the delusion that he has a mission to make life sweeter, to preach the Finer Things, to radiate Gladness. What! More gladness? Another volt or two and all civilized adults will join the Italians and Jugo-Slavs in their headlong hegira. A few more amperes, and the land will be abandoned to the Jews, the ex-Confederates, and the Bolsheviki.

These are but a half-dozen of his bloody angles:
one might with small searching find yet extremer
damnations of the régime of the democratic hive.
He has prodded every hornet in the American
swarm.   One of the "belligerent young generation,"
diagnoses Professor Sherman, and that was my own
classification once.   To every new generation the
fundamentals of forty years before seem inadequate:
that is an axiom.   When the baton of the dead
master falls into the hands of the new young leader
he at once changes the balance of saxophones and
trombones and banjos.   Periods in literature are
but generations.   The hymns of the fathers are always "pennyroyal" to the sons; jazz is always the
music of the future and *vers libre* its poetry.   The
cry of adolescence and later adolescence is always
revolutionary.   Who so "pennyroyal" now as
Wordsworth?   Yet the "Lyrical Ballads" to the
thoughtful inheritors of the eighteenth century traditions were the extreme of intolerable jazz.   Shelley
to the critics born before the French Revolution
wrote "drivelling idiocy run mad."   He was eighteen when he produced his "The Necessity of Atheism": he was not much older when he wrote his
"Defense of Poetry."   New periods in literature
always, from Sydney's day to Frank Norris's, have
been ushered in with defenses of new literary creeds
and appeals for a return to true art, as Preraphael-

ism was supposed to be a return to the naturalism that prevailed before Raphael had cast it into mold that had become classic. And these blasts invariably have been blown by men under thirty. The theory is good : it explains Mencken.

And then I found that Mencken is forty-two years old—he was born in 1880: it gave me a sensation when I saw that on the jacket of a book. It scattered my theories like an old letter discovered by a biographer. Then I did what I should have done at the start: I read Mencken, all the Mencken I could procure, and when I had read him I understood. I am clear now. In the presence of *all* his work the workman stands revealed.

II

The man began as a lyrist. At twenty-one he was Henry Louis Mencken, author of a single book, a dilettante little volume with youth writ large on every page, including the title-page, which ran: "Ventures into Verse, Being Various Ballads, Ballades, Rondeaux, Triolets, Songs, Quatrains, Odes *and* Roundels all rescued from *the* Potters' Field, *of* Old Files *and* here Given Decent Burial [Peace *to* Their Ashes], by Henry Louis Mencken with Illustrations & Other Things By Charles S. Gordon & John Siegel. . . . First (*and*

Last) Edition." At the very opening of the volume there is a

PRELIMINARY REBUKE

Don't shoot the pianist; he's doing his best.
    Gesundheit! Knockers! have your fling!
Unto an Anvilfest you're bid;
    It took a lot of hammering,
    To build Old Cheops' Pyramid!

The first third of the book is made up of ballads in the vein of Kipling:

    Prophet of brawn and bravery!
    Bard of the fighting man!

It is good work: it catches to the full the spirit of the master: Kipling himself might have written the ringing anthems that fill a dozen pages. Mingled with his "ballads of the fleet" they might deceive the pundits.

The rest of the book is prevailing in lighter vein, *vers de société,* French forms lightly fingered, love lyrics in adolescent moods. The technique for the most part is exquisite. Bunner for instance never wrote a more sparkling bit than this "Frivolous Rondeau":

    A lyric verse I 'll make for you,
    Fair damsel that the many woo,
        'Twill be a sonnet on your fan—

.That aid to love from quaint Japan—
And "true" will rime with "eyes of blue."

Ah! me, if you but only knew
The toil of setting out to hew
   From words—as I shall try to do—
     A lyric verse.

Fleet metric ghosts I must pursue,
And dim rime apparitions, too—
   But yet, 't is joyfully I scan,
   And reckon rimes and think and plan
For there's no cheaper present than
     A lyric verse.

Some of the "Songs of the City" are richly original, but in view of the later Mencken the lyric "Il Penseroso" is more significant:

Love's song is sung in ragtime now
And kisses sweet are syncopated joys,
The tender sigh, the melancholy moan,
The soft reproach and yearning up-turned gaze
Have passed into the caves without the gates,
And in their place, to serve love's purposes,
Bold profanations from the music halls
Are working overtime.

The poet of twenty-one already was passing into the sear and yellow leaf. Romantic love was made in knightly fashion once with stately vows and tall vocabulary, but now, alas,

Now to his girl the ragtime lover says,
The while he strums his marked-down mandolin,
"Is you ma lady love?" and she, his girl,
Makes answer thus: "Ah is!"
Gadzooks! it makes me sad!

That any one—except me, and that recently—ever read a line of the book there is no evidence. Evidently it is still considered valuable in certain quarters: the only copy in New York City, so far as I could discover, was stolen from the public library a year ago. The book is extinct, almost totally extinct. When it was issued it made no more impression upon the reading public than if it were a schoolgirl's yearnings published by Badger. The title was effeminate and timid; apologetic even. Had it been, say, "Hell after 8:15," some poor devil of a newspaper reviewer might have glimpsed it in the heap, but "Ventures into Verse"—it is to be rated in literary statistics as still-born. Yet show me a more promising bit of poetic workmanship put to press that year by an American.

Even the poet must live. Henry Louis Mencken became, of all things, a reporter on a city daily; a Baltimore daily. The muse drooped and faded and disappeared. *Journalism* is the antonym of *poetry,* as completely as *city* is the antonym of *country.* To set a young lyric poet to gathering gutter-sweepings and offal for the maw of the

"Gomorrah Gazette" of to-day is like harnessing an aëroplane to a swill-cart. Imagine a poet, say Swinburne, put to slavery under an American city editor whose ideal of a perfect paper is a front page covered, half of it, with red block letters and screamers. Send him out for material, say to the East Side. Contrast if you can what he might bring back with this recent picture of Swinburne by Max Beerbohm: "He spoke to us of his walk; spoke not in the strain of a man who had been taking his daily exercise on Putney Heath, but rather in that of a Peri who had at long last been suffered to pass through Paradise. And rather than that he spoke, would I say that he cooingly and flutingly sang of his experience. The wonders of this morning's wind and sun and clouds were expressed in a flow of words so right and sentences so perfectly balanced that they would have seemed pedantic had they not been clearly as spontaneous as the wordless notes of a bird in song." Swinburne was a poet and not a journalist.

Though a reporter Mencken was still a poet, but he was in protest now, in plaintive protest. At twenty-one, despite the newspaper game, he was still not wholly disillusioned. Kipling he called "Master," but he bemoaned his lapse into twentieth-centuryism. The poet of his dream was turning into "poetaster," but perhaps it was not too late to

recall him. He voiced his disappointment in a
"Ballade of Protest." I wish I had space for it
all:

> Sing us again in rhymes that ring,
>   In Master-Voice that lives and thrills;
> Sing us again of wind and wing,
>   Of temple bells and jungle trills:
>   And if your Pegasus ever wills
> To lead you down some other way,
>   Go bind him in his older thills—
> Sing us again of Mandalay.
>
> Master, regard the plaint we bring,
>   And hearken to our prayer, we pray,
> Lay down your law and sermoning—
>   Sing us again of Mandalay.

The newspaper game is as swiftly changing in
its players and their positions as collegiate foot-ball.
Youngsters are continually dropping from the line-
up, or soaring after intense periods into specialized
leadership. After four years young Mencken was
city editor—this in his native Baltimore—and a
year later he was dramatic critic. No more poetry;
criticism now, criticism for the theater pages: actors,
actresses, first nights, new plays. But the young
critic reporter's ambition soared above the newspaper column. In 1905—he was twenty-five then
and sensitive for revolt—he essayed a volume of

dramatic criticism, a study of the new Heliogabalus of the British Parnassus, Bernard Shaw, the first full-length picture to be drawn of the man. Brilliant work for a youngster, but it was mild of tone and it was received mildly. Its neglect set its author to thinking, and the final result was revolutionary. Henry Louis Mencken became H. L. Mencken. In a moment of confession, rare indeed for the man, he has told us of the evolution: "Aspiring, toward the end of my nonage, to the black robes of a dramatic critic, I took counsel of an ancient whose service went back to the days of *Our American Cousin*, asking him what qualities were chiefly demanded by the craft," and the ancient told him above all things else to be interesting: "all else is dross." It would do him, he conceded, no real harm to read the books of the great critics or even the works of masters like Shakspere,

"But, unless you can make people *read* your criticisms, you may as well shut up your shop. And the only way to make them read you is to give them something exciting."

"You suggest, then," I ventured, "a certain ferocity?"

"I do," replied my venerable friend. "Read George Henry Lewes, and see how *he* did it—sometimes with a bladder on a string, usually with a meat-ax. Knock somebody in the head every day—if not an actor, then the author, and if not the author, then the manager. And if· the play and the performance are perfect, then excoriate someone who does n't think so—a fellow critic, a rival manager, the unappreciative public. But make it hearty; make it hot! the public would rather be the butt itself than to have no butt in the ring. That is rule No. 1 of American psychology—and of English too, but more especially of American. You must give a good show to get a crowd, and a good show means one with slaughter in it.". . . The advice of my ancient counselor kept turning over and over in my memory, and as chance offered I began to act upon it, and whenever I acted upon it I found that it worked.

This is illuminating, but it explains only in part. The later Mencken unquestionably lays about him as ferociously as even his ancient friend could have desired, but the reader of all of him is impressed with the fact that his onslaughts are not yellow-journalistic, not indiscriminate and made for mere sensational advertisement. He is not a typhoon boxing the compass with his fury and tearing the whole jungle in brainless rage or assumed rage. His blasts are all in the same direction—trade winds, furious at times, but always to the westward. To read him is to discover that after he had finished with Shaw—Shaw the windy, cock-sure, iconoclastic, with eye to the box-office, perfect type of the critic described by the ancient who dated from

"Our American Cousin"—he next discovered (most unthespianic of discoveries) that devil's Messiah, the prophet Nietzsche, of the German Empire that once was. And he read Nietzsche in the bare German, and absorbed Nietzsche, and then in two diverse volumes he translated Nietzsche and explained him and rhapsodized him to an America which, save for a few scattered Ph. D.'s made in Bonn and Baesl, had never heard his name even, when indeed even the general run of the German people knew no more about him than, to quote Mencken's own words, "they knew about sanitary plumbing or the theory of least squares." And he did it brilliantly, comprehendingly—I know of no treatment more illuminating. But no man in the twenties ever plunges into that maelstrom of dogma that has swallowed empires, to emerge the man he was. After Nietzsche, no longer was Mencken poet, no longer was he critic: he was a prophet like his master, a prophet with an evangel that the "mob," the "rabble," "the proletariat," the "plain people" shall never understand, shall shudder at indeed always, and hoot at, and brand with "Antichrist."

Whatever else Professor Nietzsche may have been, critic he certainly was not; and however rhapsodic he may have been at times, and dithyrambic and seer-like of tone, he certainly was not a poet. He was a prophet (whether devil-inspired or not is another question; whether sound at philosophic base or not is a theme for another variety of investigation)—he was a prophet, a voice, a speaker-out to his generation. Prophets have always excoriated and seared their contemporaries. Consider the torrent poured out by Amos: "Hear this, O you cows, O you women of Bashan, who live softly upon the toil of the poor. . . . You shall be driven straight out through the breaches in the wall, every cow of you. . . ." And there was the Baptist "O generation of vipers," and, to come nearer home, there was Carlyle—voices in the wilderness thundering aloud, The day of the Lord is here! The methods of Nietzsche were the methods of all prophets of wrath. Thus Mencken describes his arraignment of his own Germany:

No epithet was too outrageous, no charge was too far-fetched, no manipulation or interpretation of evidence was too daring, to enter into his ferocious indictment. He accused the Germans of stupidity, superstitiousness, and silliness; of a chronic weakness for dodging issues, a fatuous "barn-yard" and "green-grazing" contentment; of yielding supinely to the commands and exactions of a clumsy and unintelligent government; of degrading education to the low level of mere cramming and examination-passing; of a congenital inability to understand and absorb the culture of other peoples, and particularly the culture of the French; of a boorish bumptiousness and an ignorant, ostrich-like complacency; of a systematic hostility to men of genius, whether in art, science, or philosophy (so that Schopenhauer, dead in 1860, remained "the last German who was a European event"); of a slavish devotion to "the two great European narcotics, alcohol and christianity"; of a profound beeriness, a spiritual dyspepsia, a puerile mysticism, an old-womanish pettiness, and ineradicable liking for "the obscure, evolving, cropuscular, damp and shrouded."

Whether it was written in hate of Germany or in love, all this torrent of vituperation had with Nietzsche one single direction: every word was a blow at what he considered German weaknesses. Again in the words of Mencken:

Even its ["Thus Spake Zarathustra's] lingering sneers at the Germans strike at weakness which the more thoughtful Germans were themselves beginning to admit, combat, and remedy. It is a riotous affirmation of race-efficiency, a magnificent defiance of destiny, a sublime celebration of ambition.

We are on the right track now: the problem of H. L. Mencken is the problem of a Nietzschean in the heart of the American democracy. What weaknesses will he find from the point of view of "blood and iron," "be hard," "death to the under dog," "not virtue, but efficiency," "the weak and the botched must perish, they should be helped to perish"—what will he find milk-and-waterish in this paradise of the proletariat? Answer: Read "Prejudices." These fulmintations seemingly against all things American are not random shots, diabolical bombs thrown by an enemy of the republic: they are prophet blasts, irritating, maddening, arousing the thoughtful, perhaps, to a conception of the America to be. The very too-muchness of his protesting classifies him: his very violence is "a sublime celebration of ambition." Those who in rage reply to him from sheltered corners of his continent-broad battle-field miss his whole meaning. To rush excitedly to the aid of Roosevelt assaulted by this most honest of Rooseveltians, to cry out in horror that the altars of puritanism have been defiled by this most jealous of all Puritans, to shriek "Antichrist" at one who sneers only at un-Christlikeness (in all of his writings I have ever read I have found no innuendo directed at Christ himself), to stone him as a vandal when he breaks open whited sepulchers and discloses corruption in the heart that had vaunted itself holy—rebuttal like this is really confession. I picture that inner padded den of the Baltimore Carlyle as a place of sardonic laughter. One does not reply with logic and with therefores when one's mother or one's wife is defamed by the prurient-souled, neither does one defend the Ten

Commandments or the moral laws that have made civilization—imperfect though it be as yet—superior to life under jungle codes wherever that jungle may be. In his heat the Nietzschean hurler of taunts goes too far; always he is too strong—one may wonder at times what the Menckenian "News From Nowhere" will really be like when he ceases to be merely destructive and formulates his creed —but at present the totality of his blasts disturbs little save weaknesses.

III

But Mencken has been branded with the herd-mark "critic"—literary critic. All the reviews I have ever read of him, some of them European, classify him only as a critic. And critic he certainly is not. To add him to the number of the real critics—not book reviewers; not book journalists; not literary muck-rakers—would require the same major treatment that were necessary if O. Henry were to be admitted to the company of the short story writers: the rules would need to be rewritten. That he has the apparatus for criticism, a dazzling knowledge of books and writers and movements and technique, no man may deny; that he has a brilliancy of style when he wills, an O. Henry-like originality of phrase and illustration and diction, a remarkable precision and range in the use of words, is evident even to sophomores; that he is curiously learned in many arts and many literatures, saturated especially with all that has poured from the presses of America for two decades, is as true as it is exceptional. I know of no man to-day more brilliantly equipped for critical expression.

But his defects are so radical and his whole attitude toward literary art so uncritical that he must be ruled out as a critic if one is to be governed at all by any of those canons which have been held axiomatic since Aristotle. He has given us at full length his own conception of the critic. It is the proper approach to this side of H. L. Mencken. Let us examine it.

It is impossible for the true critic to be a gentleman. I use the word in its common meaning, to wit, a man who avoids offence against punctilio, who is averse to an indulgence in personalities, who is ready to sacrifice truth to good manners and good form, and who has respect and sympathy for the feelings of his inferiors. Criticism is intrinsically and inevitably a boorish art. Its practitioner takes color from it, and his gentlemanliness—if he has any—promptly becomes lost in its interpretative labyrinths. The critic who is a gentleman is no critic. He is merely the dancing master of an art.

Strange astigmatism this, the flippant definition of a reviewer whose life has been spent in the muddy roil of current books. To him a blast in "The Smart Set" aimed at an effusion not yet dry in its ink is actually criticism. Substitute "newspaper book reviewer" for "critic" and there is a grain of truth in this definition—even a freshman knows that criticism should be fearless and honest whether aimed at a book or a foot-ball coach—but with this single reservation the thing is puerile. It is enlightening, however: it illumines its author. But who is Mencken that he should be lighted up for our inspection? Were this not larger than Mencken the thing might be hooted at and thrown forever into the rubbish, but the man is a type: in studying him, as in studying O. Henry and Jack London, we are studying a period, we are studying our own times.

There is a strange duality in Mencken just as there was in O. Henry: good material, but warped somehow beyond all straightening; sharp eyes beyond the average of sharpness often, but strabismic even to ludicrousness. The disease of Mencken, the disease of a growing area of our writing generation, might be diagnosed from this definition of "critic" alone: obsession by contemporaneousness. It is a city disease gendered by the lack of moral and intellectual sanitation in journalistic centers and by the steady diet of one thing never varied. It is a disease that lays hold inevitably upon the newspaper worker who remains for any length of time in the miasma of this most deadly of all extra-hazardous trades. The phosphorus of it eats into the bones and turns all the sky to mucus. The name of it? Call it the "yellows." The blight that is upon our literature to-day comes from the fact that the greater number of its practitioners have at one time or another been gassed in this deadly area and rendered unbalanced, unable thereafter to see life steadily or to see it whole.

The veteran reporter sneers at life. He has seen the feet of clay of all our idols, he has dined with the valets of all our heroes, he has learned the price of all our statesmen, he has viewed from within the ropes the totality of human sordidness and criminality and bestialness, he has visited the side-shows of all the Vanity Fairs, and found Beelzebub supreme. He has seen everything, he has been everywhere: he is disillusioned, he is blasé, he is cock-sure, he is stripped of belief in anything human or divine—he sneers. If he writes a book he entitles it, as did Mencken, "Damn!"—life for him becomes a hunt for synonyms for "Damn!" He is not a pessimist, for a pessimist is an honest philosopher who has examined *all* the sides of life, has weighed coldly both the good and the bad, and has found the evil the weightier: he is not a pessimist, he is a man who has lost his shadow, he is an apoplectic victim, one side abnormally developed, keen even to the miraculous; the other side shriveled into nothingness. To such a man the world is out of balance. To the jaundiced the whole world is yellow.

Imagine a journalist writing criticism; imagine Babe Ruth writing epics. His whole training has been centered in the contemporaneous, and criticism demands perspective; he has practised only upon the loud trumpets and the megaphone, and criticism is a thing of subtle blendings and rare shadings; he has been trained to search only for the exceptional, the instantly arresting, the sensational, and criticism demands as its very soul the entire truth. Criticism that deals with contemporaries, ruled Jules Lemaitre, is not criticism at all: it is conversation. Conversation about one's contemporaries, if one is a boor, is inevitably boorish: it makes enemies, in certain regions it makes duels. But criticism makes not enemies. Criticism is a science and science is calm, science is gentlemanly in the sense that the word "gentleman" is used outside of newspaper offices and soviets. To say that it is impossible for a true critic to be a gentleman is to classify one's self. Is the surgeon who cuts cruelly in order to save, is he a boor? May not a diagnostician tell in perfect calmness and in all gentleness facts about your physical condition that will bring you even thoughts of suicide?   Is the chemist who makes an analysis that may drive a fertilizer factory out of business a boor while he is doing his work?   Is the scientist inevitably a boor?   And is not the critic a scientist?   If one writes of the art of Shelley or of Rossetti can not one still have respect and sympathy for the feelings of one's superiors?

Unscientific, an impressionist ruled by his prejudices, Mencken is not a critic at all.   He is a bull in the literary china-shop, he is the champion of the literary off-side: let a book be damned by the prudes and he rushes blindly and furiously to gore its enemies.   He is the leading champion of his fellow-journalist Dreiser, defending him because the prudish condemned him.   "I became involved in Dreiser's cause," he says, "largely because of the efforts of the Comstocks to work up a case against him." He is to be classed not with the critics but with the literary free-lances with high-powered vocabularies, with the newspaper columnists, with the monthly appraisers of the real estate of Parnassus—up to date to the minute, cock-sure, definitive, though the ink still is smeary on the book under the knife—the criticism of the age of O. Henry. Is this too strong?   Let us examine.   Criticism, to some extent at least, is a science and obeys certain laws.

First law of all, a critic should approach his problem with honesty, with open mind, seeking truth; but the very titles of two of Mr. Mencken's most typical books bear State's evidence against him. Prejudice—*prae-judicium*—a judgment arrived at before evidence has been heard. Prejudice reads a book, not to be led to a conclusion, but to be confirmed in its own preconceptions; it picks and chooses those points that give poignancy to the already formulated verdict. It is oblivious of all else. William Dean Howells could not possibly write a book that would have merit for the author of "Prejudices," nor could Sarah Orne Jewett, nor Mary E. Wilkins. He has made his dogma and it is as inflexible as the rulings of Torquemada. Criticism with him is an exploiting of his own preconceptions and aversions, not an honest following of the truth, lead where it may. I challenge, therefore, the author of "Prejudices" when he presents himself as juryman who shall weigh evidence and pass judgment.

Again, criticism is not written in superlatives, in "C Major"—a Menckenian term; criticism does not roar in Rooseveltian strenuousness, nor raise a plain x to x^2 nor, in the very face of the evidence, to x^{10}. One need not linger here long: read "Prejudices" or "Prefaces":

I myself am surely no disciple of the Polish tuberose [Chopin].—his sweetness, in fact, *gags me,* and I turn even to Moszkowski for relief.

One *ploughs through* "Innocents Abroad" and through parts of "A Tramp Abroad" with *incredulous amazement.*

All we have in the way of Civil War literature is a few conventional melodramas, a few half-forgotten short stories by Ambrose Bierce and Stephen Crane, and a half-dozen *idiotic* popular songs in the manner of Randall's "Maryland, My Maryland."

No sound art, in fact, *could possibly* be democratic. Tolstoi wrote a whole book to prove the contrary, and only succeeded in making his case *absurd.* The *only* art that is capable of reaching the *Homo Boobus* is art that is already debased and polluted—band music, official sculpture, Pears' Soap painting, the popular novel.

The italics, in every case except the *"Homo Boobus,"* are mine.

A critic is humble in the presence of the universe of things he can never know about his subject, toil hard as he may. Seldom may he be sophomorically final or autocratically dogmatic in his generalization, but in "Prejudices" and beyond it "a campus cock-sureness"—I thank thee Shylock, for that word—an *ipse dixit* assertiveness that is as if the

Thunderer himself had descended to deliver the verdict. One may open at random:

Beethoven suffered more during the composition of the Fifth symphony than *all the judges of the supreme benches of the world* have suffered jointly since the time of the Gerousia.

We have produced thus far but *one genuine wit—* Ambrose Bierce.

New England has never shown the *slightest sign* of a genuine enthusiam for ideas.

Observe Virginia to-day. It is years since a first-rate man, *save only Cabell,* has come out of it; it is years since *an idea* has come out of it.

To wade through the books of such characteristic American fictioners as Frances Hodgson Burnett, Mary E. Wilkins Freeman, F. Hopkinson Smith, Alice Brown, James Lane Allen, Winston Churchill, Ellen Glasgow, Gertrude Atherton and Sarah Orne Jewett is to undergo an experience that is almost *terrible.* The flow of words is *completely purged* of ideas.

Phelps cites in particular an ass named Professor Richardson, whose "American Literature," it appears, "is still a standard work" and "a deservedly high authority"—apparently in colleges. In the 1892 edition of this *magnum opus,* Mark [Twain] is dismissed with less than four lines, and ranked below Irving, Holmes and Lowell. . . . Mark is dismissed by this professor Balderdash as a hollow buffoon. . . . College professors, alas, never learn anything.

Again the italics are mine.

Let the last serve as the type. Richardson's history, Volume I, from which the offending judgment comes, was written in 1885, and the publishers finally bound up the original two parts of the work as a single volume in 1892. Is a man "an ass," a "professor Balderdash," who with the perspective of 1885, a full generation ago, when Mr. Mencken was five years old, placed Mark Twain below Irving, and Holmes and Lowell? If so, then Poe was an ass, and all other critics have been asses who have ventured upon a final rating of contemporaries. He proves the asininity of Richardson apparently from this single case. I think it was Emerson who once defined *genius* as the ability to generalize from a single example.

Mencken's undoubtedly is the most raucous and the most arresting voice that has been raised to protest against the weaknesses of the Age of O. Henry, yet in all his tones and methods he is himself of the O. Henry school. The journalist must "put his stuff across" or fail miserably, and Mr. Mencken preeminently is a journalist, with the journalist's perspective and the journalist's point of view. He knows only the city, the sophisticated set, the snob-

bishly intellectual, the perpetually bored; and to
gain their attention he must be smartly original,
brilliant, violent, arresting.   The most certain sol-
vent of boredom, he realizes, is humor; the O. Henry
type of humor completely up to date and smash-
ingly original.   And he is master of the humor that
is requisite; a humor more effective indeed than O.
Henry's, since it is less obviously a straining for
effect.   Seldom have I laughed audibly over a page
of O. Henry's, never over one of Irvin Cobb's,
but I chuckled aloud the first time I read this:

The finish of a civilian in a luxurious hospital, with
trained nurses fluttering over him and his pastor
whooping and heaving for him at the foot of the bed,
is often quite as terrible as any form of exitus witnessed in war.

The O. Henry likeness is largely a matter of style
and expression, a disregard for exactness and truth;
journalistic cleverness, vulgar sensation.   One may
open at random now: note the O. Henry paradox,
the O. Henry triplets, the O. Henry smartness:

A Scotch Presbyterian with a soaring soul is as
cruelly beset as a wolf with fleas, or a zebra with the
botts.   Let a spark of the divine fire spring to life in
that arid corpse, and it must fight its way to flame
through a drum fire of wet sponges.   A humming bird
immersed in *kartoffelsuppe*.   Walter Pater writing for
the London Daily Mail.   Lucullus travelling steerage.

He [Shaw], founded, in England the superstition that Ibsen was no more than a tin-pot evangelist—a sort of brother to General Booth, Mrs. Pankhurst and the syndics of the Sex Hygiene Society.

Here we have a situation in comedy almost exactly parallel to that in which a colored bishop whoops "Onward, Christian Soldiers!" like a calliope in order to drown out the crowing of the rooster concealed beneath his chasuble.

Down there [in Dixie] a poet is now almost as rare as an oboe-player, a dry-point etcher or a metaphysician. It is, indeed, amazing to contemplate so vast a vacuity.

Good health in man, indeed, is almost invariably a function of inferiority. A professionally healthy man, *e. g.,* an acrobat, an osteopath or an ice-wagon driver, is always stupid.

If that time ever comes, the manufacture of artists will become a feasible procedure, like the present manufacture of soldiers, capons, right-thinkers and doctors of philosophy.

The truth about Dreiser is that he is still in the transition stage between Christian Endeavor and civilization.

One by searching may find still smarter examples:

One would not be surprised to hear that, until he [George Ade] went off to his freshwater college, he slept in his underwear and read the Epworth Herald.

Oppenheim . . . stands, as to one leg, on the shoulders of Walt Whitman, and, as to the other, on a stack of Old Testaments.

It is a sort of college town *Weltanschauung* that one finds in him [Howells]; he is an Agnes Repplier in pantaloons.

Here [in Bennett's novels] we have a sweet commingling of virtuous conformity and complacent optimism, of sonorous platitude and easy certainty—here, in brief, we have the philosophy of the English middle classes—and here, by the same token, we have the sort of guff that the half-educated of our own country understand. It is the calm, superior numskullery that was Victorian; it is by Samuel Smiles out of Hannah More.

And this last from the author who finds in Poe "congenital vulgarity of taste":

This man, for all his grand dreams, had a shoddy soul; he belonged authentically to the era of cuspidors, "females," and Sons of Temperance.

It is unnecessary to comment. To some, perhaps, this is literary criticism. Perhaps.

IV

The professor is nothing if not a maker of card indexes; he must classify or be damned. His masterpiece is the dictum that "it is excellent, but it is not a play."

Yes, I am listening. But what if it is not excellent? what if it is labeled a play on its yellow jacket and made emphatic by adjectives in the superlative? What if it is sold as a play, and whooped up as a play on all the bill-boards, and reviewed as a play by all the reviewers, and what if it is not a play at all, but a mere vaudeville stunt? The whole transaction becomes then a sign of the times. It is felony under the pure food laws to brand a package "California honey" when it is Missouri corn syrup, even though the corn syrup is excellent. Am I concerned only with the name, only with niceties of technique, with manner and traditions? If that were all then I would deserve all the sarcasm that the tribe of Mencken has heaped upon my profession. The very foundations are in question. Criticism should be rulings of a supreme court of literature. Whatever else is extreme and impassioned, criticism should be serene; whatever else is distorted, criticism should be the truth. And Mencken, touch him where you will, is extreme and distorted. He leaves sacrifice and service out of his philosophy of life and thus reduces it to a mere zero. He is the Nietzsche of our literature, and of Nietzsche, as we have already quoted, "no charge was too far-fetched, no manipulation or interpretation of evidence was too daring, to enter into his ferocious indictment." He was not seeking the truth: he was hurling his dogmas.

Mencken is a journalist, and the curse of the journalist, as already we have seen, is that he has lost his horizon. His work he pitches ever to the almighty Now. He must be heard instantly: he must bring methods and materials startlingly new or see his work drop dead from the press. When he speaks he must speak in falsetto; when he means three he must say nine. When Mark Twain—a journalist to his finger tips—wished to convey the fact that the characters in Cooper's novels are stiff and wooden, he expressed it this way: it is impossible to tell in his novels the living people from the corpses save that the corpses are more lively. It is not true: it is farce, pure and simple, and not criticism, but "it is what you must write if you are to be read in these days." The journalist is prone to forget that the history of literature is the history of a long evolution, that there are fashions in literature as surely as there are fashions in dress, and that the fashions of 1850 are no more asinine than the fashions of 1922. Shall one call one's grandfather an ass because he enjoyed literature that to-day would not be accepted by "The Smart Set"? Mencken damns George William Curtis as a "shoddy mediocrity," but a generation ago Curtis was the Mencken of his time, the leader of the Mugwumps, champion stone-slinger at the Blaine Goliath.

The man, then, is a literary Nietzsche who has been evolved from American journalism during the age of O. Henry. I write of his failures not to try to reform him—that would be like preaching to Eugene Field in the presence of Nye and Riley: he would be pinning a tail on the solemn old ass and winking from behind his hand—I simply describe a literary disease of the times. · H. L. Mencken at forty is training a surprisingly large group of youngsters, who should be the future makers of American criticism, into a kind of literary jazz band. Their writings confront one everywhere. Pick up the latest assessment of our literature, "Letters on Contemporary American Authors," by MacCollough—Mencken and water. Follow it through the newer reviews. Just as the trail of O. Henry has been beaten into a highway through the jungle of the American short story, so the sensational vogue of Mencken is creating a new type of criticism. Is it to endure and become the type of the criticism of the next literary period? Is it to dominate the picture, or are we to-day simply living through a rag-time interlude?

Muck-raking may endure for a night, but the morning comes always swiftly. Destructive criticism is the most ephemeral of all literary things. It is narrowly limited by its very nature. It must have quick results or cease. The muck-rake era of twenty years ago, with its "shame of the cities" and "corrupt and contented," endured not long and is to-day forgotten. Undoubtedly it accomplished some good. An eruption of superlatives will rout certain classes of criminals often as effectively as a machine-gun. According to Mencken, it is the only way some intrenched lawbreakers may be reached. In an "Atlantic Monthly" paper he defends the fierce vice-scourgings and the furious boss-baitings periodically indulged in by the daily papers because of the positive results that often are achieved.

The white-slave agitation of a year or so ago was ludicrously extravagant and emotional, but its net effect is a better conscience, a new alertness. The newspapers discharged broadsides of 12-inch guns to bring down a flock of buzzards—but they brought down the buzzards. They have libeled and lynched the police—but the police are the better for it. They have represented salicylic as an elder brother to bichloride of mercury—but we are poisoned less than we used to be. They have lifted the plain people to frenzies of senseless terror over drinking-cups and neighbors with coughs—but the death-rate from tuberculosis declines. They have railroaded men to prison, denying them all the common rights—but fewer male-factors escape to-day than yesterday.

Agreed! It is like a Methodist sermon. But what do these methods accomplish when applied to the literary field? It is not a felony punishable under State or Federal statutes to write a "mushy" book. Harold Bell Wright or Henry Sydnor Harrison or Gene Stratton Porter cannot be convicted, after a newspaper hue and cry, and sent to prison for feeding literary "Peruna" to the willing multitude. There is no law on any of the statute-books to convict Robert W. Chambers of literary boot-legging and send him to the reformatory. No depths of denunciation, no machine-gun crackle of adjectives however hot and original, no expression of contempt of the twaddle-swallowing multitude however withering, no threatenings of hell however sulphurous will ever send these authors to the Menckenian mourners' benches, not at least while the multitude pays for their creations in figures that would delight a "patent" medicine manufac-turer.

But what of the mass itself, the abysmal brain-less monster that battens on Wright and Chambers and "Pollyanna" books—can this be reformed by our new literary Amos? Not in the slightest. The people, "the proletariat," "the masses," do not read him; they could not were it to save their lives read a line of him. I lent "Prefaces" to a sophomore, and he said it certainly "stumped him": he could not find, he said, all the words even in the dictionary. "Prefaces" is for the few, not for the herd.

And what of the few, the "saving remnant," "the forlorn *intelligentsia*," some of them professors, many of them book reviewers, some of them publishers' readers, some of them decayed old "Atlantic" Brahmans? What can he accomplish by harrying this bedeviled little forlorn hope? The herd can be stampeded into violence of many kinds, but it cannot be driven with a rush to higher literary levels. America is paying the penalty inseparable from democracy. To compel *all* the people of a nation to attend school until into their teens, their late teens in some States, to lift the *totality* of the mass—all of it—up toward the reading level, means inevitably the bringing down of the literature of that nation toward this average plane. Literature until democratic times, until yesterday in fact, was an aristocratic thing, made by the inspired few for the civilized few who could enjoy and comprehend it. Mencken, so far as literature is concerned, has never been democratized. Read his "Men versus the Man." His contempt for the literary crudeness of the democratic mass, and for those who prostitute their powers in order to fatten upon its demands, is the source of much of his sarcasm. But American democracy is what it is. Shall we ignore the mass, have a distinctive literature worthy of the civilized few, and be as oblivious of what the "Homo Boobus" reads as we are of what he eats? Who will have the powers and the sacrificing soul to write it? Literature has become a commercial product. When prepared for the mass which has learned to read in our schools and colleges, it means for its creator motor-cars, and winters in Florida, and country estates, but when made on the high classic levels of beauty and art it means the attic and celibacy, and, if fame finally, then posthumous fame. To raise the mass to the appreciation of real art requires time: it is a matter of evolution. It cannot be done by shouting and reviling or arguing. To stand and damn a mud-turtle will not make him a sprinter. Only remove the obstructions that hinder him, and be patient; he will get there in time.

Why then all this sound and fury? It accomplishes nothing worth the accomplishing. It furnishes entertainment to a few sophisticated souls who have exhausted the round of sensations, and it provokes a few devil-ridden professors to retort, but that is all. It is a tempest in a Volstead beer-mug; it is a wicked new home-brew, strangely exhilarating at first, but requiring, like a narcotic, ever a stronger and stronger dose. X must be raised to x^2, then to x^9, and then to x^n. There is small variety in the Mencken box of tricks, as small as in Irvin Cobb's, and the show is beginning to tire one by its monotony. Like O. Henry's work it deadens its readers for the more subtle tones of art. Moreover, it creates nothing: its whole course is destructive. At the close of his "Yale Review" diagnosis of the ailments afflicting our "National Letters" he can bring only this consolation to the patient: "I have described the disease. Let me say at once that I have no remedy to offer." He has revealed to the astounded sufferer that he has cholera infantum, rubeola, pink-eye, and cerebral peritonitis, but he refuses to prescribe even a palliative, and he will not suggest to the patient even that he smile serenely and say at frequent intervals, "I am in perfect health."

At forty comes the philosophic mind. Is it too much to hope that a Sainte Beuve may be lurking under this vulgar and furiously erupting Stromboli? Is it stretching credulity too far to believe that real meat may at last come out of this ferocious eater of men—even "Causeries du Lundi," penetrating, brilliant, constructive? May we not even hope that the fires of romance, genuine romance, still smoldering, we believe, smokily in this crematory furnace,

may yet flame up clear and produce for us creative
work, rather than destructive work unworthy of
his undoubted powers? And may we not address
him even as he addressed the wavering Kipling
when he also was hovering about forty:

Unsung the East lies glimmering,
Unsung the palm-trees toss their frills,
Unsung the seas their splendours fling
  The while you prate of laws and tills.
  Each man his destiny fulfils:
Can it be yours to loose and stray,
  In sophist garb to wash your quills—
Sing us again of Mandalay.

Master, regard the plaint we bring
  And hearken to the prayer we pray.
Lay down your law and sermoning,
  Sing us again of Mandalay.

THE PROPHET OF THE LAST FRONTIER [1]

FROM the first year of the new century, when he burst upon the consciousness of the reading world, until the year before America entered the World War, when he as suddenly disappeared, for sixteen years Jack London, like an unheralded comet, shocked and horrified and thrilled the American people. That the majority of them liked to be shocked and thrilled and horrified is shown by the demand for his work. A stream of checks from more than eighty different magazines poured in upon him; six of the foremost publishing houses of America were eager to gamble on the financial coup that might come from his next book, and he gave them forty-eight chances; forty-eight books in sixteen years, some of them heading the list of the best sellers of their period. The sixteen years were his. He was the startling figure in that loud-voiced, Kipling-swayed *fin de siècle* decade before the war; the voice crying in the wilderness, "Make ready for the reign of the brute"; the ax laid at the foot of

[1] Delivered before the Phi Beta Kappa of Ohio Wesleyan University, March 16, 1922.

98

the tree of sickly sentiment and effeminate swash-
buckling romance and the "mollycoddle" life. He
learned his art of Kipling and of Gogol, and he
wrote in the Presidency of Theodore Roosevelt, in
the era of the strenuous life. From Jack London
learn of Jack Londonism, learn the spirit of the
epoch that could make him possible. No other
American writer has had a career more representative of his time; none certainly has had one that
is more remarkable.

To study Jack London is to be impressed first
of all with his (Americanism.) He was as indigenous as Mark Twain; the culmination of a century
and a half on American soil, a figure impossible
save in the California of the opening decade of the
twentieth century. His family, both sides of it,
was of old American stock: English adventurers
with a dash of Puritanism, Welsh settlers in New
Jersey, Teutonic refugees in Pennsylvania, the most
restless souls of a restless age. They fought in
all the wars, they surged westward with the settlement, they lived in emigrant trains, they were mas-
sacred by Indians, they were in all the perils of that
century-long march across the continent. One of
them, "Priest" Jones, tarried behind in Ohio as a
circuit-rider through regions where physical prowess
was the chief prerequisite for spreading the Gospel,
and he became the grandfather of our novelist. By

the time of the Civil War both branches of the family had reached the Gold Coast, but they had got no gold. With empires all about them to be had for the taking, they were pressing excitedly on for something better.

In more than one of his books London has pictured this iron race from which he sprang. "The Valley of the Moon" is the epic of the descendants of the Argonauts halted in their westward march by the Pacific, too restless to settle down, and allowing their hard-won prize to be taken from them by the more patient tribes of toilers and grubbers for whom they had broken the way. And the race had degenerated into dreamers, revolutionists, bolshevists, aimless adventurers. The father of Jack London, instead of settling upon lands that easily would have brought him wealth, had turned northward from the westward march and had spent his young manhood as a trapper and adventurer in the Canadian wilds. London's super-man *Jacob Wilse* in "A Daughter of the Snows" is an idealized picture of him.

The trapper father had come out of the sturdy Welsh stock which had trickled into early Ohio out of the jostling East, and the mother was a nomadic daughter of the Irish emigrant settlers of Ontario. From both sides came the wanderlust of the blood, the fever to be moving, **to be** pushing on to the edge of *things.*

In 1873 he was in San Francisco, a member of the police force, and here it was that three years later, January 12, 1876, was born his tenth child. Jack London, the most restless soul of all his restless line. He was reared in a nursery for restlessness: his first years were a perpetual moving-day. When he was four, the family was living on a truck farm in Alameda; three years later they were on a desolate ranch in San Mateo County, south of San Francisco. The squalid moving scene burned itself into the lad's memory: "We had horses and a farm wagon," he tells us, "and onto this we piled all our household belongings, all hands climbing up on the top of the load, and with the cow tied on behind." A desolate region at best, to the solitary boy it was lonely beyond description. "Ours was the only American family. I had no companions." A year later the scene changed to a truck farm at Livermore. "I was very much alone. Had I been as other children, 'blessed' with brothers and sisters and plenty of playmates, I should have been mentally occupied, grown up as the rest of my class grew, become a laborer and been content. But I was alone, very much so. This fostered contemplation."

Until his eleventh year there was nothing in his life to refine him or to quicken his powers. No childhood could have been more squalid: "I never had toys nor playthings like other children. My first memories of life were pinched by poverty." Forced to a round of labor that he hated, driven in upon himself, he became dwarfed in all save the physical, but this, as if to compensate, became at length perfect. Everything in his life watered and fertilized the wild individualism that was his birth-right: it bred day-dreaming and discontent, an Indian-like impatience of control, and that wild sense of freedom to work his solitary will which is the heritage of the border-born. Of the religious and the moral in his early training there was nothing and worse than nothing. He was reared in an atmosphere of coarseness: "All the inconceivable filth a child running at large in a primitive country-side may hear men utter was mine." A little schooling there was, ludicrously narrow and crude, and a few books: "dime novels borrowed from the hired men," Irving's "Alhambra," a life of Garfield, du Chaillu's African travels—that was all. At eight he chanced upon a mutilated copy of Ouida's novel "Signa" and was thrilled and set to day-dreaming by its opening sentence: "It was only a little lad, but he had dreams of becoming a great musician, and having all Europe at his feet."

When he was ten came the final move of the family, this time to Oakland—a veritable new world for the starved lad. Now he could attend the public schools and draw books from the city library. At first he plunged into an orgy of reading, but without knowledge of books or guidance. "Nobody at home bothered their heads over what I read. I was an eager, thirsty, hungry little kid." Juveniles he passed in contempt. He wanted books telling of life in the world of action of which he had dreamed. He read books like Prescott's "Conquest of Peru"; and records of voyages into the great ocean that lay beyond the Golden Gate.

But time for reading grew ever more and more limited. The family poverty had flung him literally into the streets, and in hours out of school, on Saturdays and Sundays, he worked as he could find jobs; setting up pins in bowling-alleys, assisting on ice-wagons, sweeping out saloons, and selling newspapers. When he was eleven he was given a newspaper route along the water-front of the city, then as now the Tenderloin of Oakland. Here his education moved rapidly. He became a member, then leader of a boys' gang, and then the most notorious fighter in his district: his fight with the slum gamin "Cheese Face," as narrated in "Martin Eden," was as primitive and as ferocious as even the dog-fight in "White Fang." Soon he grew to be precociously wise in the lore of street and saloon; he knew the dives of the water-front, in Oakland and San Francisco, the last frontier in the march across the continent, where, halted by the Pacific, so many of the Argonauts had abandoned their dreams and had settled down to rottenness and despair or else had turned their restlessness into lawlessness and piracy on the bay.

Upon completing the work of the grammar grade, he considered his school days over. He had enlarged the field of his restlessness. "When I was fourteen," to quote his own words, "my head filled with the tales of the old voyagers, my visions with tropic isles and far sea-rims, I was sailing a small centerboard skiff around San Francisco Bay and on the Oakland estuary. I wanted to go to sea. I wanted to get away from monotony and the commonplace. I was in the flower of my adolescence, a-thrill with romance and adventure, dreaming of wild life in the wild man-world. . . . And the winds of adventure blew the oyster pirate sloops up and down San Francisco Bay, from raided oyster beds and fights at night on shoal and flat, to markets in the morning against city wharves where peddlers and saloon-keepers came down to buy."

For a time he found work in a salmon cannery

but his blood revolted at the drudgery. There was no withstanding the restless desire within him to be off and away, and impulsively, with the savings of his black mammy gladly lent to him, he bought himself a sloop, the *Razzle-Dazzle*, hired a crew of one man, "Spider Healey," "a black-whiskered wharf-rat of twenty," and joined the poachers who lived by night raids upon the oyster-beds of the lower bay. No longer would he live at home: he slept in the cabin of his sloop like other pirates and was at home upon the bay. Again his progress was rapid. By his skill and ingenuity and dare-devil fearlessness he became in true dime-novel fashion leader of the gang: "When I was sixteen I had earned the title of 'Prince,' but this title was given me by a gang of cutthroats and thieves, by whom I was called 'The Prince of the Oyster Pirates.'" He was sailing partner now of the heroes of the bay: "Clam" and "Young Scratch Nelson." "Clam was a dare-devil, but Nelson was a reckless maniac. He was twenty years old with the body of a Hercules. When he was shot in Bernicia a couple of years later, the coroner said he was the greatest-shouldered man he had ever laid on a slab." It was fame to be accounted the equal and the superior of men like these. After a mad exploit he was invited to the bar by the father of "Young Scratch" himself. Fame indeed!

" 'Old Scratch' was a blue-eyed, yellow-haired, raw-boned Viking, big-bodied and strong-muscled despite his age. And he had sailed the seas in ships of all nations in the old savage sailing days. . . . His nickname 'Scratch' arose from a Berserker trick of his, in fighting, of tearing off his opponent's face." To get the full madness of the period one must read "John Barleycorn." His wild exploits are still remembered. "Along the Oakland water-front," writes one who knew him at that period, "the old salts will even now be recounting ripping tales of the 'young dare-devil London' who could drink any man down at the bar, and knock any two of them down at once who had the temerity to refuse his invitation to 'line-up.' "

At seventeen, to use his own words, he was "a drunken bum." "I practically lived in saloons, became a bar-room loafer and worse. For weeks at a time I did not draw a sober breath." And all this because of the heritage of his race, because of his starved boyhood, and his eagerness to live what he conceived to be the life of a man. "I was just human, and I was taking the path in the world that men took—men whom I admired if you please: full-blooded men, lusty, breedy, chesty men, free spirits, and anything but niggard in the way they foamed life away." His philosophy at this period is the philosophy of the water-front saloon: "Better to reign among booze-fighters, a prince, than to toil twelve hours a day at a machine for ten cents an hour. There are no purple passages in machine toil, but if the spending of $180 in two hours is n't a purple passage, then I 'd like to know what is."

The road is a short one. All that saved him was that very restlessness of his race which had brought him into the danger, and that thrill of romance in his blood which had come from a century and a half of wandering toward the west, for that winter there came to the Oakland saloons "the skippers, mates, hunters, boat-steerers, and boat-pullers of the sealing fleet wintering in San Francisco Bay." Their tales of adventure fired his besotted imagination until in January, 1893, when he was seventeen, he signed for a voyage in the three-topmast sealing schooner *Sophe Sutherland* to the North Pacific and Japan. It was a turning-point in his career. Coming back in August, the liquor driven from his system by the seven months' cruise, he was horrified to find that most of his boon companions were either dead or in prison. Impulsively he found a job, resolved to listen to his mother's advice and consider his wild oats sown. The winter he spent first in a jute mill, and then in a boiler-room as a coal-beaver, but the work became steadily more intolerable, until one day when the springtime was opening he dropped everything by a sudden impulse

Kelley'

and boarded a freight-car with Coxey's army bound for the East. "I became a tramp, begging my way from door to door, wandering over the United States and Canada sweating bloody sweats in slums and prisons. I was in the pit, the abyss, the human cesspool, the shambles and the charnel-house of our civilization." He went not at all to study sociology as did Josiah Flint. "I became a tramp," he explains, "because of the life that was in me, of the wanderlust in my blood that would not let me rest; because I could not keep away from it."

The Jack London that the world knows dates from this experience; it was while tramping with tramps that Jack London awoke. He was in his nineteenth year; his whole life had contained nothing that had not fed his rampant individualism. "I could see myself only raging through life without end like one of Nietzsche's *blond beasts,* lustfully roving and conquering by sheer superiority and strength." But suddenly he found himself in a world of which he had never dreamed. "On rods and blind baggages I fought my way from the open West where men bucked big and the job hunted the man, to the congested labor centres of the East where men were small potatoes and hunted the job for all they were worth. On this new *blond beast* adventure I found myself looking upon life from a new and totally different angle." He was converted—"reborn" as he has expressed it—to the doctrine of socialism, which to him in those early days meant simply a square deal for the under dog. In his contacts with worn-out laborers on city benches, men who had once been just as "blond beastly" as he and who now were mere rubbish on the dumps of a city, he made the discovery that the rewards of the world go, not to the muscle-workers, but to the brain-worker. It stirred his imagination: something awoke within him. "I resolved to sell no more muscle, and to become a vender of brains. Then began a frantic pursuit of knowledge. I returned to California and opened the books."

For a year he was a student in the Oakland High School, paying his way by working as janitor and spending all of his spare time reading or else preaching in the parks his new gospel of socialism. The slow pace of the school disgusted him: it would be two years more before he could enter the University of California, and characteristically he wanted to enter at once. To think was to act. "I gritted my teeth and started to cram myself. There were three months yet before the university entrance examinations. Without laboratories, without coaching, sitting in my bed-room, I proceeded to compress that two years' work into three months and to keep reviewed on the previous year's work.

Nineteen hours a day I studied. For three months I kept this pace, only breaking it on several occasions." And he passed the examinations. Some have declared that the swift, super-man-like progress of London's hero *Martin Eden* was an impossible feat, but London swept away all such objections by the single statement: "I was *Martin Eden*. At the end of three working years, two of which were spent in high school and university, and all three in studying intensely and immensely, I was publishing stories in magazines such as 'The Atlantic Monthly,' was correcting proofs of my first book, issued by Houghton, Mifflin & Co., and selling sociological articles to the 'Cosmopolitan' and 'McClure's'."

He remained in the university a little more than a semester, leaving in January, 1897. "The pressure from lack of money, plus a conviction that the university was not giving me all that I wanted in the time that I could spare for it, forced me to leave." He had determined to make a writer of himself, and with characteristic impetuosity he sought the nearest way. His comments on university methods are enlightening:

I had to unlearn about everything the teachers and professors of literature of the high school and university had taught me. I was very indignant about

this at the time; though now I can understand it.
They did not know the trick of successful writing in
the years of 1895 and 1896. They knew all about
'Snow-Bound' and 'Sartor Resartus'; but the American editors of 1899 did not want such truck. They
wanted the 1899 truck, and offered to pay so well for
it that the teachers and professors of literature
would have quit their jobs could they have supplied it.

By sheer main force he would teach himself the
writing art and would enter the literary profession
as he had entered the university—perchance in three
months. He would take the kingdom of letters
by storm. "Heavens, how I wrote! The way I
worked was enough to soften my brain and send me
to a mad-house. I wrote, I wrote everything—
ponderous essays, scientific and sociological, short
stories, humorous verse, verse of all sorts from triolets and sonnets to blank verse tragedy and elephan-
tine epics in Spenserian stanzas." His manuscripts
were returned as regularly as they were sent out,
but like *Martin Eden* he toiled on.

In the midst of these efforts there came, like a
repetition of the days of '49' sudden news of a
gold strike in the Klondike region of Alaska, and
as impulsively as he had joined Coxey's army, he
was off with the first wave of adventurers. A
year later, compelled by an attack of scurvy, he

fought his way out in an open boat, a 1900-mile trip down the Yukon made in nineteen days. Arriving in Oakland, he found that his father had died and that the care of the family had shifted to his shoulders. Work was scarce; in desperation he turned again to literary efforts and during the following three or four years he fought the battle for recognition that he has described, undoubtedly in heightened terms, in "Martin Eden." Whatever one may think of his literary product, one can but admire the pluck and the perseverance that brought his final success. No one ever succeeded with heavier odds, and no one with more of toil. His first recognition came in January, 1899, when "The Overland Monthly" of San Francisco published his first story "The Man on Trail," following it during the year with seven other Alaska stories. Then "The Atlantic Monthly," repeating the Bret Harte episode of thirty years before, accepted his story, "An Odyssey of the North," and early in 1900 issued the nine tales under the title, "The Son of the Wolf." Success, however, was far from won: his first five books were issued by five different publishing houses. It was not until 1903, with his sixth book, "The Call of the Wild," that he may be said fairly to have arrived as a writer of fiction.

II

With this introduction one is prepared in a measure for the after career of the man, the career that made picturesque the opening years of the new century, the swift era before the German explosion. Such a nature must have constant stimulus, adventure, movement. Now he is in the slums of London in rags and without money to study the conditions of the underworld of the modern Babylon. He emerged with pictures so extreme that they outraged the sensibilities of all who read them.

Strange vagrant odors come drifting along the greasy wind, and the rain, when it falls, is more like grease than water from heaven. The very cobblestones are scummed with grease.

. . . We went up the narrow gravelled walk. On the benches on either side was arrayed a mass of miserable and distorted humanity, the sight of which would have impelled Doré to more diabolical flights of fancy than he ever succeeded in achieving. It was a welter of rags and filth, of all manner of loathsome skin diseases, open sores, bruises, grossness, indecency leering monstrosities, and bestial faces. A chill raw wind was blowing, and these creatures huddled there in their rags, sleeping for the most part, or trying to sleep.

When the season for picking hops comes around for two or three weeks all the slum dwellers who can possibly get loose from London, "their guts a-reek with pavement offal," flock like vultures into Kent:

Out they come, obedient to the call, which is the call of their bellies and of the lingering dregs of adventure-lust still in them. Slum, stews, and ghetto pour them forth, and the festering contents of slum, stews, and ghetto are undiminished. They overrun the country like an army of ghouls, and the country does not want them. They are out of place. As they drag their squat, misshapen bodies along the highways and by-ways, they resemble some vile spawn from underground. Their very presence, the fact of their existence, is an outrage to the fresh bright sun and the green and growing things. The clean, up-standing trees cry shame upon them and their withered crookedness, and their rottenness is a slimy desecration of the sweetness and purity of nature.

His life was a succession of rapid changes: everything, like his pictures of the People of the Abyss, always in extreme. Now he is in the Far East as war correspondent; now he is in Mexico. He will make a journey around the world in his own boat especially made after his own specifications, and to pay for it he will pour out feverishly story after story. He will have a ranch that is a veritable kingdom: there shall be planted thirty thousand eucalyptus-trees, there shall be a big house, and there shall be great herds of choicest stock, and again the feverish writing of stories and magazine articles and letters hot-footed to his publishers for advances upon royalties. The mere quantity of his work is staggering. In the sixteen years of his literary life he wrote nineteen complete novels, eighteen short story collections with a total of 152 stories, three plays, and eight other books, auto-biographical or sociological—forty-eight volumes already in print, besides six or eight others to be collected from the periodicals or from unpublished manuscripts.

After the quantity one is next surprised by the heterogeneousness of his output, its unevenness of texture and of content, its vagaries, its wide domain of subject. To read Jack London straight through is to emerge in confusion: a swift-running film of vignette-like pictures; hobbies furiously ridden; headlong narrative; wild snapshots of jungle and borealis, of naked head-hunters and fur-muffled dog.drivers. Everywhere superlatives and extremes; everywhere antithesis: soap-box shrillness and har-monious music; poverty of style and sonorous or-nateness; vulgarity, sublimity; realism, romanticism; brutality and humanitarianism; always superlatives and exaggerations in wild riot—the astonishing hodgepodge we call Jack London's writings.

If we do not understand the man it is not because he has not put himself upon record. His confessions bewilder us by their quantity and by their brutal frankness. How dare one open one's soul as he has done in "John Barleycorn" and "The Road"? He does not apologize, he does not qualify the record wtth extenuation, he does not even present the story as a warning to others. "The Road," for instance, is an amazing book: the point of view from cover to cover is that of the hobo. Organized society is a thing to be preyed upon with as clear a conscience as one would have in preying upon the wild forest for its fruits and its game. He goes into detail about the web of lies unblushingly told kind-hearted old ladies who pitied him, lies told the police, lies told along every mile of ten thousand miles of road, and he does it with the air of one who expects to be applauded for his smartness. He can even hold up his hobo period with commendation as a seminar in which he learned the art of fiction. "Art is only consummate artfulness," he says, and by artfulness he means lying with imagination and artistic detail. And he illustrates the point with the story of how he escaped from the police court in Winnipeg, by telling on the impulse of the moment a detailed and realistic story of his escape from the hell-ship *Glenmore*. So adroitly and creatively did he lie, he declares, that a veteran sailor who was called in as an expert to cross-examine him could find no flaws. "The successful hobo must be an artist. He must create spontaneously and instantaneously—and not upon a theme selected from the plenitude of his own imagination, but upon the theme he reads in the face of the person who opens the door, be it man, woman, or child, sweet or crabbed, generous or miserly."

To read any of London's work is to be in the presence of his own biography: few authors have drawn so freely upon their own experiences for literary material. We know every phase of his life: "Martin Eden," "The Game," "The Valley of the Moon," "The Little Lady of the Big House" are autobiographical in their revelations. He was as egocentric as Byron. All his characters—*Jacob Wilse, Wolf Larsen, Martin Eden, Burning Daylight, Billy Roberts, Dick Forest*—are Jack London in masquerade, or Jack London as he dreamed of himself. Like Byron's, his imagination was kindled only by life translated into his own experience.

His confessions help us to classify him. We know that he was not a genius driven to creation by fires within him: he was a journalist. He selected literature deliberately as a profession and learned it as one learns a trade. Speaking of himself as *Martin Eden,* he discloses the method of his training:

Reading the books of men who had arrived, he noted every result achieved by them, and worked out the tricks by which they had been achieved—the tricks of narrative, of exposition, of style, the points of view, the contrasts, the epigrams; and of all of these he made lists for study. He did not ape: he sought principles. He drew up lists of effective and fetching mannerisms, till out of many such, culled from many writers, he was able to educe the general principles of mannerism, and, thus equipped, he cast about for new and original ones of his own, and to weigh and measure and appraise them properly.

And so on and on. Thus in cold blood he learned his trade, and as he learned it he tested and studied his market, like a manufacturer of collars or a maker of breakfast-foods. What did the literary market demand in 1898? Listen to *Max Irwin* in London's story, "Amateur Night":

Get the atmosphere, the color, strong color, lots of it. Dig right in with both hands, and get the essence of it, the spirit, the significance. What does it mean? Find out what it means. That's what you're there for. That's what the readers of the "Sunday Intelligencer" want to know. Be terse in style, vigorous of phrase, apt, concretely apt, in similitude. Avoid commonplaces and platitudes. Exercise selection.

Seize upon things salient, eliminate the rest, and you have pictures. Paint these pictures in words—the "Intelligencer" will have you. Put a snapper at the end, so if they are crowded for space they can cut off your contents anywhere, reattach the snapper, and the story will still retain form.

Thus did Jack London, vagabond and adventurer, make himself into a literary artist.

III

It was his Alaska stories that gave him his first hearing. He had the good fortune to speak at the one moment when all would listen. In 1898 the imagination of the world had been stirred by the Klondike gold strike, and everywhere there was demand for material that was concrete, circumstantial, hot from first-hand observation. Of London's first six books all save one, a juvenile in "St. Nicholas," were tales of the Alaska gold fields, vivid with pictures, breathing everywhere actuality; and it is upon these five—"The Son of the Wolf," "The God of His Fathers," "A Daughter of the Snows," "Children of the Frost," and "The Call of the Wild," the last issued in 1903—that his ultimate fame must rest. All are of short story texture: even the novel "A Daughter of the Snows" is a series of episodes, and "The Call of the Wild" might have for its sub-title "Seven Episodes in the Life of the Dog Buck."

His method was the method of Kipling, as Kipling's had been that of Bret Harte. He would present a field new to literature by means of startling pictures; swift scenes flashed upon a screen with emphasis, even to exaggeration, upon the unique and unusual. Everywhere Bret Harte paradoxes: *Hay Stockard* is accused by the missionary of breaking all the commandments, and he is a blasphemer until "From the slipping of a snow-shoe thong to the forefront of sudden death his Indian wife would gauge the occasion by the pitch and volume of his blasphemy," and yet he dies rather than renounce the God of his Puritan fathers. In all this early fiction the rush of the narrative is compelling and the seeming fidelity to nature in the background convincing. For instance the opening chapters of "A Daughter of the Snows," picturing the landing in Alaska of *Frona Wilse,* the baggage-strewn beach, the excited mob gathering for the march, the horrors of the long trail, the discarded dunnage and crippled victims strewn along the miles, the squalid night camps, and over it all the madness and lure of the goal that stripped men to the primitive elements of character—all this the reader accepts without question as a living document in the history of a vanished era.

We are won at the start by the positiveness of the author. We must take him on faith: few of us know how civilized men behave in the areas beyond the bounds of civilization, how men die of starvation, how dogs deport themselves in the Arctic night. He tells us in minute detail, with Defoe-like concreteness of touch upon touch. But are we certain it *is* the truth? We are not. He is no more a realist than was Harte. Like Harte he is writing from memory and imagination the story of a vanished period, a brief and picturesque day in a new environment, where youth is supreme and alone, and his fancy hovers over it fondly, and paints it and exaggerates it and idealizes it even to romance.

It was a weird scene; an anachronism. To the south the nineteenth century was reeling off the few years of its last decade; here flourished man primeval, a shade removed from the prehistoric cave-dweller, a forgotten fragment of the Elder World. The tawny wolf-dogs sat between their skin-clad masters or fought for room, the firelight cast backward from their red eyes and slavered fangs. The woods in ghostly shroud, slept on unheeding. The White Silence, for the moment driven to the rimming forest, seemed ever crushing inward;

the stars danced with great leaps, as is their wont in the time of the Great Cold; while the Spirits of the Pole trailed their robes of glory athwart the heavens.

His characters are not actual men whom he has himself seen and known: they are demigods, the unsung heroes of a heroic age now put into epic setting. For all of them might be inscribed the epithet given to one: "So, many an unsung wanderer fought his last and died under the cold fires of the Aurora, as did his brothers in burning sands and reeking jungles, and as they shall continue to do till the fulness of time and the destiny of their race be achieved."

Moreover, he adds to this the romance of a fading race. He dates "The God of His Fathers" at "the moment when the stone age was drawing to a close." His Indian women are a remarkable group: *Ruth,* wife of *Mason,* in "The White Silence"; *Madeline* in "An Odyssey of the North"; *Unga* in "The Wife of a King"; *Passuk,* wife of *Sitka Charley; Zarniska,* wife of *Scruff Mackensie; Sipsu,* the Chief's daughter, in "Where the Trail Forks"; and *Killisnoo,* wife of *Tomm,* introduced with the remark: "Takes a woman to breed a man. Takes a she-cat not a cow to mother a tiger." By no means are they realistic studies. They are drawn from imagination rather than from notes made after observation; they are the type of primi-

tive super-woman their author's imagination delighted in—*Jees Uck* for instance, with her "great
blazing black eyes—the half-caste eye, round, full-
orbed, and sensuous," or *Winapie,* the Koyokuk girl,
whom *Philip Payne* married and was true to even
when the San Francisco belle, once his fiancée,
came to Alaska to find him:

Eyes piercing black and large, with a traditionary
hint of obliqueness, looked forth from under clear-
stencilled, clean-arching brows. Without suggesting
cadaverousness, though high-boned and prominent, the
cheeks fell away and met in a mouth, thin-lipped and
softly strong. It was a face which advertised the
dimmest trace of ancient Mongol blood, after long
centuries of wandering, to the parent stem. This effect
was heightened by the delicately aquiline nose with its
thin trembling nostrils, and by the general air of eagle
wildness which seemed to characterize not only the
face, but the creature herself. She was in fact, the
Tartar type modified to idealization, and the tribe of
Red Indian is lucky that breeds such a unique body
once in a score of generations.

Romanticized and overdrawn as unquestionably
they are, nevertheless these women are the most
vital and convincing of all Jack London's characters.
They are his only additions to the gallery of original
characters in American fiction. Their doglike fidelity and honesty, their loyalty and self-sacrifice, their
primitive resourcefulness in danger and privation,

excite unconsciously our admiration and our pity.

It is not too sweeping to say that the primary purpose of all London's early fiction was pictorial. He would reproduce for us the White North. Everywhere pictures, flash-lights not only upon the surfaces of the scene but into the heart and meaning of it. One might fill a book with vignettes as sharply cut as figures in a frieze:

It was midday. To the south, just clearing the bleak Henderson Divide, poised the cold-disked sun. On either hand the sun-dogs blazed. The air was a gossamer of glittering frost. In the foreground, beside the trail, a wolf-dog, bristling with frost, thrust a long snout heavenward and moaned.

Or again:

Overhead, the Aurora, a gorgeous wanton, flaunted miracles of color, beneath lay the sleeping town. Far below, a solitary dog gave tongue. The king again began to speak, but the Kid pressed his hand for silence. The sound multiplied. Dog after dog took up the strain till the full-throated chorus swayed the night. To him who hears for the first time this weird song, is told the first and greatest secret of the Northland; to him who has heard it often, it is the solemn knell of lost endeavor. It is the plaint of tortured souls, for in it is invested the heritage of the North, the sufferings of countless generations—the warning and the requiem to the world's estrays.

And this voice of the wild he has tried to interpret. He would, like Thoreau, peer behind the scene and catch a glimpse of the sources of it.

With the Aurora Borealis flaming coldly overhead, or the stars leaping in the frost dance, and the land numb and frozen under its pall of snow, this song of the huskies might have been the defiance of life, only it was pitched in minor key, with long-drawn wailings and half-sobs, and was more the pleading of life, the articulate travail of existence. It was an old song, old as the breed itself—one of the first songs of the younger world in a day when songs were sad. It was invested with the woe of unnumbered generations, this plaint by which Buck was so strangely stirred. When he moaned and sobbed, it was with the pain of living that was of old the pain of his wild fathers, and the fear and mystery of the cold and dark that was to them fear and mystery. And that he should be stirred by it marked the completeness with which he harked back through the ages of fire and roof to the raw beginnings of life in the howling ages.

His affinity is with Conrad; with him he might have said, "My task which I am trying to achieve is, by the power of the written word, to make you hear, to make you feel—it is, before all, to make you *see.*"

He achieved this end most fully in "The Call of the Wild," the crowning work of his first period and indeed of his whole career. [His zest of life is in it and the undiminished enthusiasm of youth. It is his most perfect balance between the realistic and the romantic.] There are no digressions; there is no social philosophy protuberant and no propaganda. One who reads it surrenders to the romance of the North as completely as one surrenders to the romance of medievalism when one reads Scott. Its success was instantaneous as it should have been; from the moment it first appeared its author's literary place was secure in all the English-speaking world. Jack London had arrived: and yet, even as we say this, we must add that the very year of his arrival is the date of the beginning of his literary decline.

The causes of this decline lay in the author's temperament and in the nature of his literary field. In reality, after the first five books, he exhausted his Alaska claim; his lode petered out. Harte and even Kipling had discovered that to confine oneself to the recording of a primitive society is soon to run out of material. London had added nothing to Harte's outfit save a new set of drop scenery, a new fresh vigor of treatment, and a Gogol-like gruesomeness of detail, and these now had grown familiar. But the enormous vogue of "The Call of the Wild" gave him at once new latitude. He cleared his desk of early material—"The Faith of Men," "The War of the Classes," "Moon Face,"

and the like—and then began to write as he pleased:
his market allowed it. By nature and training he
was an extreme idealist; a revolutionist, indeed.
The blood of "Priest" Jones, the circuit-rider, was
in his veins. He, too, was a preacher, though not
of conventional religion, which to him was anath-
ema, but of an individualistic brand of social philosophy. From this time on he was constantly astride
of hobbies, some of which he rode furiously. He
had discovered in his tumultuous reading the evolu-
tionary theory, the recapitulation theory, Gogol,
Spencer, Karl Marx, Nietzsche. At the time of
his death he was, to quote his wife's words, "enormously interested in psychoanalysis," and had he
lived would have written a series of novels concerned with "research into the primitive, into the
noumenon of things, in order to understand the
becoming of what man is to-day," novels undoubtedly of the type of "The Star Rover."

He rode his theories into the fiction of this period
with the unction of the novitiate who has discovered
what to him is a new world. He would entertain
his readers, but he would teach them at the same
time; he would reform the world while it believed
it was playing. He has explained his theory in
"Martin Eden":

Apparently it was to be a rattling sea story, a tale of

twentieth century adventure and romance, handling real characters, in a real world, under real conditions. But beneath the swing and go of the story was to be something else—something that the superficial reader would never discern and which, on the other hand, would not diminish in any way the interest and enjoyment for such a reader. It was this, and not the mere story, that impelled Martin to write it.

His theory is wrong. To realize how wrong it is one needs but to read "The Sea Wolf." The story begins tremendously: the opening chapters are as moving as anything in American fiction, but before it has reached its middle point its failure is so apparent that it is used in college classes as one of the best examples to be found of extreme faultiness in novel construction. It was so with all his later novels, "Burning Daylight," for example, brilliant as it occasionally is in episode, is a mass of materials for fiction rather than a novel. The first half of it might be called "Miscellaneous Adventures in the Life of a Super-man": his way of celebrating his birthday, his record-trip with the Yukon Mail, his fight with starvation, his discovery of Klondike gold, his adventure with the stock market, his sensational hold-up of the New York brokers, etc. The heroine, as in "The Sea Wolf," is not introduced until the story is half told, and she seems to be necessary then only to teach the super-man in long lectures the elements of socialism. The last half of the book is propaganda. "The Valley of the Moon" is three stories: how *Billy Roberts*, prize-fighter, wooed and married *Saxon*, the laundry worker—excellent; the story of the Oakwood Strike and the brutalization of *Billy;* and the flight from the city and the idealization of the country—nauseatingly sweet. The second part is painted black to serve as the foil to the third part. As with "The Little Lady of the Big House," the book is not a novel but propaganda. Even "White Fang," his second dog book, is a tract in disguise.

Unquestionably he was not a novelist: he was too impatient, too headlong, to round out a large plan. He had not the patience to revise; he refused to read his earlier chapters day by day as he proceeded. As a result, the novels grew by accretions, and became, like "The Little Lady of the Big House," masses of loosely-bound material for novels. Had patience been granted him, and restraint, he might, perhaps, have enlarged his vignettes into careful wholes; into novels even. One cannot deny power to an artist who can cut a cameo like this:

And then, suddenly, before his eyes, on the foul plaster-wall appeared a vision. He stood in front of a gloomy tenement house. It was night-time, in the East End of London, and before him stood Margey, a little factory girl of fifteen. He had seen her home after the bean-feast. She lived in that gloomy tene-ment, a place not fit for swine. His hand was going out to hers as he said good night. She had put her lips up to be kissed, but he was n't going to kiss her. Somehow he was afraid of her. And then her hand closed on his and pressed feverishly. He felt her callouses grind and grate on his, and a great wave of pity welled over him. He saw her yearning, hungry eyes, and her ill-fed female form which had been rushed into a frightened and ferocious maturity; then he put his arms about her in large tolerance and stooped and kissed her on the lips. Her glad little cry rang in his ears, and he felt her clinging to him like a cat. Poor little starveling! He continued to stare at the vision of what had happened in the long ago. His flesh was crawling as it crawled that night when she clung to him, and his heart was warm with pity. It was a gray scene, greasy gray, and the rain drizzled greasily on the pavement stones. And then a radiant glory shone on the wall, and up through the other vision, displacing it, glimmered Her pale face under its crown of golden hair, remote and inaccessible as a star.

His range, however, is small. Of one whole rich area of human society he knew only the surface. The sordid misery of his childhood had warped his sense of values and narrowed the circle of human characters that he knew intimately enough to portray as a novelist should portray characters.

His world, therefore, is lopsided and misleading. His socialism, unrelieved as it is by humor, is often ludicrous. His gospel, as one finds it in "The Sea Wolf," for instance, and "Martin Eden," is frankly and outspokenly materialistic, and materialism is the antipodes of all that we denominate art.

Moreover, within his own chosen field he is limited of range. After the voyage of the *Snark* he added the South Seas to his literary area and tried to do for them what he had done for Alaska, but it was only a changing of scenery. Instead of intense cold, intense heat; instead of the aurora, the glamour of the tropic night. The novel "Adventure" is "A Daughter of the Snows" transferred to the Solomon Islands, and *Frona Wilse* changes her name to *Joan Lackland*. *Smoke Bellew* becomes the *David Grief* of "A Son of the Sun." But there is a falling off in zest and vision. The South Sea tales do not leave so wholesome an impression as the earlier tales of the Arctic. He has chosen only the loathsome, the sensational, the unique; and one feels that he has chosen them simply to make salable copy. There is an excess of glamour and color expressed by a profusion of hyphenated adjectives:

Aloft at giddy mast-heads oscillating above the decks of ships, I have gazed on sun-flashed water where coral growths iridesced from profounds of turquoise deeps, and conned the ships into safety of mirrored lagoons where the anchor rumbled down close to palm-fronded beaches of sea-pointed coral rock, etc.

Or this from "A Son of the Sun":

But over and beyond was his love of all the other things that go to make up a South Seas rover's life— the smell of the reef; the infinite exquisiteness of the shoals of living coral in the mirror-surfaced lagoons; the crashing sunrises of raw colors spread with lawless cunning; the palm-tufted islets set in turquoise deeps; the tonic wine of the trade-winds; the heave and send of the orderly crested seas; the moving deck beneath his feet, the straining canvas overhead; the flower-garlanded, golden-glowing men and maids of Polynesia, half children and half gods; and even the howling savages of Melanesia, head-hunters and man-eaters, half-devil and all the beast.

Or again:

I have loved princesses of royal houses in the tropic-warmed and sun-scented night, where black slaves fanned the sultry air with peacock plumes, while from afar, across the palms and fountains, drifted the roaring of lions and the cries of jackals.

His sea tales are contemporary with Conrad's and at many points there is parallelism. Both deal largely with outcasts; both exalt their leading characters into super-men—*Captain MacWhir* in

"Typhoon," *Razumov* with his "men like us leave
no posterity"; both tell graphically of typhoon and
violence; both are sonorous and gorgeous of diction.
But Conrad is objective and London is prevailingly
subjective; Conrad knows the sea better and he
loves it with his whole soul. And he is more
human. To him sailors are "an unorganized
brotherhood": in such work as "The Nigger of the
Narcissus" there is almost a grotesque display of
tenderness. London could never close a novel or a
short story with a passage like this: "Good by,
brothers! You were a good crowd. As good a
crowd as ever fisted with wild cries the beating
canvas of a heavy foresail; or tossing aloft, invisible in the night, gave back yell for yell to a
westerly gale." The reason, perhaps, lies in Conrad's own dictum: "Failing the resolution to hold
our peace, we can talk only about ourselves."

IV

The final literary style of Jack London—and
doubtless it is true of all men—was the product of
his own temperament. He was too individualistic,
too impatient long to follow the lead of other
men. Directed as he was at first by Kipling and
Gogol and O. Henry, he soon divested himself of
their mannerisms and voiced only himself. He

was writing now furiously for money and only for money. In an interview published with his sanction at the height of his career, he declared that he did not write because he loved writing. He hated it.

Every story that I write is for the money that will come to me. I always write what the editors want, not what I'd like to write. I grind out what the Capitalist editors want, and the editors buy only what the business and editorial departments permit. The editors are not interested in the truth.

Everything in his life during the last decade of his work called aloud for money, and his only source of income was his pen. For a man of his temperament there could be but one result: one finds almost nothing in his writings that has been brooded over, that, like ripened wine, has body to it and bouquet. One thousand words a day, every day in the week, without vacation or rest, excited work unrevised and unreturned to, is journalism, the ephemeræ of the Sunday supplement.

His temperament is everywhere visible. His sentences are short, often mere members of a sentence—the unit of measure of one excitable and headlong. There is no reserve, no restraint: everywhere exaggeration, superlatives; everything in extreme. In his later work he used the adjective "abysmal" until it became a mannerism that could even creep into one of his titles; "The Abysmal Brute." His hero catches a mountain trout:

He hooked a monster steelhead, standing to his neck in the ice-cold water of the Roque and fighting for forty minutes, with screaming reel, ere he drew his finny prize to the bank, and with the scalp yell of a Comanche jumped and clutched it by the gills.

Everything at this intense pitch. Is he in the Arctic? "It was very warm, barely ten below zero." "It was a clear cold night, not over cold—not over forty below." "It was the land where whiskey freezes solid and may be used as a paper-weight the greater part of the year." Does he need a central figure for his tale? He must have a superman, a *Burning Daylight* or a *Wolf Larsen*. The *Wolf* is wholly unschooled; he has lived his whole life among ignorant and brutal seamen on sailing vessels; he is muscled like a gorilla and has the gorilla's code of ethics; yet he is an authority on the Bible and he has Herbert Spencer at his tongue's end. Even on literary topics he can render tongue-tied and silent *Humphrey Van Weyden,* "the Dean of American Letters the Second," Van Weyden "the cold-blooded fish, the emotionless monster, the analytical demon." Are we convinced? On the contrary we begin to doubt the accuracy even of his autobiographical confessions. *Can* this man tell the truth? Will his imagination and melodramatic impulses permit him, even if he tries? Can we believe, for example, that a healthy country boy—not a De Quincey under the influence of drugs—can have dreams as extreme and as circumstantial as those he describes in the autobiographical parts of "Before Adam"?

That London devoutly believed that he was a realist and that his extreme pictures came only from his thoroughness, there can be no doubt. In "Martin Eden" he has said: "Realism is imperative to my nature, and the bourgeois spirit hates realism. The bourgeois is cowardly. It is afraid of life." But realism is science, and scientist London was not. Surely his is not the realism of the French school that filled endless note-books with careful observations before it began to write. He has been on the spot, to be sure, and the reader is never allowed for a moment to lose sight of the fact, but he works not from scientifically collected data. He can weave a glorious web of impressions of an era over which time is throwing a mellowing haze, he can heighten its picturesque places and exaggerate its lights and shades, but this is not realism. Wherever he touches the things that we know, we are likely to find him even grotesquely unrealistic. His dialogue seldom rings true, never, indeed in his later novels. *David Grief* in "Feathers of the Sun" is met by a trader and accosted in this O. Henry-like manner: "You'll have to pay your legitimate import duties same as any other trader with mind intent on robbing the gentle Polynesian savage on coral isles implanted." The half-breed *Sitka Charley* talks dialect through the first half of the tale and then at the climax launches out in Addisonian balances like these: "Brothers, my blood is red with Siwash, but my heart is white. To the faults of my fathers I owe the one, to the virtue of my friends the other. When I speak harshly to one of your own kind, I know you will not take it amiss," and so on to the end of the speech. It is London in his study, not *Sitka Charley.* The costume may deceive us, but the voice is the voice of London.

We may make the same observation upon his feminine characters: they are not nature; they are Jack London. A single illustration will suffice. The novel is "A Daughter of the Snows." It is in the middle of the Arctic night. The spirit thermometer registers sixty-five degrees below zero, and *Frona Wilse* from sheer excess of vitality has harnessed her dogs and taken an eight-mile run at top speed. Out in the frozen waste across the river from Dawson she happens by pure luck to stumble upon *Lucile,* a fallen woman, a professional dancer in saloons, a former vaudeville performer, sitting alone and disconsolate in the snow, presumably lost. One would suppose that the finding of a feminine cabaret stranger lost in the snow, away in the Arctic waste, the thermometer sixty-five below, would arouse in the finder curiosity or at least instantly-expressed emotion of some kind. But *Frona Wilse* is not conventional. She simply stops her dogs and asks the forlorn stranger in the snow—the mercury still at sixty-five—a question in esthetics. Is "stern" or "somber" the proper adjective to apply to the landscape they see about them? They differ instantly in their opinions and, the girl not rising from the snow, they begin their debate.

"That is because the lines of our lives have been laid in different places," the other ventured reflectively. "It is not what the landscape is, but what we are. If we were not, the landscape would remain, but without human significance. That is what we invest it with,

"'Truth is within ourselves; it takes no rise
From outward things, whate'er you may believe.'"

Frona's eyes brightened, and she went on to complete the passage:

"Where truth abides in fulness, and around—
There is an inmost centre in us all,

"And—and—how does it go? I have forgotten."

" 'Wall upon wall, the gross flesh hems it in.' "

The woman ceased abruptly, her voice trilling off into silvery laughter with a certain bitter recklessness which made Frona inwardly shudder.

In all his stories, whenever a woman goes away to school, even for a brief period, she comes back quoting Browning and Bergson and Ibsen and talking of the decadence of the French symbolists. He lacked humor, and he knew no more of the social realm in which Thackeray, for instance, lived, than did Dickens.

In the field of action, however, especially action in the primitive areas of life, he stands with the masters. Few have surpassed him in power to present vivid moving-pictures: records of fights— dog-fights, prize-fights, bull-fights, the fight of a bull moose with a wolf pack, the battle of a *Scruff Mackensie* with a whole Indian tribe, the over-powering single-handed of a mutinous crew by a *Wolf Larsen,* the stand of a band of island lepers against the authorities. Scenes of battle and tempest arouse his imagination as nothing else: typhoons in the Solomon Islands, races with the Yukon mail, mutinies at sea, Arctic heroes conquering single-handed a whole firm of Wall Street sharpers. Chapter XXXVIII of "The Mutiny of the Elsinore," where *Pike* single-handed fights the ship off

the Horn, is as stirring a bit of adventure as there
is in the literature of the sea.

In his own estimation London was never a hap-
hazard worker. It was a part of his literary creed,
learned in the days of his laborious apprenticeship
and strengthened by the socialism that became his
religion, that behind all art which is worthy of the
name must lie something more than appears on the
surface. "There must be the *major motif*," he
says, "the big underrunning *motif*, the cosmic and
universal thing. I tried to make it keep time to
the story itself." This cosmic theme underlies the
work of all the great artists. "There must be a
cosmic quality to what they sing. They must seize
upon and press into enduring art forms the vital
facts of our existence. They must tell why we have
lived." Applying his test to Kipling, he says he
has sung "the sweat and blood and toil of the Anglo-
Saxon race, and back of it the genius of the race.
And this is the cosmic quality." Of his own
work he says:

It was the apotheosis of adventure—not the adventure of the story books, but of real adventure: the
savage task-master, awful of punishment and awful
of reward, faithless and whimsical, demanding terrible patience and heartbreaking days and nights of
toil, offering the blazing sunlight glory or dark death
at the end of thirst and famine or of the long drag

and monstrous delirium of rotting fever, through blood and sweat and stinging insects, leading up by long chains of petty and ignoble contacts to royal culminations and lordly achievements.

And again:

He felt the stress and strain of life, its fears and sweats and wild insurgencies—surely this was the stuff to write about. He wanted to glorify the leaders of forlorn hopes, the mad lovers, the giants that fought under stress and strain, amid terror and tragedy, making life crackle with the strength of their endeavor. And yet the magazine short stories seemed intent on glorifying the Mr. Butlers, the sordid dollar-chasers, and the commonplace little love affairs of commonplace little men and women.

At one time—about 1903 it was—O. Henry threw his influence over London's short stories, notably those in "The Faith of Men" and "Moon Face," but between London and O. Henry there is this fundamental difference: London was passionately in earnest; he wrote without humorous intent; he wrote with a motif, and this he never forgot even in his most headlong moments of copy production. Behind his work was a principle that he fought for, a conviction that was Puritanic in its intensity. O. Henry, and also Bret Harte, lacked this element, and lacking it, they are in danger, despite their literary cleverness and their humor, of falling among the mere entertainers, useful people but not a class to be placed high in the major scale of values.

V.

Were it not for this cosmic quality in London's work, we might dismiss him at this point or even declare it not worth while to consider him at all save as a picturesque incident in the history of American literature, but, like Mark Twain, he is the interpreter of a region. In his underrunning motifs we find the underrunning motifs of a whole new era of our western civilization. He was not an entertainer merely any more than Mark Twain was a humorist merely: he was a voice, the voice of the new America emergent beyond the Rockies, the first really Californian writer worthy of our study, for Harte and his circle were Easterners who were temporarily in the West. London was indigenous, a voice Californian and only Californian. He was from the pioneers and the Argonauts, the blond race in the first van of the march into the unknown beyond the horizon, and with them he lifted his voice decrying the decadent days that had followed the age of the heroes. It was the same voice that coined the phrase "the effete East," the old voice of the northern blond beasts who had smitten in contempt the softness and effeminacy of declining Rome.

He voiced the romance of California, its feet amid the ruins of the stately Spaniards, its face turned to the Golden Gate and the Pacific. Still on its horizon lay the frontier—the new Eldorado to the north, and beyond the sea-rim the islands of the South Seas, the last domain of mystery, the last unconquered bits of the primitive world.

Moreover, London voiced the recklessness and the headlong venturesomeness that came as a heritage from the Argonauts. These early Titans had gambled with the horizon. "The Valley of the Moon" is a sermon with this text:

Whenever a man lost his stake, all he had to do was to chase the frontier west a few miles and get another stake. They moved over the face of the land like so many locusts. They destroyed everything— the Indians, the soil, the forests, just as they had destroyed the buffalo and the passenger pigeon. Their morality in business and politics was gambler moral- ity—the loser chased the frontier for fresh stakes. The winner of to-day, broke to-morrow, on the day following might be riding his luck to royal flushes on five-card draws. So they gobbled and gambled from the Atlantic to the Pacific.

In all that he wrote was the spirit of this new empire of the Pacific; its magnificent distances, its recklessness and exaggeration, its adolescent dreams. It was the spirit of his own biography: "What we want," says his heroine *Saxon*, really his wife Charmian, "is a valley of the moon; and we'll just keep on looking till we find it."

In atmospheres like this are born the giants of the race. London's super-men are only Californians as Californians dream of men. They came from his Western expansiveness, his life in camp and forecastle where the masculine predominated, and from the romance of the border that creates from the material about it its own mythology. On the westward-looking borders always iconoclasm, always fierce individualism that erects self-reliance into a religion. Note the philosophy of *Jacob Wilse:*

Conventions are worthless for such as we. They are for the swine who without them would wallow deeper. The weak must obey or be crushed! not so with the strong. The mass is nothing; the individual everything; and it is the individual always that rules the mass and gives the law. A fig for what the world says.

All of London's leading characters are of this type: super-men, super-women, dreams of their creator, half real, half mythical. All of them are blonds even to the golden degree. They have blue or gray eyes and bodies that are perfect. His men have muscles that creep and knot like living things, and skins like silk. We think of *Wolf Larsen,* of *Burning Daylight* who had "that super-strength that is the dower of but one human in millions," of *Axel Gunderson*:

In the making of Axel Gunderson the gods had remembered their old-time cunning, and cast him after the manner of men who were born when the world was young. Full seven feet, he towered in his picturesque costume which marked a king of Eldorado. His chest, neck, and limbs were those of a giant. To bear his three hundred pounds of bone and muscle, his snowshoes were greater by a generous yard than those of other men. Rough-hewn, with rugged brow and massive jaw and unflinching eyes of palest blue, his face told the tale of one who knew but the law of might. Of the yellow of ripe corn silk, his frost-incrusted hair swept like day across the night, and fell far down his coat of bearskin.

His women are mates for his men: super-women of the border type, the half-mythical idealizations of a young man whose life has been passed largely in masculine society. *Miss Caruthers* in "Under the Deck Awnings" could stay under water two minutes, could gather forty-seven coins before coming up, and do other physical feats as extraordinary. And besides this, "Men were as wax in her hands. She melted them, or subtly molded them, or incinerated them, as she pleased. . . . As a man-conqueror she was supreme. She was a whip-lash, a sting, a flame, an electric spark. At times there were flashes of will that scorched through her beauty and seduction and smote a victim into blank and shivering idiocy and fear." To one who objects to the picture, or to other super-women like *Maud Sangster* or *Joan Lackland,* their creator would say in the words of *Frona Wilse,* who would voice both herself and the virile new land of which she was a part: "You are unused to consistent, natural women; because more like you are only familiar with the hot-house breeds—pretty, helpless, well-rounded, stall-fatted little things, blissfully innocent and criminally ignorant. They are not natural or strong; nor can they mother the natural or strong."

Everywhere in his work the Western energy, virility, enthusiasm, expansiveness, the ability to see things and do things in the big, in the world of the impossible made possible by super-energy and self-reliance. His super-men are not all in the realms of savagery and frontier squalor. *Dick Forest* in "The Little Lady of the Big House" is a business super-man, master of a super-ranch, in the Valley of the Moon—London's own ranch and London's own self as he dreamed and planned in his study. The despatching of a train-load of pedigreed stallions and three hundred registered bulls to South America is but one episode of a single day. Thousands of men are employed, each group superintended by the world's leading expert and these experts instructed and directed by *Forest*. He is supreme master of the masters of every branch of knowledge required upon the ranch.

A manager, at the end of a five or ten minute session, often emerged sweating, limp and frazzled. Yet for a swift hour, at high tension, Forest met all comers, with a master's grip handling them and all the multifarious details of their various departments. He told Thompson the machinist, in four flashing minutes, where the fault lay in the dynamo of the Big House refrigerator.

And in the same way he went down the whole line of his super-specialists. Is it enough? He does this by working one hour a day. The rest of the day he spends as a bronco-buster, marksman, swimmer, defeater of the champion diver of the whole South Seas, composer of music and poetry, and quoter of Browning and Bergson.

Youth is the key to it all. In the glorious youth of his native region he was an adolescent, driven, as he has said of one of his own heroes, by "the urge of life healthy and strong, unaware of frailty and decay, drunk with sublime complacence, ego-mad, enchanted by his own mighty optimism." When he died at forty he was still, like his California, in the flower of his adolescence, still dreaming over the vision that had glorified his squalid boyhood: "It was only a little lad, but he had dreams of becoming a great musician and having all Europe at his feet." It put the thrill of romance into all that he wrote, a thrill like that in the climax of "The Call of the Wild":

When the long winter nights come on and the wolves follow their meat into the lower valleys, he may be seen running at the head of the pack through the pale moonlight or glimmering borealis, leaping gigantic above his fellows, his great throat a-bellow as he sings a song of the younger world, which is the song of the pack.

It is the soul of Western individualism, the spirit of the young, free West of our America.

That London should have been a socialist was inevitable: iconoclasm and revolt were in the air he breathed, as also that extreme individualism that chafed under authority from any source whatever. The point of view in his sea stories is that of the forecastle to which authority is synonymous with tyranny; in "The Road" it is that of the hobo to whom all organized society is tyrannical, and in "The Iron Heel" it is that of the modern bolshevist who would destroy everything in authority and begin anew. "The Iron Heel" is the "News from Nowhere," just as "Martin Eden" is the "Alton

Locke" of later socialistic literature, with this difference, however: Morris could bring his reader into the sunshine beyond the revolution, but London could offer only failure and suicide. The very violence of his emotions and the radicalness of his remedies left him powerless to close otherwise. His own life and his later novels offer his only solution that is not merely destructive: flee away from the cities and the gathering-places of men, he says, and in a Valley of the Moon create an empire of your own over which you can rule supreme.

All this reveals to us much. To read Jack London is to understand, perhaps for the first time, the soul of the great Northwestern empire on the Pacific, that bred the I. W. W., that has turned the tide of Presidential elections, that single-handed embroils the nation with Japan, and that ever must be reckoned with in all national councils; and also it is to feel in vivid reality the power and the vitality of that Western tide that is bound to overflow to the enrichment of all areas of our American life.

VI

But not only was London the embodiment of the spirit of a vibrant locality, he was during a brief period a voice that was national and international. The war has thrown the nineteenth century into new perspective. The years before 1914 already seem to belong to a bygone era. No one smiles now when we speak of "the remarkable rightness of Rudyard Kipling," or even when we pronounce Jack London the most widely representative American literary figure, the more arresting literary voice during the decade preceding the war.

London was swept into notice upon the crest of the Kipling wave, that protest of the nineties against Tennysonian sentiment, Preraphaelitism, Oscar Wildeism, Aubrey Beardsleyism. In 1903, while he was still fighting for recognition, London reviewed Kipling who was then under his first eclipse, taking as his text the pronouncement of a Chicago reviewer that Rudyard Kipling, "prophet of blood and vulgarity, prince of the ephemerals, and idol of the non-elect," was dead. London hailed him as the most living writer of the nineteenth century: "When the future centuries quest back to the nineteenth century to find what manner of century it was, to find not what the people of the nineteenth century thought they thought, but what they really thought; not what they thought they ought to do, but what they really did do, then a certain man, Kipling, will be read and read with understanding."

It was inevitable that he should have taken his

own stand with prophets of blood and vulgarity: his birth and his training had fitted him for nothing else. Moreover, it was his good fortune that the time was ripe for such prophets. Roosevelt, ranchman of the Northwest, wilderness hunter, roughrider, apostle of the free air and the out of doors, was in the fierce light of the Presidency. A generation of young men excited by the call of war and then thwarted of their desire by the quick collapse of the foe was on the scene. To gratify their heroic desire they turned perforce to swash-buckling romance—thin food and soon intolerable. A reaction such as Kipling headed in the eighties was inevitable. From the White House flew Jack-London-like phrases: "mollycoddle," "race suicide," "the strenuous life," "red-blooded men." The "muck-rake" and "Ananias Club" schools of criticism arose and flourished; the out-of-doors movement changed overnight from a fad to a religion; Seton's "Wild Animals I Have Known" started a whole group of writers. Frederick Remington published "Men with the Bark On"; the title is redolent of the times. It was the period of Stephen Crane and "The Red Badge of Courage," of Frank Norris and "The Pit," of Elbert Hubbard and the "Message to Garcia," of Davis and "Soldiers of Fortune," of Sinclair's "The Jungle," and—like a sudden jazz note—the short stories of O. Henry: surely no period in our literary history was ever more various or more sensational. (Note: this 19

And it was into this excited group of young men of the nineties of the dying Victorian period, who had come down upon the literary metropolis like the wild university group upon London in the nineties of the Elizabethan age, that Jack London projected himself, and, at the one moment in our history when it would have been possible, he seized the baton and led the orchestra. And it was a leadership no man may call conventional. A contemporary English critic characterized him as a literary runner amuck.

It was as if he foresaw the reign of savagery that was to come with the German uprising. His cry was: Face the truth. Why refuse to see what is straight before your eyes? Soft-living peoples have always been awakened by blond beasts of the North. Civilization is not to be depended upon; it is but a veneer that hides the abysmal brute. *Pathurst,* the esthetic club man, gone to sea because of ennui, becomes a man of the viking age when he awakes one day to find himself in command of a mutiny-stricken ship. Instantly he becomes blood and iron, knocks men right and left, shoots mutineers in cold blood, rules with brutality a crew that is "the sweepings of hell," and single-handed brings his ship to port. And the motif of the book is this: *Pathurst* is *you.* The blond beast of Nietzsche lies only skin-deep within *you* and needs but circumstances to set it free. Like *Smoke Bellew,* the veriest mollycoddle has it in him to be in the right environment a sea-wolf and a trampler upon all save the strong.

From the first London had to fight against the contention that his pictures were too strong and brutal. Eight years before the rape of Belgium he wrote in anger his essay "The Somnambulists." What is the matter with the world? he cried. It is asleep.

Civilization has spread a veneer over the surface of the soft-shelled animal known as man. It is a very thin veneer; but so wonderfully is man constituted that he squirms on his bit of achievement and believes he is garbed in armor-plate. . . . Yet man today is the same man that drank from his enemy's skull in the dark German forests, that sacked cities, and stole his women from neighboring clans like any howling aborigine. The flesh-and-blood body of man has not changed in the last several thousand years. Nor has his mind changed. . . . Starve him, let him miss six meals, and see gape through the veneer the hungry maw of the animal beneath. Get between him and the female of his kind upon whom his mating instinct is bent, and see his eyes blaze like any angry cat's, hear in his throat the scream of wild stallions, and watch his fists clench like an orang-outang's. Maybe he will even beat his chest. Touch his silly vanity, which he exalts into high-sounding pride, call him a liar, and behold the red animal in him that makes a hand clutching that is quick like the tensing of a tiger's claw, or an eagle's talon, incarnate with desire to rip and tear.

The same rule applied to nations:

The Anglo-Saxon is a pirate, a land robber and a sea robber. Underneath his thin coating of culture, he is what he was in Morgan's time, in Drake's time, in William's time, in Alfred's time. The blood and the tradition of Hengist and Horsa are in his veins. In battle he is subject to the blood lusts of the Berserkers of old. Plunder and booty fascinate him immeasurably.

And so on and on. We called him brutal when he wrote this in the serene days before the war; we called him gruesome disciple of Gogol, parader of horrors that civilization had outgrown. We are not so sure now. And his point of view was the German point of view. Over and over again in all his volumes he proclaimed shrilly his soap-box doctrine that the world belongs to the strong. *Martin Eden* proclaims it in every chapter.

Nietzsche was right. The world belongs to the strong—to the strong who are noble as well and who do not wallow in the swine-trough of trade and exchange. The world belongs to the true noblemen, to the great blond beasts, to the non-compromisers, to the "yes-sayers." And they will eat you up, you socialists who are afraid of socialism and who think yourselves individualists. Your slave morality of the weak and lowly will never save you.

And again:

In the struggle for existence the strong and the progeny of the strong tend to survive, while the weak and the progeny of the weak are crushed and tend to perish. The result is that the strong and the progeny of the strong survive, and, so long as the struggle obtains, the strength of each generation increases. That is development. But you slaves dream of a society where the law of development will be annulled, where no weaklings and inefficients will perish, where every inefficient will have as much as he wants to eat as many times a day as he desires, and where all will marry and have progeny—the weak as well as the strong. . . .

Your society of slaves—of, by, and for slaves—must inevitably weaken and go to pieces as the life which composes it weakens and goes to pieces. I am enunciating biology and not sentimental ethics. . . .

To *Jacob Wilse*—

Battle was the law and the way of progress. The world was made for the strong and only the strong inherited it and through it all there ran an equity. To be honest was to be strong. To sin was to weaken. To bluff an honest man was to be dishonest. To bluff a bluffer was to smite with the steel of justice. The primitive strength was in the arm; the modern strength in the brain. Though it had shifted ground, the struggle was the same old struggle.

And all this in the days long before the war in books eagerly republished in Sweden and Germany and Russia.

London out-Kiplinged Kipling for the reason that he knew more than Kipling. The author of the "Plain Tales" is as brutal and bloody and vulgar as the life that he saw and described, but London saw depths of brutality that Kipling was ignorant of. Like *Martin Eden,* "he had sighted the whole sea of life's nastiness that he had known and voyaged over and through. . . ." When Kipling would write "Captains Courageous," he went to Gloucester and studied the fishing fleet and interviewed the sailors; but when London wrote of the sea he drew his material from his own blood and sweat in the forecastle of a grimy seal-oil-soaked schooner in Arctic waters. He had himself known the lowest depths to which drunkenness and vagrancy bring men. He had seen the naked brute, he had seen what men become when the restraints of civilization are relaxed, and he told his generation, in words as strong as his generation would bear, the naked truth. And to the last he complained that he was not allowed to tell the whole truth. Even when he was at the height of his fame he had stories rejected by magazines because the editors considered them too brutal for their readers to bear. We can imagine his sardonic chuckle when the "abysmal brute" broke loose in Belgium and his squeamish countrymen shuddered in such ghastly horror. For ten years he had been telling them of the blond beast. More even than Kipling was he the "prophet of blood and vulgarity" in the smug epoch before the outburst of the war.

VII

The popularity of London in Europe during his decade cannot be overlooked. In Sweden translations of twenty-four of his books were sold to the number of 230,000 in nine years. Many editions were taken by Russia, especially of his later social-istic books. When he died in 1916 more space was devoted to him in the European papers than to the Emperor Francis Joseph, who died at the same time. His socialism undoubtedly was taken more seriously in eastern Europe than at home. We tolerated his pictures of the burning and rape of Chicago in "The Iron Heel" and of the blotting out of American civilization in "The Scarlet Plague" as graphic bits of fiction, but bolshevist Europe accepted them as solemn prophecy and as all but accomplished fact. For London, when he defined his position and his program, spoke with no uncertain voice. To him socialism meant war to the limit: "It is its purpose to wipe out, root and branch, all capitalistic institutions of present-day society." And only shortly before his death he resigned from the Socialistic party in disgust "because of its lack of fire and fight, and its loss of emphasis on the class struggle."

Richard Henry Little, who was with the Russians during the period after the fall of Germany when the Red army was coming into power, has given a glimpse of the influence of Jack London upon the Russian people:

I was n't left long in doubt as to who the Russians considered the greatest living American. It was "Yakclunnen." For the life of me I could n't figure out for a while just who Yakclunnen was, although I eagerly agreed that he was the greatest American of them all. Then they brought out a great many treasured and tattered volumes, and I realized they were talking of Jack London.

Never was an author so idolized as Jack London is among the Russians. Apparently all of his works have been translated into Russian, and I found them everywhere. Officers passed them around from one to another, and often I have seen little groups of soldiers sitting in the woods, while the man who could read was doing so aloud to the eager delight of the awestruck group around him. At every mess the officers wanted me to tell them all I knew about Jack London.

I wanted to talk about Lenin and Trotzky, but they wanted to talk about "Yakclunnen."

To what extent his voice is still directing the great soviet uprising we may not say.

We do know, however, that he can be but a temporary disturbance. His philosophy was materialistic, based upon the Nietzschean omnipotence of force, and the World War, if nothing else, has shown its fallacy. Beyond "The Sea Wolf" materialism cannot go, and that "Martin Eden," which purports to trace the evolution of a life under the workings of this philosophy, could be ended only by suicide, reveals its fatal weakness. The thunder and the earthquake were all this Californian Nietzsche could understand: of the philosophy of the still small voice he knew nothing at all. He could run away from the problem and fancy he had found a solution in his unsocialistic Valley of the Moon experiment, but of the meaning of life expressed in terms of sacrifice he was as ignorant as his Alaskan savages.

Undoubtedly he will be rated as a picturesque incident in the decade that closed an era. His social philosophy and his pseudo-science will disappear early. If anything of his writings is to survive its day, it will be a few fragments from his novels, a dozen or two of his short stories that are wholly American in scene and spirit, and "The Call of the Wild," which has in it not only the freshness and the realism of the living North, but the atmosphere and the thrill of romance, which is the eternal spirit of youth.

THE EPIC OF NEW ENGLAND

SOME day the history of New England will be written as an epic.

I hesitate to confess it, for I am New England born, but the *Mayflower* and the Pilgrim Fathers and Plymouth Rock do not move me as once they did. Niagara stuns and terrifies one at first, but at length it lulls one to sleep. It is time perhaps to change the subject, and yet there is one thing about the episode that holds me against my will: there once lived men so fearfully in earnest that they could take their wives and children straight off the map into the blank vault of the west and without a thought of ever returning. They sought no port, no definite land: they sailed simply into the west and the first landfall they made was to be their home. They headed only for America three thoussand miles away.

And here I pause. When you aim at random at America you have a wide mark. After weeks and weeks of zigzagging and uncertainty, headed this way and that by contrary winds, swept leagues to the south or the north by fierce tempests, blown out of all reckoning for days, at the mercy of a sailing-master eager only to land his cargo at the earliest possible moment, he cared not where, why of all points should New England have been the landfall? Why not Newfoundland? Why not Florida? Any one of a thousand chances would have veered them away from the New England coast. We say to-day that sheer chance flung them there. The Pilgrim said it was the hand of God on the tiller.

But whether it were chance or Providence, one thing is certain: that landfall decreed the settlement of a region as inhuman as any that ever engaged the powers of man. Had those Pilgrims possessed an accurate chart and had they known what we know in these later times, that landing never would have been. Indeed, had the seventeenth century known the real facts about the Atlantic coast and the territory inland, whole great areas of New England would have remained unsettled to this day. Where else in the world, save in Scotland, perhaps, or Switzerland, can one find under cultivation an area to match it? Mazes of boulders and glacial drift tilled with all seriousness as farms; dizzy hillsides jagged thick with rocks turned into corn-fields; veritable sloughs bottomed with polypod and sweet-flag made into meadows; vast stretches of granite ledges snarled with hardhack turned into pastures; wrenched from nature with incredible toil, fenced with heavy stone walls that called for the labor of Titans; winters Arctic cold with snow often for six months; roads eternally up and down at sharp angles, buried under great drifts in winter and washed into ragged trenches by the cloudbursts of summer—where else will one find a farming region like that?

The old Puritan hive, those earliest-settled towns near the mouths of the larger rivers and along the sea, sent out its first swarm during the mid-years of the eighteenth century. It was that sturdy brood that fought the Seven Years' War and the Revolution; a restless, free-born race, full-lunged and mighty-limbed, that crashed into the northern woods far up into Maine, New Hampshire, and Vermont, founded towns by every water-power, surveyed the land into lots, and carved out the first farms along the flats and river-courses. For forty years the wilderness rang with their axes, the crash of their old-growth pines, their mighty bonfires, and their shouts to their toiling oxen. Clearings became farms; trails were plowed into roads; wild mountain torrents were turned upon saws and mill-stones. That was the first generation of the New England hill lands; demigods who did each the work of five; who toiled every moment of the daylight and far beyond, a generation that wrestled barehanded with brute nature in her strongest fastnesses and won. And the women did no less than the men. They it was who under sternest conditions and amid elemental surroundings bore and reared those families of twelve and fifteen children, washed and baked and mended, prepared the great meals, spun the yarn, wove the cloth, made the garments, did the thousand little chores which a farm and a household demand, and died at last worn out, their work all undone lying in heaps about them.

The great families swiftly outgrew the home farm and scattered into the hills and the farther valleys to clear other land. This second generation completed the organization of the hill towns, pulled out the last stumps in the earlier meadows, built the great farmhouses with enormous chimneys and wainscoting of clear pine boards four feet in width, and completed the early highways, running them without thought of compromise straight over the steepest hills, oblivious of the fact, not discovered until a century later, that "the kettle bail is no longer when it lies down than when it stands erect." They multiplied the settled land by ten and they made of the northern hills a neighborhood with growing villages and fast improving farms.

The third generation, which came upon the scene in the early years of the new century, completed the expansion. When they had done their work, every acre of land that could by human effort be wrung from nature had been taken. All the steep hillsides were dotted now with farmhouses. Everywhere were little neighborhoods: far in the mountain fastnesses, deep in the back valleys, high on the wild north slopes where the winter sun scarcely ever shone after mid-afternoon, or clustered like Swiss villages about the very bases of the bare peaks sometimes ten and fifteen miles from post-office and store. It was this generation that completed the stone walls, running them for miles over hills and through forest, surrounding every field with a barricade like the outworks of a fortress, and heaping up rock heaps that to-day stand like the pyramids, imperishable monuments to a race forever gone.

Again great families of twelve and even eighteen children, that marvelous fourth generation about which our epic centers. Born in the thirties and forties, they saw New England in its prime. During their childhood the hills swarmed with life. Nowhere was place so remote that one might not find there a neighborhood with fifty and even seventy pupils in its red schoolhouse. Sprung from generations of hill-born men, toilers in the open air, feeders upon the wholesome fruits of the soil, lovers of the woods and the hills over which they scurried like the red foxes, reared in the great farmhouses where sleeping rooms were unheated and abundantly ventilated, this generation was as sturdy a race as the earth ever produced. They were as free as the hill winds they breathed; they looked one straight in the eye; they depended solely upon their own brain and muscle and will; they were self-confident and undismayed by difficulties; they could adapt themselves to circumstances and improvise new methods; and they had in them a love of work that had been ground into their very bones.

Those were the days when the little back towns which to-day number scarce two hundred souls numbered twelve and fifteen hundred, and sent often two representatives each to the General Court of the State. Then it was that a town-meeting day at the Center was the event of the year. The whole town was there; hoary old grandsires of the second generation bent and feeble who chattered of the strength of their youth and told tales of their childhood in the forests, the third generation in its prime talking of cattle and corn and the coming spring's work, and lastly, flocking by itself, the center of it all, the young men under twenty-one, a hundred of them with massive shoulders and mighty limbs, clad in coarse and strong garments, and with heavy cowhide boots with tops that reached almost to the knees. What a magazine of stored-up energy! They are not still a moment; crowding and pushing each other, boasting, fighting, wrestling, laughing boisterously at rough jokes, jumping, lifting each other by the heels with main strength, massing together to crash down the inner partition of the town hall; a "rough lot," a band of young Titans, with energy enough and self-confidence enough to shake the very foundations of the republic. What outlet was there to be for all this pent-up power?

It was time for New England to swarm again; the hive was full to bursting. Had there been no vent beyond the home domain it is hard to imagine what might have been. Land already was being worked against the very protest of nature, and this new brood would have had to turn the ledges and the very pastures into farms and expend itself in making into a garden what nature had intended for a golf-links and a quarry.

The first overflow consisted of the older girls who found work in the cotton mills of Lowell and Fall River, and of the older boys who found employment in the machine shops and in the growing city of Boston. But this was a mere nothing. The pressure in the northern districts was increasing. Something must happen, and suddenly the something came.

The great West opened all in a moment as if the

curtain had arisen for the first act. Gold had been found on the far Pacific, fabulous masses of gold to be had for the mere gathering—in California, a region as vague and as far away as the valley of diamonds which Sindbad entered. How it thrilled the northern farms! Then had come the Kansas-Nebraska call that sounded over New England like a trumpet blast; for every settler sixty acres of flat land and a yoke of oxen free. Iowa, Minnesota, Wisconsin, Illinois; men talked of nothing else. Whole families started westward; young boys stole from their homes at dead of night and worked their way toward the Mississippi, their imaginations set on fire by the tales they had heard.

Then suddenly, like a fire alarm at night, rang out the call to war. Seventy thousand, five hundred thousand, two million men must come from the North, and there must be a thousand leaders raised instantly, leaders of the first rank, for this was to be a war such as the world never before had seen. Never has there been such a call for men, men for the armies of the North, men to break the vast West, men to develop the iron and the oil and the coal, men to bridge rivers and streams and to tunnel mountains and build cities. And they were to be picked and perfect men, of heroic mold, iron-limbed and self-reliant, men that nothing could quench and nothing dominate, who could grapple with a whole continent and wrestle with problems as wide as the world itself. And it was not a mere dozen or a score that was wanted; it was thousands and tens of thousands. And they must be had instantly. There was no time to train this army, to discipline and college it for the new work. It must be picked from material already at hand. And to the glory of the New World, all was ready. In 1838 Emerson had written: "This country has not fulfilled what seemed the reasonable expectation of mankind. Men looked, when all feudal straps and bandages were snapped asunder, that Nature, too long the mother of dwarfs, should reimburse itself by a brood of Titans who should laugh and leap in the continent, and run up the mountains of the West with the errand of genius and love." And even as he wrote, the race of Titans which he described was in its cradles all about him, and now they are ready. In twenty years New England sent forth a brood that not even America will ever equal again. Emerson himself in later years could say, "We shall not again disparage America, now we have seen what men it will bear."

It was this fourth generation that carried through the great Civil War, that conquered the vast West of America and turned it in a single lifetime from a raw wilderness stretching over a quarter of the earth's girdle into a garden and an empire. To these marvelous men nothing was impossible. They spanned the vast distances with railroads, penetrated the Rockies and the Sierra Nevadas as if they had been molehills, crushed the Plains Indians, exterminated the great buffalo herds, opened up all the rivers, built Chicago and the cities of the Plain, organized the iron works of Pittsburg, uncovered the coal and the oil and sent them broadcast over the earth, and in their old age left the West they had found in their boyhood a dream that to their grandsons seemed as wild and romantic and as far away as the tales of the "Arabian Nights."

But alas for the old hive. A visit to New England to-day is a sad pilgrimage to one who knows aught of the early years. There hangs over it forever an atmosphere of melancholy and tender regret. The very winds and the waters seem to murmur, "They are gone." [The Civil War destroyed for the South the old plantation life and the only aristocracy in the European sense of the word that America has ever known, and it left behind it that vague sadness and longing that are the soul of romance; but the war destroyed just as surely the old régime in New England, the old patriarchal life, the sense of family and of home that comes only in perfectly organized neighborhoods untouched by the world, and it left behind it the same "before the war" atmosphere of a golden age forever gone. For North and South alike the war ended an era, and behind it lies the only romance this garish republican land of ours has ever known.

In New England it vanished almost literally in a night. It was like the bursting of a barrier behind which the waters have been silently gathering. Now vast stretches of the land are again wildernesses; everywhere silence save as the hawk screams over it and the fox arouses the night echoes. Whole neighborhoods have been abandoned; school districts where sixty and seventy scholars plowed through the winter snow deserted completely. Again as in the days of the earlier generations are the farms confined to the river bottoms and the easier worked plains. Those hillside fields over which the fathers toiled so terribly are distant pastures now, wild and seldom visited, or else they are veritable forests, and the deer, an animal unknown to the third and fourth generations, swarm again as in the days of the first settlers. Slowly but surely the wilderness again is claiming its own. As the hunter crashes though the thick woods he comes constantly upon the great stone walls and the rock heaps of that race which has vanished almost as completely as the mound-builders. Sometimes he finds the cellar hole and the old well, and near by perhaps a few ghastly skeletons of apple-trees, but there is nothing else to tell him that here only a lifetime ago was a home that had rung with the happy voices of children.

That exodus never has been recorded. There is in it the material for a thousand tragedies. What heartburnings in the old homes from which the children had all departed! Here the father and mother abandoned the farm and went, too; here the mother died first and the father lived alone for a time in the home that once had been so full of joyous life; and here perhaps it was that the father died first. Almost every one of these little abandoned farms has a tragedy written over its latter days. No one can tell the longings, the heartburnings, the loneliness of two parents growing old, their children all in distant lands, their farm which had always been their home no longer a thing of value. A few years they struggle along in the old round, but the end is inevitable. The farmhouse door closes forever when it shuts behind the little funeral procession. The son who has come for a few sad days from the West would gladly sell the old place, but there is no one to buy. For a time the hay is sold to those who will buy it, but the gray birches grow swiftly over the walls, the grass is no longer worth the cutting, and the farm becomes a pasture. The old buildings, their roofs tumbled in, furnish shelter for a while to the sheep and the young cattle until a spring fire clears the place of the rubbish. The forest returns with swiftness, and it blots out at last the final vestige of the labors of man.

To-day this Northland is the country that God forsook. A curse seems to have fallen upon it. A blight has fallen upon its fruit-trees; the brown-tail and the gipsy moths have blasted it; the gray birch is in the old pastures; the lumber-man and the forest-fire have swept off its pines and spruce and pointed firs. The churches are all but abandoned. What few farms there are are taken more and more by French Canadians and other aliens who know no more of the history of the land than did the old Teutons who settled amid the Celtic monuments. To them the great stone cairns, relics of the first clearing, and the double stone walls runing for miles over the hilltops and through tangled forests, and the abandoned cellar holes and wells in distant pastures are as unintelligible as are the relics of the mound-builders to the farmers of the Middle West.

The cultivated lands are every year decreasing. In the State of New Hampshire, according to Sanborn, its historian, "More than a million acres cultivated in 1850 had gone back to pasturage and woodland in 1900." The native race is swiftly dying out. In 1900 almost half of the population of Massachusetts were born of foreign parentage. The hill towns are losing in population steadily. Let me take as a type my boyhood town in Grafton County. In 1860 its population was 1273; in 1870, 876; in 1880, 728; in 1890, 679; in 1900, 630; in 1910, 559; in 1920, 480. In 1861 in a single day a hundred young men enlisted from this town for the war, and the greater number of them never returned as permanent dwellers. Whole neighborhoods in the seventies migrated to Minnesota and to Iowa. In 1860 there was scarcely a foreign-born person within the limits of the township; to-day of the small remnant that remains nearly 25 per cent. are of alien birth. It is so in the whole State. Again to quote Sanborn: "In one generation the foreign-born in New Hampshire have trebled and those of foreign parentage considerably more than doubled."

The epic of New England centers about four generations, and the greatest of them was the last, that marvelous single generation that burst from its borders like another wave of vikings from the north and tamed a raw continent. It is a new epic of a new Jason who burst into the unknown West and wrung from it the marvelous golden fleece which we pigmies of the later years must look at forever in wonder.

ON THE TERMINAL MORAINE OF NEW ENGLAND PURITANISM [1]

ONE may not dwell long with the biography or the writings of Mary E. Wilkins Freeman without being reminded of Nathaniel Hawthorne. There is suggestive parallelism at the start. Both traced their lines of descent to old Salem, Massachusetts, and to families which had persisted there since colonial days. In the line of the one was William Hawthorne, a grim magistrate who ordered the lashing of Quakers and itinerant preachers and vagabonds; and in the line of the other was Bray Wilkins, a judge in the witchcraft trials of a later day. That the two grimmest recorders of Puritan tragedy and its inherited results should have originated in this town of dark tradition is, we somehow like to feel, not a coincidence. It sets us to looking for other parallelisms; it furnishes us with a key.

A descendant of Bray Wilkins, Warren E. Wilkins, born in the generation which began in the

[1] By permission of Harper & Brothers, publishers of "A New England Nun," Modern Classics edition.

thirties of the last century, was the first of his line to break permanently from the Salem home and to render himself unfixed of hearth, a man, in the American fashion, of many environments. Despite his restlessness, he was a gentle soul. Joseph Chamberlain, collaborator with Miss Wilkins on the novel "The Long Arm," has said that "the Puritan seemed to survive in him, as it does in thousands of other Yankees of the finer and unsordid type, merely in a sort of exaggerated nervousness, conscientiousness, and general unworldliness. He was an architect of the old kind, trained in the building trades rather than in the schools; and he varied this, his true occupation, with a little unsuccessful store-keeping up at Brattleboro. Miss Wilkins' mother's people were of the Holbrooks of Holbrook—fine 'genteel people of the old sort,'" survivals of an early New England aristocracy. We shall find many of them depicted with tender care as we read "A Humble Romance" and the tales which followed it.

From this union of two branches of primitive New England stock was born Mary Eleanor Wilkins on January 7, 1862, at Randolph, a little village half an hour by rail out of Boston, in a home next door to the mansion which her grandfather Holbrook had built with his own hands.

There is little to record of her early years. A

frail and sensitive child, unable to attend school, she
was much by herself, a dreamer and an eager reader
in the seclusion of her home while other children
were playing at active games in the out of doors.
One thinks of this when one reads of the lonely and
imaginative children scattered throughout her stories:—*Nancy Wren* in "A Gentle Ghost"; *Diantha*
in "The Prism"; and the pathetic little soul in "Big
Sister Solly." When she was eight her parents
tried the experiment of sending her to Mount Hol-
yoke Seminary, but in a year her health had become
so precarious that she was withdrawn. Two years
later, in 1873, she removed with her parents to
Brattleboro, Vermont, a larger town at the base of
the Green Mountains and near the Connecticut River.
"Sometimes I wonder," she has written, "if the
marvellous beauty of that locality was not largely
instrumental in making me try to achieve anything."
Here again she saw a little of school life, this time as
a day pupil in a boarding-school at West Brattleboro, but not for long. Like Emily Brontë, with
whom in so many ways she may be compared, she
was almost wholly self-educated and that in her
own home. She was an imaginative child and early
she created for herself a world of her own from the
materials of her reading. "I read Dickens and
Thackeray and Poe," she says, "and some translations of Goethe. I also read translations from

the Greek. I remember being delighted at a very early age with some of the Greek philosophers, I cannot remember which. I was on very intimate terms with mythological people. I read Ossian; I read a lot of poetry."

This Hawthorne-like seclusion during a shy and dreamy childhood, this perpetual reading of poetry and old romance and far-off literatures, made upon her an indelible impression. Being "on very intimate terms with mythological people" meant that the world of fairies became to her as real as it was to her own heroine of "The Prism," who, through the cut-glass pendant which she had appropriated from the parlor lamp, saw the whole fairy world, and who, as she told of her visions, had "in her eyes a light not of her day or generation, maybe inherited from some far-off Celtic ancestor . . . a strain of imagination which had survived the glaring light of latter days of commonness." And then one remembers that the author of the story has spoken of her own ancestry as "straight American, with a legend of French lineage generations back." Two distinct strains, indeed, we shall find in this daughter of New England: the Puritan with tyrannical conscience and grim repression of soul, and the Gallic with lightsomeness of fancy and exquisite sensitiveness to beauty.

The Gallic element was the first to manifest itself. It was only natural that a child of her temperament and rearing should begin to write early, and that her first attempts should be lyrical, should be fanciful little songs for childhood and ballads of fairy-land. One may find them in early volumes of "St. Nicholas," lyrics like "Cross-Patch" and "Rock-a-bye Baby," or in "Wide Awake," fairy-tales in prose like "The Cow with the Golden Horns," which furnished the title for her first published book, or "The Princess Rosetta," or "The Silver Hen." "Given perfect freedom of choice, which I was not given," she has said, "I might have been a lyrist, but the notes would certainly have been intense." Even as a child she had reveled in the song-books of the Elizabethans, and that she had read the more modern masters, like Rossetti, is evident from such lyrics as "Banbury Cross":

> "Pray show the way to Banbury Cross,'
>   *Silver bells are ringing;*
> "To find the place I 'm at a loss,"
>   *Silver bells are ringing;*
> "Pass six tall hollyhocks red and white;
> Then, turn the corner toward the right—"

and so on and on. Her fairy ballads ring with conviction. She is at her best in dainty works like "The Fairy Flag"; in some of her climaxes, indeed, she is almost perfect:

There came a twang o' pearly harp,
　There came a lilting loud and sweet;
And softly o'er the fairy bridge
　There came the dance o' slender feet.

In September, 1881, when she was twenty, she began a series of *vers de société* lyrics in "The Century Magazine"—"Sweet Phyllis," "Boy's Love,"
"It was a Lass," and others, lyrics that were not
dimmed by their proximity in the magazine to
similar work by James Whitcomb Riley, Frank
Dempster Sherman, H. C. Bunner, and Andrew
Lang. A lyric like this, for instance, written a
little later, would enrich any collection:

Now is the cherry in blossom, Love,
　Love of my heart, with the apple to follow;
Over the village at nightfall now
　Merrily veers and darts the swallow.

At nightfall now in the dark marsh grass
　Awakes the chorus that sings old sorrow;
The evening star is dim for the dew,
　And the apple and lilac will bloom to-morrow.

The honeysuckle is red on the rock;
　The willow floats over the brook like a feather;
In every shadow some love lies hid,
　And you and I in the world together.

The last of the "Century" series, "A Maiden Lady,"

is the transition from her period of poetry and
dreams to that of prose.   From its opening stanza,

> Of a summer afternoon,
> In a parlor window there,
> She would sit, her meek face showing
> Delicately long and fair,
> Sewing on some dainty garment, no one ever saw her
> wear,

to the last,

> When she cried, poor, shy old maiden,
> Her artless secret saw the sun:—
> She had been with love acquainted,
> Always, just like anyone:—
> But had kept him in a closet hidden, as a skeleton,

we have the material and the method of the short
stories which were even then beginning to come: their
swift characterization, their touch of humor and gentle pathos, and their telling close.   The lyric marks
the end of one period and the beginning of another.

II

The second period in her life came with the
death of her father in 1883.   Her last years at
Brattleboro had been filled with the bitterest experiences of bereavement.   Her only sister had

died and then her mother. For a time she kept house for her father; then he too died, and, virtually alone in the world, she returned to the home of her girlhood and took up her residence with Miss Mary Wales, a friend of her earlier years. "I returned to Randolph, Massachusetts," she says with typical incisiveness, "and made my home with friends. I was forced to work for my mere living, and of course continued writing, which I had already begun, although when my father, the last of my family, died, I had earned very little. . . . I wrote no more *vers de société,* no more 'Cherries in Blossom.' I had to earn my living. I also had an aunt to support. . . . I had written only three stories, that is real stories for adults. One was a prize story, fifty dollars, the others were accepted by Harper & Brothers."

The prize-winning story, "A Shadow Family," was printed in the Boston paper which had conducted the contest; the second story, "Two Old Lovers," was accepted by "Harper's Bazar," then edited by Mary L. Booth, who was the first to discover the new short story writer; and the third, "A Humble Romance," was published in "Harper's Monthly" in June, 1884. From now on she became a writer of short fiction, a literary craftsman, writing to the limit of her strength, not what she would, but what she must if she was to sell her product and win immediate success, which in her case was necessary. "Circumstances," she has said, "seemed to make it imperative for me that I do that one thing and no other. I did not at the time think much about the choice. I think more now."

She was influenced, perhaps molded, by her times. The eighties, at the opening of which she began to work, stand in American fiction for "local color." In 1884, when her stories began first to appear in the Harper publications,—the literature-of-locality tide, with its dialect and its strangeness of materials, was at its full. During this single year there were published "In the Tennessee Mountains" by Charles Egbert Craddock, "Mingo and Other Sketches" by Joel Chandler Harris, "On the Frontier" by Bret Harte, "Doctor Sevier" by Cable, "Huckleberry Finn" by Mark Twain, "Old Mark Langston" by Richard Malcolm Johnston, "The Story of a Country Town" by Edgar W. Howe, "Tompkins and Other Folks" by Philander Deming, "A Country Doctor" by Sarah Orne Jewett, and "The San Rosario Ranch" by Maude Howe. Thomas Nelson Page's story "Marse Chan," written entirely in the negro dialect, was now brought out and published after having been held by the magazine timidly for several years, and immediately it was hailed by the reading public as a modern classic. The period of dialect was at its height; no wonder that Miss

Wilkins's second story in "Harper's Monthly," "An Honest Soul," began, as most assuredly it would not have begun in Hawthorne's day, with the sentence: "Thar's Mis' Bliss's pieces in the brown kaliker bag, an' thar's Mis' Bennett's pieces in the bed-tickin' bag." There are fashions in literature as there are fashions in wearing apparel, and one who would live by literature must be aware of them or else write for posterity. The new writer was in no position to become a rebel even if she had desired, and she therefore began to make localized studies of the life about her, even as Miss Murfree was doing, and Page and Harris and Cable.

The New England of the eighties seemingly had been exhausted as a background for fiction. Mrs. Stowe had used it freely and Rose Terry Cooke and Sarah Orne Jewett and Howells and others, but there had been little attempt as yet to study it with the new focus, to seek for the strange, the unique in background and character. The times demanded *Colonel Starbottles* and *Yuba Bills, Ramonas* and *Colonel Sellerses, Posson Joneses* and *Mingos,* and to find them in New England one must seek for them in that terminal moraine of human specimens which the New England glacial period of puritanism had left in its wake: abnormalities of conscience, freedom of will become narrow wilfulness, unswerving allegiance to an idea degenerated into balkiness, frugality engendered by a scanty soil warped into a *Silas-Berry*-like meanness of soul, the sensitiveness born of isolated environment became the very essence of sullen pride and egotism, and added to all this a patriarchal sense of masculine superiority and headship of households, based on a narrow interpretation of the Hebrew Scriptures, which has resulted in a type of womanhood often so individual and so peculiar in its tragic problems as to be classifiable as unique.

It was into this field of investigation that Miss Wilkins threw herself with all the intensity of her lyric soul. She chose the short story form of expression partly because it was the fashion of the time but chiefly because it promised the most immediate results. "What directed me to the short story? I think the answer is very simple. The short story did not take so long to write, it was easier, and of course I was not *sure* of my own ability to write even the short story, much less a novel. I consider the art of the novel as a very different affair from that of the short story. The latter can be a simple little melody, the other can be grand opera." Her New England conscience demanded moral basis for her art, her lyric soul could express itself only with intensity; therefore the seriousness of her themes, the swift rush of her narrative without pause for ornament or background, the absorption of soul that forgot itself in its eager contemplation of the drama unfolding before her. Her vogue came not from any new information that she gave concerning her material or life in general: it came from her originality of method, her gripping intensity, her power to move the reader's emotions.

In 1887 twenty-eight of her short stories were published in a collection entitled "A Humble Romance and Other Stories." Her first real books, "The Cow with the Golden Horns" and "The Adventures of Ann," collections of early juvenile stories for "Wide Awake," had been published without her knowledge. The book produced no such sensation as did the first collections of Harte and Miss Murfree and Cable and Harris. The New York "Critic," the leading critical journal of its day in America, dismissed it with seven lines, half of them patronizing praise and half protest against the grotesque impossibility of one of her characters. Holmes and Lowell, however, felt the power of the new writer and congratulated her. General recognition came slowly. The year 1890 may be set as the date of her final triumph. The "Critic" again noticed her, this time with the simple announcement that "There is something like a craze in England over Mary E. Wilkins." Then had come the full tide of her popularity. When a year later, in 1891,

"A New England Nun and Other Stories" appeared, most of the American critics echoed the review of the London "Spectator": "The stories are among the most remarkable feats of what we may call literary impressionism in our language, so powerfully do they stamp on the reader's mind the image of the classes and individuals they portray without spending on the picture a single redundant word, a single superfluous word."

The decade from 1887, the year of "A Humble Romance," to "Madelon: a Novel," 1896, was the golden period of her genius. It was the period of short stories in her first manner: stories bare of all save the absolute essentials, staccato in style, often crude even to incorrectness, yet so vibrant with human life that they hold their reader now with intense sympathy, now with indignation, now with pleasure, now with something like fear. "Young Lucretia and Other Stories," juvenile tales from "St. Nicholas," came in 1892, and "Jane Field," which by every standard of criticism is a short story, began as a serial in "Harper's Monthly" the same year. Two years later, in 1894, in "Harper's Weekly," came "Pembroke," nominally a novel, but really a series of short story episodes. All the stories in "Silence and Other Stories," 1898, were written during this period, the last of them being "Evelina's Garden," which appeared in "Harper's" in June, 1896. It was the decade of her most spontaneous work, the period of her young enthusiasm.

In the joy and the wonder of her success her youthful dreams of literature came again. "Miss Wilkins informs me that she has always had a desire to write a play," wrote Mr. Charles E. Wingate in one of his Boston letters of the period. She had actually begun upon one and like Hawthorne she turned for her material to old Salem and its great tragedy. In 1890 she had finished "Giles Corey, Yeoman: a Play," and it had been read with high approval at the Deerfield summer school of history and romance. Later on, completely re-written, it was given a trial on the Boston stage, and, to be brief, it failed, completely and definitely. Undoubted power and literary beauty it had, but its writer knew nothing of stagecraft, and moreover its sponsors handled it with awkwardness, and its failure was total. Poetry, too, still called to her. In 1897 she issued "Once Upon a Time and Other Child Verses," and more and more infrequently she sent lyrics to the leading magazines. One may find as late as 1900 such sonnets as "Cyrano de Bergerac" in "Harper's" and "The Lode Star" in "Scribner's," lyrics that make us wonder what might have been had she been able to dedicate all of her powers to the elder muses.

III

It was in this second period then, the period which ended with "Pembroke" and the exquisite story "Evelina's Garden," that Miss Wilkins made her strongest and most original contribution to American literature. But criticism had been doing its work. Almost every reviewer since her first book had closed his review by pointing out her bareness and repression of style, her short, almost gasping sentence structure and, in the case of "Pembroke," which had run serially as a novel, had noted its looseness of structure. They declared it to be like "Jane Field," of short story texture rather than a novel, and they bade her back to her earlier field, often with the observation that the short story by its very nature unfits one who has long used it for any other form of fiction.

That Miss Wilkins was aware of this criticism cannot be doubted. In the only bit of literary criticism that I can find from her pen, a critique of Emily Brontë written in 1903, she has expressed the opinion that had the author of "Wuthering Heights" "lived longer she might have become equally acquainted with the truth and power of grace; she might have widened her audience; she might have attracted instead of repelled, but she could not have written a greater book, so far as the abstract quality of greatness goes." Were Emily Brontë alive to-day she might reply to her critic: "Your own experience would seem to show that this is true. You lived longer than I, you sought to become acquainted with the truth and power of grace, you strove to attract and please, you widened your audience, but unquestionably you wrote nothing so great as your first work, so far as the abstract quality of greatness goes." The retort would sum up the quality of her final period, her period of novels, beginning with "Madelon," of experiments in style and technique, of conscious art.

One's first impression as one approaches the work of Mary E. Wilkins Freeman is a feeling of surprise at its bulk. Her industry has been remarkable. "Edgewater People," 1918, was her thirty-eighth book. Beginning with "Madelon," 1896, she wrote nine major novels in twelve years, the most of them for serial publication in magazines, and during the same time she issued nine collections of short stories. The total of her short stories in all her collections is 173, and in addition she has written about sixty-five more which have never been republished from the magazines. Seventy-one of her short stories appeared in "Harper's Magazine" alone. Moreover, in addition to the nine novels mentioned above, she has written either wholly or in part six other stories which are generally rated as novels. When her physical frailness is considered and the ill health that she has struggled with her life long, the quantity of her literary output is not the least of her claims upon our wonder.

One is next impressed by the variety in her work, especially in the output after "Pembroke." It seems like the work of an experimenter, of one who is careful to adapt her products to the standards of the various markets that may care to buy them. In 1895 came a detective novel founded on the Borden murder case in Massachusetts, "The Long Arm," which, revised by Mr. Chamberlain of the "Youth's Companion," won the first prize of $2000 from three thousand competitors. The next year came "Madelon," an intense love story with a heroine not of New England ancestry, a maiden partly French and partly Indian, who in her savage, unreasoning cleaving to her lover reminds us of the lovers in Emily Brontë's romance. Quickly following it came "Jerome, a Poor Young Man," the longest and most elaborate of her fiction, a novel of purpose for "Harper's Weekly," a sermon for the times. Abandoning her early method of standing detached from her material, she became a propagandist, a sentimentalist with a theory, a pleader for the under dog in the industrial battle.

With her next novel, "The Jamesons," contributed as a serial to "The Ladies' Home Journal," she tried still another experiment. We may call it a "period story," a serio-comic satire upon the fads and foibles of its time. From its very nature it is ephemeral work, as ephemeral as a fashion-plate. Mrs. Jameson, a city woman who sets out to reform a little country town and to give it city ideals, is a caricature. No sane woman in America, no matter what has been her training, will be so ignorant of country life as to feed her pigs on alternate days so the bacon may have alternate streaks of fat and lean, 'or will insist on setting hens on hard-boiled eggs so that the nests may be thoroughly antiseptic. It is not even good comedy. This was in 1899. The next year, the year of "To Have and to Hold," "When Knighthood was in Flower," and "Alice of Old Vincennes," she, too, wrote a historical romance, "The Heart's Highway, a Romance of Virginia in the Seventeenth Century," vibrant with passion, in flowing, gorgeous sentences that, compared with those of her earlier work, are as hot-house roses compared with the wild violets of a New Hampshire springtime. A passage like this certainly has little in it to remind one of the stories in her first collections:

As we followed on that moonlight night, she and I alone, of a sudden I felt my youth and love arise to such an assailing of the joy of life, that I knew myself dragged as it were by it, and had no more choosing as to what I should not do. Verily it would be easier to lead an army of malcontents than one's own self. And something there was about the moon-light on that fair Virginian night, and the heaviness of the honey-scents, and the pressure of life and love on every side, in bush and vine and tree and nest, which seemed to overbear me and sweep me along on the crest of some green tide of spring. Verily there are forces of this world which are beyond the overcoming of mortal man so long as he is encumbered by his mortality.

IV

After her marriage in 1902 to Dr. Charles M. Freeman, whom she had first met in the home of Dr. Alden, and her removal to Metuchen, New Jersey, where she has since made her home, she devoted herself for several years to short story work, but in 1905 she published in "Harper's Bazar" a long novel, "The Debtor," then the next year in "Harper's Weekly" "By the Light of the Soul," and since that time she has issued "Doc Gordon," 1906, "The Shoulders of Atlas," 1908, "Butterfly House," a serial in "The Woman's Home Companion," and finally, in collaboration with Mrs. Florence Morse Kingsley, "The Alabaster Box"— surely a miscellaneous collection. One need not linger long with these books. Almost without exception they lack constructive art: the plot in many of them is improbable, it does not steadily and inevitably grow to a culmination, the ending often is weak. Their power, and all of them have unquestioned elements of strength, lies in parts instead of wholes, in passages and episodes, in vivid characterization, in pictures, however, of completed character rather than in tracings of gradual character development; in short story technique, in short, rather than in novelistic art. In many of the novels there is a distinct gain in sentence length and fluidity of style, yet one feels every such gain has been at the expense of spontaneity and convincingness.

Much better may one linger over the ninety-five and more short stories which she wrote during the period. Like her novels they show a surprising variety of types of fiction and like them a surprising unevenness. That they are not all of them on the level of her earlier work is not to be wondered at; no literary crop so quickly exhausts the soil as the short story. A single collection of studies of localized environment is all that most writers can make with profit, as witness Harte and Cable, Miss Murfree and Page. Mrs. Freeman in her short story work has clung to her New England themes and characters as tenaciously as Harte clung to California and with something of the same result.

Some of these later stories have about them, like so many of her novels, the odor of the market-place. They were made to order. In "People of Our Neighborhood," for instance, published in a domestic journal, she seems deliberately to have exploited her powers of characterization. Often, moreover, there is evidence of haste, of jaded enthusiasm, of diminishing returns from an over-cultivated area. And yet, despite all this, one may say with confidence that the general average of her later short story work is higher than that of the later short story average of any American contemporary, and that here and there in her later collections one may find a story that comes fully up to the highest achievements of her time.

In many of her later short stories she tried, as in her novels, to enrich her style, to rid herself of the mannerisms of the eighties, and, in some of her collections, to change the key of her work, and to attempt themes more in accord with her earlier ambitions. "The most of my work," she has said, and there is a touch of the pathetic in her words, "is not really the kind that I myself like. I want more symbolism, more mysticism. I left that out because it struck me people did not want it, and I was forced to consider selling qualities." A faint trace of symbolism, Hawthorne-like in its suggestiveness, pervades all her best work. One sees it in the gradual stoop that came to the stubborn *Barney Thayer* and that was overcome when once he threw off his burden of pride, and one sees it in a story published as late as 1917, "The Cloak Also," in which the condition of the neighboring river is constantly mentioned in connection with the leading character, *Joel Rich,* the defrauded storekeeper, who suddenly, like the river after the hot spring day, broke the bonds that so long had held him and swept over his customers with a torrent of truth about themselves. The story ends thus: "There was a breaking-up of human meanness and dishonesty greater than the breaking-up of the ice in the great river." One might illustrate, too, with *Amarina,* in the story "Amarina's Roses," the "last of the *Deering* women" who was herself a rose, "an instance of endurance instead of degeneration. She was as perfect as one of the roses in her garden, which had come of the reproduction of many generations of bloom." This is the theme of her volume "Understudies," poetic exercises in symbolism, flowers and animals so treated as to suggest women and men, and also of her collection "Six Trees," stories of people who are not only analogous to certain trees, but in some subtle way are bound to them in their lives and destinies. Her treatment of the mystic world is also Hawthorne-like in its subtle art. No literary theme is so disastrous to

the unskilful; none requires of its user more consummate skill. As a teller of ghost stories few
have surpassed her. She has no tales of vulgar
horror; the usual machinery of such stories she
throws away; the boundaries between the seen and
the unseen she does not set. Of her ghosts one
may hardly say whether they are of the earth or
not: they are maidens who have merely faded
away from their ghostlike lives. There is a gentle
mystery in her very titles: "The Southwest
Chamber," "Shadows on the Wall," "Luella Miller,"
"The Vacant Lot," "The Wind in the Rosebush."

Not all her stories deal with the New England
environment. Some of them are parables like many
of Hawthorne's. "A Slip of the Leash," for instance, which may be compared with the elder
romancer's "Wakefield," makes us wonder what
might have been had she earlier confined herself
to such themes. The story is universal. The head
of a prosperous family in the far West becomes
more and more oppressed by the chains of convention that have bound him hand and foot to one
spot and one round of life. The eternal monotony
of civilization lays more and more hold upon his
soul, until one day in the restlessness of the early
springtime, "rasped beyond endurance," he drops
everything by an impulse and disappears into the
perfect freedom of the forest. Month after month

he lingers upon the outskirts of the settlement, watching the slow adjustment of his family to their new life without him. Year after year goes by. The subtle changes in the woman who was his wife as the sense of widowhood comes upon her and then gradually fades into a new sense of freedom, and the consequent changes in the characters of his children, all are noted by the man as he stands unseen and silently protects them. Then finally, by another impulse, he returns like *Wakefield,* takes up the thread of his life where he had dropped it so long before, and all moves again in the old channel, but in the meantime the souls of the man and the woman have been laid open to our gaze, and with a start we find ourselves asking the ancient question, "Lord, is it I?" She has done nothing stronger. It is enough in itself to warrant our statement that in her last period, the period that has been so consistently assailed by her critics, her powers as a writer of short stories did not wholly decline. As late as 1909 the New York "Nation," reviewing her book, "The Winning Lady and Other Stories," could call it the best of all her collections.

VI

It is, however, the short stories of her earliest collections, "A Humble Romance" and "A New

England Nun," with "Pembroke" which followed, that will give her her final place among American writers. In these we have her first spontaneous work; work that is hers alone, and that has furnished a short story type which no one may imitate without detection any more than one may imitate the work of Irving or of Poe. This element of originality is the first that must be considered by the critic. We of a later day, to whom the manner has become familiar, do not realize how startlingly novel these tales appeared to their first readers. In 1887, the year of "A Humble Romance," Kipling was unknown in America: the first mention of his name in the "Critic" was in March, 1890. It was in 1893, ten years after Miss Wilkins's removal, that he also took up his residence in Brattleboro and that his loud trumpet began to dominate the fiction of the decade. The first surprise at the work of Miss Wilkins came from her method, her peculiar perspective, her style, her startling originality. She appeared suddenly, almost without forebears; seemingly she had been influenced by no one. "Concerning any influence of other writers," she has written of herself, "it may seem egotistical, but there was none. I did, however strange it may seem, stand entirely alone. As a matter of fact, I would read nothing which I thought might influence me. I had not read the French short stories; I had not read Miss Jewett's stories. I will add that, although I have repeatedly heard that I was founded on Jane Austen, I have never read any of her books."

This independence accounts for many crudities in her earlier work, and it accounts also for most of those elements in her short stories that have given her the place that is hers. She was herself and no one else. Her short sentence structure is a part of her personal equation; it is her literary length of stride. When she attempts more elaborate structure she becomes self-conscious and unconvincing. All her efforts in her novels to gain a more flowing style have been unable to give her the long sentence habit. As late as 1913 she could begin a story with a paragraph like this:

Jim Bennett had never married. He had passed middle life and possessed considerable property. Susan Adkins kept house for him. She was a widow and a very distant relative. Jim had two nieces, his brother's daughters. One, Alma Beecher, was married; the other, Amanda, was not. The nieces had naïvely grasping views concerning their uncle and his property.

It is as bare and as disjointed as a scenario. The writer has concentrated upon four persons and a situation, and she presents her material intensely with no more thought of ornamentation than had her Puritan ancestors when they poured out their burning convictions of sin and salvation. Everywhere repression. The dialogue moves swiftly without explanation; every coloring adjective is primly removed.

The center of her art, the beginning and the end of it, is humanity, the individual soul. She plunges at once *in medias res,* usually with the name of her leading character. Her backgrounds are incidental. There is as little description in her best stories as there is in an old ballad. Swiftly she introduces her two or three or four characters: they reveal themselves by means of dialogue, they become often fearfully alive, they grip at the heart or the throat, and then suddenly with a throb the story is done, like a ballad. Unlike Bret Harte or Miss Murfree or Hardy, with whom the physical landscape is often one of the characters in the tale, she so strips her narratives of background that they become universal in their atmosphere and setting. The grim story "Louisa" might be a translation from the Russian; "A Village Lear" might be passed as a story of Egdon Heath. The most of her stories are localized only by the fact that her characters are such as are found solely within the confines of the old New England puritanism. Her chief use of landscape, as has been suggested, is Hawthornesque—the use of it symbolically, poetically, as an interpreting or contrasting touch in her human tragedy or comedy. Thus the closing sentences in "A Village Lear": the old man, dying, sees in imagination his cruel daughters transfigured, coming to him over the meadow with love in their faces, "jest as they did when they was young":

"Jest see 'em, Sary." The old man laughed. Out of his ghastly, death-stricken features shone the expression of a happy child. "Jest look at 'em, Sary," he repeated.

Sarah looked, and she saw only the meadow covered with a short waving crop of goldenrod, and over it the September sky.

This intensity, repressed with New England severity, is the only style that could fitly treat the material that her conscience and her stern sense of truth furnished her—the only material that she knew. Her characters are like plants that have sprung up from a sterile soil. As subjects for fiction in the older interpretation of fiction they seem impossible: tillers of rocky hillsides, their natures warped by their poverty-stricken environment; old maids, prim and angular, who have erected a secret shrine in their hearts in commemoration of a moment in the long ago to which a more sophisticated maiden would never have given a second thought; workhouse inmates, forlorn children, work-worn wives of driving men, stern, practical-minded women

whom generations of repression have rendered sex-
less—the descendants of come-outers, noncomform-
ists, dissenters, sons and daughters of the men who
survived the earlier régime with its blue-laws, its
interminable dialectic, its grim bareness, and, added
to all this, generations of solitude on hillside farms
tilled in the face of nature's protest. The result
was survivals, not of the fittest, but of the worst
elements—abnormalities, reliance upon inherited
dogma, stubbornness of head and meanness often.
Moreover, the accumulated habits of generations
of wrestlers with moral problems had begotten an
uneasiness of soul whenever there was a stepping
out of the ruts plowed by the fathers—the New
England conscience. In the stories of Miss Wilkins
even the children are victims: little *Anna Eliza*
finally confesses to her grandmother that she lost her
patchwork on purpose; little *Patience,* after a heroic
struggle with herself, braves the terrors of the old
Squire's presence and gives him back the sixpence
prize he had awarded the best scholar in the school
because at the critical moment some one had whispered to her the answer to his question. In these
tales we see not the New England of Mrs. Stowe,
the New England of the high tide period, nor that
of Miss Jewett, the New England of the transition:
it is the picture of the swift decline and the final
wreckage, the distorted fragments of what once had

been glorious. It is the fifth act of the Puritan drama. A half-century before, the minister would have been the central figure of a New England village picture; in "A New England Nun" there are only four ministers mentioned, all of them minor figures, spineless and effeminate.

How did this young girl of twenty-five know of all this human tragedy, of all these grim and desolate lives, of all these curious abnormalities of soul? There are pages in her work as remorselessly gripping as anything in modern realism. One might gather them into a New England "Spoon River Anthology"—pictures of senility almost terrifying, as in "Louisa"; of the parish workhouse as depressing as Zola, in "Sister Liddy"; of human cruelty as harrowing as Balzac's "Père Goriot," in "A Village Lear." One may reply in the words of her own critique of Emily Brontë: "Hedged about by great spaces of loneliness and insuperable barriers of religion, in an isolated parsonage with more of the dead than the living for neighbors, . . . how she ever came to comprehend the primitive brutalities and passions, and the great truth of life that sanctifies them, is a mystery. The knowledge could not have come from any actual experience. The book is not the result of any personal stress. She had given to her a light for the hidden darkness of human nature, irrespective of her own emotions.

A lamp was set to her feet in the beginning. If a girl of twenty-eight could write a novel like 'Wuthering Heights,' no other conclusion is possible."

This impression is strengthened by another, an almost Shaksperian, element in her work: she stands external to her material and seemingly she is irresponsible for it. She makes no comment; her characters seemingly are alone responsible for the story —they develop themselves. It is the art of the old ballad which was anonymous; the subjective is absent. To quote again from her critique: "All that Emily Brontë is intent upon is the truth, the exactness of the equations of her characters, not the impression which they make upon her readers or herself. She handles brutality and coarseness as another woman would handle a painted fan. It is enough for her that the thing is so. It is not her business if it comes down like a sledge-hammer upon the nerves of her audience, or even if it casts reflections derogatory to herself."

Only in parts and passages is her work of "Spoon River Anthology" texture. In soul she is a romanticist and a poet. Even in her most depressing material there is little of realism in the Zola sense of the term. Her New England critics declare that her vision, so far as at least New England character is concerned, is astigmatic; that she has given caricatures rather than realistic studies from the life. They are wrong and they are right. In reality, her characters are of the Dickens type, not photographs but paintings, idealizations of the truth, individuals intensely alive, yet drawn not from the life, but from the heightened images projected by their creator's imagination. They are therefore, in reality, like the characters of Dickens, mythological creations. Their author, a nunlike soul who has lived her whole life like an Emily Brontë in the seclusion of a little village, frail of body and delicate of health, over-imaginative, poetic, intense, creates in the quiet of her study her own world. Her materials are indeed scanty. She has, like the Brontë sisters, known little of the actual lives of men save as feminine talk of a small town has brought them to her. Her own heart, however, she has known, and her own dreamings and hopes and idealizings. With these she did her work. How far unconsciously she has written autobiography we may never know, and yet we know this, that the writer of fiction which is at all worth our study can have no secrets, and that inevitably he spins his web from his own heart. One need say no more. Her characters mostly are unmarried women. Of the central figures in the twenty-four stories of "A New England Nun" nineteen are unmarried females and all but five of them are past middle age. Or, to go still wider, there are in the book, leaving out merely incidental personages, sixty-seven characters, all but sixteen of whom are women, just half of them unmarried.

With such material there are infinite possibilities for depressed realism, and yet seldom are we sent away depressed. Almost all her stories, and some of them against the very protest of nature, end happily. The lover returns; the hapless maiden, pathetically patient through years of waiting, is married at last; justice is done and all is well. Even "Louisa" turns out happily. The Puritan conscience seems to consider it a duty to justify the ways of God to man. Unconsciously it is impressed with the idea that it is compelled to be a defender of God and to make life's plots come out in strict equity, with no injustice done. It is not too much to declare that no descendant of the New England Puritans can be an absolute realist.

Her favorite theme is revolt. Her tale opens with a study of repression. The central figure is bound by inherited forces which hold him as with steel. Sometimes the force is external, as in the case of *Mrs. Penn* in "The Revolt of 'Mother,'" but more often is it internal. On the surface of the life there is apparent serenity and reserve, but beneath there is an increasing fire. Then suddenly the barriers break and the strength of the recoil is in proportion

to the strength of the repression. *Jane Field,* once
the barrier of her deception is down, spends the
rest of her life in an insane iteration of her story
of weakness; *Selma Woodsum* in the fierce impetuosity of her repentence can scarce be restrained
from publishing in all the papers the story of her
violation of her conscience. It is the central topic
of "Jane Field"; it furnished the most gripping
episode in "Pembroke"—the midnight coasting of
Ephraim; it is the theme of four stories in "A
New England Nun": "A Village Singer," "Sister
Liddy," "Amanda and Love," "The Revolt of
'Mother'"; and it is central in many later stories
like "Evelina's Garden," "The Givers," "A Slip
of the Leash," "The Cloak Also," and "The Liar."

She does not present her material merely to entertain. In all her stories there is far more than
the story. "The Revolt of 'Mother,'" for instance,
might furnish a thesis on the homes of farmers,
and yet no one may call it a purpose story. There
are times when the preacher that is within every
descendant of New Englanders gets the better of
the artist, but it is not often. In "The Amethyst
Comb," for example, she can launch out like this:

When a man or a woman holds fast to youth, even
if successfully, there is something of the pitiful and
the tragic involved. It is the everlasting struggle of
the soul to retain the joy of earth, whose fleeting

distinguishes it from heaven, and whose retention is not accomplished without an inner knowledge of its futility.

But more often these deeper truths of the story are gold that is far from the surface. Never does she present unlovely pictures simply to display them. Kipling's robust cynicism is in a world apart from hers. She thinks well of life; she hates oppression with her whole New England soul, and she sends her reader away always more kindly of heart, more tolerant, more neighborly in the deeper sense of the word.

Her kinship is with Hawthorne rather than with the realists. Both worked in the darker materials of New England Puritanism; both were romancers and poets, both were seekers after truth, and both were able to throw over their work a subtle atmosphere that was all their own. Hawthorne, writing as he did in the mid-nineteenth century, in the mild noon of later German romance, suffused his work with the rich glow that the later writer, bound by her more prosaic times, was unable to find; she, however, equal to him in her command of pathos and of emotional intensity, was able to surpass him in her command of gripping situation and her powers of compelling characterization. Of the generation born since the war she alone may be compared with this earliest depicter of the New England soul.

THE SHADOW OF LONGFELLOW

IN the third number of his "Hymns to the Night," Novalis records that once while he was weeping on the grave that had swallowed up his very life, "alone as no other mortal ever had been alone," suddenly there had come upon him a kind of shuddery twilight, a new atmosphere, that swept from him forever all desire for day. He stood in a new world, the transfigured world of night. Then through the mist there had appeared to him the glorified figure of his beloved who henceforth was to be an abiding presence, and from that moment he had had "an eternal, unchanging faith in the heaven of Night."

It is well known that the death of his betrothed, followed a few weeks later by the death of his favorite brother, made of Novalis a dreamer and a mystic. It swept away from him the boundaries between the worlds of matter and of spirit until he was no longer sure that there were boundaries at all. Henceforth for him the only reality was the unreal. There were to be for him no more sharp outlines; life was to move in a delicious mist, amid the half-seen and the dreamy, in a "holy, inex-

pressible, mysterious Night." Twilight with its
grotesqueries and shadows, allowing the imagination free rein, moonlight soft and ethereal, delicious
sadness, longing for something vaguely felt yet
inexpressible, crumbling ruins, dim cathedrals, the
dream-world of medievalism—all things where the
senses and the reason lose perspective and must be
supplemented by the fancy—these became for him
the real.   Day with its commonplaces was the unreality.   In a word, he became a romanticist and
a leader in that strange choir which sang the decadence of the German *Sturm und Drang*.

Almost identical was the experience of our own
Longfellow.   The shock, the utter bereavement,
the unutterable loneliness, the brooding, the vision,
the ministry of night, the mysticism—the parallel
is startling.   He ran, it is true, into no fantasti-
cisms, he exploited no revolution, he curbed no con-
suming genius, yet, for all that, he was the true child
of Novalis—mystic, dreamer, poet of the Night.
While all about him were the din and the shoutings
of a lusty young nation carving with might a new
commonwealth from raw nature, he steadfastly
held true to his vision, for, says Novalis, "he who
has once stood on earth's borderland and perceived
that new county—the dwelling of Night—returns
no more to the tumult of life, to the land where
light reigns amid ceaseless unrest."

The year 1836 marks the opening of the second period in the life of Longfellow. All that he produced before it when compared with the product of his later pen is as different as if written by another. An earnest, somewhat sentimental youth, never a boy among boys, horizoned only by his father's library, he had grown up like Hawthorne in a world created by his imagination from fragments of his reading.

College widened his opportunities for knowing books; it did little more. The ancient classics—Homer, Herodotus, Vergil, Horace—impersonal creations that seem as if a part of nature herself, not the deliberate work of man; the English bards—Milton, Pope, Dryden, Gray, Goldsmith—great shadowy names, almost abstractions; and then, all of a sudden, a book with the ink scarce dry, the last numbers not yet written perhaps—"The Sketch-Book," marvelously modern, marvelously beautiful, the work of one who was an American and a contemporary: it set his pulse to running. He records that he "read each succeeding number with ever-increasing wonder and delight, spellbound by its pleasant humor, its melancholy tenderness, its atmosphere of reverie—nay even by its gray-brown covers, the shaded letters of its titles, and the fair clear type, which seemed an outward symbol of its style." Following hard upon it had come that chaste little book of poems by Bryant, then "The Spy" by Cooper, that first "seller" among American novels.

Authorship at last had become a concrete thing in the young student's mind. He, too, would make books. And it was now that he began to dream of a wider horizon; to turn with longing toward that vague land over which Irving had thrown his haze of romance. "If I were in England now," writes the college junior, "(and I have been wishing myself there all the day long so warmly that if my wishes could but turn to realities I should have been there), I should become a bacchanalian for a while. I do not believe that any person can read the fifth number of the Sketch-Book without feeling at least, if not expressing, a wish similar to my own." But Europe and literature were utterly out of the question. The father was in only moderate circumstances, and he had, moreover, a supply of hardheaded Yankee wisdom. "A literary life," he wrote the ambitious senior, "to one who has the means of support, must be very pleasant, but there is not enough wealth in this country to afford encouragement and patronage to merely literary men." It was time for the boy to settle down to the studying of his profession. A time there was of heart-burning and mild rebellion, but there was no help for it. The young graduate settled down to the study of the law with no prospects save those that concerned the humdrum of his deeds and conveyances and routine of the law office.

Then like a flash out of clear sky came the miracle. Where else can you find a little, struggling country college sending a boy of nineteen to Europe to fit him for a chair in an utterly new subject, one that even Harvard has only just recognized? But no such thoughts engaged the youth. Away he sailed into the land of his dreams, into the region that "The Sketch-Book" had made for him "a kind of Holy Land lying far off beyond the blue horizon of the ocean."

For three years he wandered over enchanted ground—France, Spain, Italy, Germany, England —a *Wunderreise,* a kind of glorified day-dream come true. He came back an enthusiast, an interpreter, a missionary. There had been no single overmastering impression, but a broadening, a revealing, an educating in the broadest sense. His travel had come at the precise moment in his life when it could be most effective. It had taken from him the Puritan narrowness and intolerance that had been his birthright, and it had given him horizon, perspective, and degrees of comparison.

For the next six years he moved amid an atmosphere of perpetual wonder and mild excitement. To talk with him, to listen to his glowing lectures, even to sit in his class-room, was to get a veritable whiff from that Old World which to the little provincial village was so far off and wonderful. He began his work at Bowdoin as one opens a mission in a heathen land. He threw himself into the work with all the enthusiasm of youth. There were no adequate text-books—grammars, readers for learners of French, Spanish, Italian. He would make them himself. He gave voluntary courses of lectures; he taught with unction and conviction. Bowdoin was too small for his mission work; he would broaden his field. He wrote studies and introductions and appreciations of the Romance languages and sent them abroad to his countrymen in the best review that America then possessed.

But the vision that had come to him in boyhood over those gray-brown numbers of "The Sketch-Book" was not forgotten amid all this mission work. He, too, would be an Irving; he, too, would issue books in numbers with shaded letter titles and fair, clear print. Even while he had been in Göttingen he had outlined his literary plans —a series of sketches after the "Sketch-Book" pattern. Poetry, after his first few echoes of Bryant, he had laid aside; his vocation was to be prose. "I am writing a book," he confides to Greene, during his fourth year at Bowdoin, "a kind of Sketch-Book of France, Spain, Germany,

and Italy." The book was "Outre Mer," half
Spain, a little of Italy, and the rest France. It
was, indeed, a kind of "Sketch-Book"; it even appeared in numbers with "gray-brown covers,"
"shaded letter titles, and fair, clear type." Irving
speaks from every chapter; a shadowy, emaciated
Irving to be sure, stripped of much of his "pleasant
humor," his "melancholy tenderness," his "atmosphere of reverie"; yet unmistakably Irving. It was
a young man's book full of high spirits, didactic,
"flowery," at times even inflated; every book is a
"tome," every clock a "horologue." In the history
of American literature it has little significance; it
was simply one of the swarm of books that fluttered
for a time about "The Sketch-Book." It is worth
noting, perhaps, that the same year that witnessed
its publication in book form produced also Cooper's
"Sketches in Switzerland," Willis's "Pencillings by
the Way," and Tuckerman's "Italian Sketch-Book."

This, then, was the Longfellow who, in April,
1835, in his twenty-ninth year, started joyously with
his young wife for his second *Lehrjahre.* The
world was good; he had been called to Harvard,
to the most influential chair of modern languages
in America; his mission field had been increased
a thousandfold. The world was good. It was
quite another Longfellow who, late the next year,
came back alone and took up a solitary residence

among strangers at Cambridge. On November 29 his wife had died at Rotterdam.

We know very little of this crisis in the poet's life. With a brother's delicacy his biographer passes over it with five lines. What it meant in a foreign land, then immeasurably more foreign than to-day, among utter strangers, in strange surroundings, alone, we can imagine. Four days after her death, with her last words in his ears, "O Henry, do not forget me. I will be with you and watch over you," he was again on his wanderings. "All that I have left me," he cried, "is the memory of her goodness, her gentleness, her affection for me." Hardly caring what he did, he pushed on to Heidelberg as he had planned, and tried to drown his memory in work.

Then came the second blow even as it had come to Novalis—the death of his brother-in-law, his dearest friend. It is from this point that we trace the beginning of the later Longfellow. He was alone. "Oh, George," he writes to his friend Greene, "what have I not suffered during the last three months, and I have no friend to cheer and console me." His solitude, his brooding, his natural sentimentality drove him in upon his own soul; the image of his lost one was ever before him. "Hardly a day passes," he wrote a year later, "that some face, or familiar object, or some passage in the book I am reading, does not call up the image of my beloved wife so vividly that I pause and burst into tears—and sometimes cannot rally again for hours."

Everything was turning him to romanticism: his naturally subjective, sentimental temperament; his mystic tendencies, heritage of all descendants of Puritans; his wrought and receptive condition; his utter loneliness; the old medieval town with its castle ruin; the romantic nooks and groves and legends; the opening springtime with all its German softness and beauty; and, above all, the atmosphere of romantic poetry that was shimmering all about him. No wonder that the world lost its sharp outlines; that the unseen drew nearer, that the misty past became the reality; that dreams and longings dominated at length his soul.

The life of the poet by his brother, that book of strange omissions, is almost silent here. We see little of the processes which, during those months at Heidelberg, made of Longfellow the poet that we know. The biographer's comment implies a copious journal, or, at least, a wealth of self-revealing letters, but we are allowed to see nothing, though otherwise it is impossible fully to know the poet.

We do know, however, that during the winter and spring he read almost incessantly, and that his favorite authors were from that earlier school which even then was still dominating German literature. In Bonn, we know, he had met personally the venerable A. W. Schlegel, and had conversed with him. We know that he read fully the prose of Goethe, Tieck, Hoffman, and Jean Paul. "Many hours were spent in solitary rambles in the neighboring woods . . . in sketching among the castle ruins, or enjoying the magnificent views from its terraces." Under the garden trees he read Herder. Sitting on the benches of the road that climbs to the Wolfsbrunen, Richter's *"Kampaner Thal* is his companion." "Hyperion" reveals fully the nature of his reading. He was familiar with Tiedge's "Urania," Bettina Arnim's "Goethe's Correspondence with a Child," Arnim and Brentano's "Boy's Wonder-Horn," Novalis's "Heinrich von Ofterdingen," Hoffmann's "Tales," Fichte's "Destiny of Man," Schubert's "History of the Soul," Goethe's "Faust," Müller's "Songs of a Wandering Horn Player," Jean Paul's "Titan," Uhland's "Poems," Werner's "Dramas," Tieck's "Poems," Carové's "Story Without an End," Salis and Matthisson's "Lyrics." These, save some few casual allusions, are all the writers mentioned and criticized in "Hyperion," and it is notable that with the single exception of Goethe they belong, all of them, to the romantic group. It is almost a roll-call of the school.

The influences that were shaping the new poet did

not end with the months at Heidelberg. The lonely journey into Switzerland, with Uhland in his pocket, the meeting with Frances Appleton at Interlaken, the solitary room in the old Cragie House at Cambridge, the continued reading of Goethe, Jean Paul, Tieck, Hoffmann, the brooding and dreaming over "Hyperion"—the three years from that November day at Rotterdam were the crucible from which emerged the Longfellow which we know. "Most of the time I am alone," he writes to Greene two years after his return. "I want to travel. Am too excited, too tumultuous inwardly and my health suffers." He records in his journal September 8, 1838: "Moped and groped about unwell. Dejected—no sunshine in the soul." His college work no longer inspired him. At Bowdoin he had written: "I am delighted more and more with the profession I have chosen. . . . I have such an engrossing interest in the studies of my profession that I write very seldom except in connection with those studies." Now he complains constantly of interruptions, of having his mind a playmate for boys. "This dragooning of schoolboys in lessons is like going backward." He longs for the evening hours when, with no one to disturb him, he can read and write and dream deliciously of the world he loves.

To get the full meaning of this period in Longfellow's life we have only to read "Hyperion," which was published in July, 1839. The events of the romance may be "mostly fictitious" even as the author declared to Greene; but the events are the smallest part of "Hyperion." "It contains my cherished thoughts for three years," he declared; he might have said: It contains my naked soul. The shock, the brooding, the unutterable longing and heart-hunger, the vision of angels, the ministry of night, the shadow-land of the romantic poets, the new love, the struggle of this love with the specter of the past—it is all here.

The Longfellow of "Outre Mer," and the Bowdoin days is a thing of the far past. The book is a German book, like a translation of one of those thousand shoots that sprang up about the trunk of "Wilhelm Meister." Even the conception of the book is German and romantic. Hölderlin had written the first "Hyperion," so naming it, he explains, because he stood "like the geese flat-footed in the water of modernity, impotently endeavoring to wing his flight upward toward the Greek heaven." Like all the Tieck-Richter romances, Longfellow's book is a rambling, chaotic creation, full of Jean Paul interludes and digressions, with the slenderest thread of plot, and without climax or dramatic force. In every way is it typical of its class. Everywhere romance; atmosphere above all: "the mingling of daylight and starlight," "a dreamy, yearning, ideal indistinctness." We can visualize nothing. The heroine, after two pages of description, is simply voice and eyes. It is a book written at night to be read "the evening having come and the tall candles being lighted"—a book without predecessors on this side of the water, an exotic, a pale and marvelous night-moth that has fluttered over somehow from the ruins of the Old World. Everywhere night scenes and twilight. The plot moves, when it moves at all, from moonlight to moonlight. To get its atmosphere, read of *Emma of Ilmenau*, who shunned "the glare of daylight and society, and wished to be alone. Like the evening primrose, her heart opened only after sunset; but bloomed through the dark night with sweet fragrance."

Longfellow wrote the book with a purpose. "It is a sincere book," he writes Greene, to whom, more than to any one else, he confides his inner life, "showing the passage of a morbid mind into a purer and healthier state." To find what this morbid mind was we have only to read the chapter entitled "The Fountain of Oblivion." Here the student *Hieronymus,* who has suddenly been dazzled by the beautiful *Hermione,* until, like one who has looked at the sun, he can see nothing else, thinks to drown his new love in the Fountain of Oblivion. As he stood and gazed into its waters "he beheld far down in their silent depths, dim and ill-defined outlines, waving to and fro, like the folds of a white garment in the twilight. Then more distinct and permanent shapes arose—shapes familiar to his mind, yet forgotten and remembered again, as the fragments of a dream; till at length, far, far below him, he beheld the great City of the Past, with silent marble streets, and moss-grown walls, and spires uprising with a wave-like, flickering motion. And amid the crowd that thronged those streets, he beheld faces once familiar and dear to him; and heard sorrowful, sweet voices singing, O, forget us not! forget us not! and then the distant mournful sound of funeral bells, that were tolling below, in the City of the Past." But despite this call from the old days he is powerless to surrender his new love, and the struggle between the quick and the dead goes on. Even at the close nothing is settled. The hero does, indeed, during the last few pages, resolve no more to look "mournfully into the past," "to be a man among men, and no longer a dreamer among shadows," but it comes as a swift impulse, a mere mood. The book shows no gradual growth of character, no steady leading up to this crisis. There is effect, but no cause. There can be no transformation of soul at the mere sight of an epitaph.

All through this period we find evidences of a

struggle in the poet's life—a wrestling, not only with the new love that confronted the jealous past, but with the moodiness, the aimlessness, the idle dreaming, the vain regrets which had begun during those solitary months at Heidelberg. His Puritan conscience and the teaching of the later Goethe were protesting against mere dreaming and moonlight and lack of definite aim. That Longfellow was inclined to moodiness and dreaming, with a tendency even to the purposeless, we have only to read his journals to know. He was, indeed, the *Mr. Churchill* of his own "Kavanagh"—"a dreamy, poetic man." "Life presented itself to him like the Sphinx, with its perpetual riddle of the real and the ideal. To the solution of this dark problem he devoted his days and his nights. He was forced to teach grammar when he would have written poems; and from day to day, and from year to year, the trivial things of life postponed the great designs, which he felt capable of accomplishing, but never had the resolute courage to begin. Thus he dallied with his thoughts and with all things, and wasted his strength in trifles; like the lazy sea, that plays with the pebbles on the beach." And after years the old schoolmaster had done nothing —"the same dreams, the same longings, the same aspirations, the same indecision . . . While he mused the fire burned in other brains." This is the picture of the true romanticist, of a Brentano or a Tieck—it is the confession of a weakness of the whole school.

Against this extreme Longfellow had constantly to struggle. He wrote the "Psalm of Life" with the same quill that had produced that penultimate chapter of "Hyperion," and the inspiration of both was the same. He first made public the poem during a lecture on Goethe—doubtless to illustrate the spirit of "Wilhelm Meister." Goethe, too, had had his period of dreaming, of melancholy, of irresolution. "That the life of man is but a dream," he had written in "The Sorrows of Werther," "has come into many a head; and with me, too, some feeling of that sort is ever at work." But the Goethe of the "Wilhelm Meister" period is another man. Life is no longer a dream, but a place for work. Be self-reliant, self-forgetful, he cries; away with introspection and morbid dreams;

> Life's no resting, but a moving;
> Let thy life be deed on deed.

He could say now to the *Werther* of his youth:

Once more then, much-wept shadow, dost thou dare
  Boldly to face the day's clear light,
To meet me on fresh blooming meadows fair,
  And dost not tremble at my sight?

Act, then, as I, and look with joyous mind,
 The moment in the face; nor linger thou!
Meet it with speed, so fraught with life, so kind
 In action, and in love so radiant now.

The very soul of "Wilhelm Meister" is the message, "art is long, life is short, judgment difficult,
opportunity transient—therefore, be doing."

> Keep not standing fixed and rooted;
> Briskly venture, briskly roam!
> Head and hand, where'er thou foot it,
> And stout heart are still at home.
> In each land the sun does visit
> We are gay whate'er betide;
> To give space for wandering, is it
> That the world was made so wide.

The message came to Longfellow, as, indeed,
it had come to all Europe, like a breath from the
living North. Frederick Schlegel expressed his
belief that the nineteenth century was molded by
three great tendencies: Fichte's "Wissenschafs-
lehre," Goethe's "Wilhelm Meister," and the French
Revolution, and there's a grain of truth in it.

It was this ringing message of action, of stirring
self-reliance, this challenge of the aimlessness, the
idle dreamings, the sentimentality of the age, that
Longfellow put into verse for his own soul discipline. His first intent was that it should be for

no eyes but his own. Read, with this thought in mind, "The Psalm of Life" becomes immediately significant. There is no haziness about even the first stanza, though it has been said that a prize was once offered to any one who could interpret the stanza, and no one succeeded in winning it. The poem is everywhere full of crudeness. But despite defects, the poem marks a crisis in Longfellow's life, and, in some ways, a crisis in American thinking. This is the substance of what he wrote:

Life's no time for dreams; the soul that simply slumbers and dreams is not living at all. The world, it is true, seems to me to be a mere shadow or dream even as it did to *Werther,* but it is not —("things are not what they *seem*") life is real. Art is long; life is short—act; look the moment in the face. It is not for me to muse idly on the future, building castles, nor to be the slave of the past. It is for me to be up and doing to-day.

It was the first real breaking of the spirit of "Wilhelm Meister" on our shores, and it quickened the heart-beat of the nation. In an era of sentimentalism, of Wertherism, of Byronism, of graveyardism—Wendell suggests as a general name for Bryant's works "Glimpses of the Grave"—it came indeed as the clash of steel. No wonder it gripped the American conscience, even as it had stirred Germany and Europe.

It was not in poetry, however, that the Longfellow of the Heidelberg era sought to express himself publicly. Months after the issue of "Hyperion" he was doubtful as to his work. "Meditating what I shall do next. Shall it be two volumes more of Hyperion, or a drama on Cotton Mather?" Poetry he had reserved for expressing his own innermost soul. What he wrote was for no other eye. The earliest stammer of his new mood he had written during that first solitary winter at Cambridge, a Novalisque lyric confided a year later to his journal, and then, later still, after the startling success of "The Psalm of Life," given to the public as "The Footsteps of Angels." One cannot understand the later Longfellow without a study of this earliest of his lyrics. I shall quote it entire in its earlier version: it brings us nearer to the poet:

When the hours of day are numbered,
   And the soul-like voice of night
Wakes the better soul that slumbered
   To a holy calm delight;

Ere the evening lamps are lighted,
   And like specters grim and tall,
Shadows from the fitful firelight
   Dance upon the parlor wall,

Then the forms of the departed
  Enter at the open door;
The belov'd ones, the true-hearted
  Come to sit with me once more.

And with them the being beauteous
  Who unto my youth was given,
More than all things else to love me,
  And is now a saint in heaven.

With a slow and noiseless footstep
  Comes she like a shape divine,
Takes the vacant chair beside me,
  Lays her gentle hand in mine.

And she sits and gazes at me,
  With her deep and tender eyes,
Like the stars so still and saint-like,
  Looking downward from the skies.

Here we have the soul of Novalis. The life of the night has become the only real life. Day is the unreality; the "better soul" sleeps until the twilight comes. As with Novalis, the partitions between the material and the spirit world have all but vanished. Again and again do we catch this note in Longfellow:

Have I dreamed or was it real
  What I saw as in a vision,
When to marches hymeneal

In the land of the ideal.
Moved my thoughts o'er fields Elysian?

The two worlds of waking and of dreaming, of flesh and of spirit, lie very close together in Longfellow's poems. There is no need to give a list: "Haunted Houses," "Song of the Silent Land," "The Two Angels," "The Haunted Chamber," "Auf Wiedersehen," are enough to illustrate. Years later, after his early romanticism had become modified somewhat, the poet could still say: It is at night that the better life begins; the day is the time for phantoms and ghosts, not the night; the things of day are trivial and commonplace, and without the reality of night, life would be unendurable.

Into the darkness and the hush of night
  Slowly the landscape sinks, and fades away,
  And with it fade the phantoms of the day,
The ghosts of men and things, that haunt the light.
The crowd, the clamor, the pursuit, the flight,
  The unprofitable splendor and display,
  The agitations and the cares that prey
Upon our hearts, all vanish out of sight.

The better life begins; the world no more
  Molests us; all its records we erase
From the dull commonplace book of our lives,
That like a palimpsest is written o'er
  With trivial incidents of time and place,
And, lo! the ideal, hidden beneath, revives.

The success of the "Psalm of Life" and the few lyrics that had followed it, joined with the importunities of his friends, induced Longfellow, late in the year 1839, to issue a collection of his lyrics and translations. The very title, "Voices of the Night," is significant. It was two books in one: the Bryantesque poems and the translations of the early Longfellow, and the psalms and translations of the Heidelberg mystic. The nine original poems are the soul of the book, and they are shot through and through with the softness and the sentiment of German romanticism. The "Prologue," which opens the collection with a bit of Tieck's "Waldeinsamkeit," finds the poet amid the shadows of a solemn and silent wood, dreaming under a patriarchal tree. He determines that hereafter his songs must be not of the external and the objective, things of the daylight, but of the world within him, and the solemn voices of the night. In the next poem we are in the full current of romanticism: "the manifold, soft chimes that fill the haunted chambers of the night"; "from the cool silence of the midnight air, my spirit drank repose"; and

> O holy night, from thee I learn to bear
> What man has borne before;
> Thou layest thy finger on the lips of care
> And they complain no more.

It is in the selfsame key as Novalis's "Hymns to

the Night": "But sacred Night, with her unspoken mysteries draws me to her . . . Dost thou not feel pity for us, O holy Night? . . . My whole being awakes. I am thine and thou art mine. Night has aroused me to life and manhood." It is a dominant note in Longfellow: "The Light of the Stars," "The Beleaguered City," "I Stood on the Bridge at Midnight," "The Day is Done," "The Rainy Day," "Daylight and Moonlight," "Afternoon in February," "Curfew," "The Wind Over the Chimney"—their spirit pervades like an atmosphere all of the poet's work.

It was this element that gave to Longfellow his instant popularity, both in America and in England. The people were ready for the "sadness and longing," and the dreamy mysticism of the German school. They had been prepared by the sentimentalism of Byron and Moore, by the medievalism of Scott, by the lacrymose poets, by "The Sorrows of Werther." Germany had had no small influence in molding the English writings of the early century, but it had been the Germany of Bürger and the *Sturm und Drang*. It had touched Scott and Coleridge and Byron, but none of them, even Coleridge, had cared much for Tieck. The work of the *Spätromantiker*, especially the softened romance of Uhland, had come not at all to English and American readers. It was brought in by Longfellow as something utterly new. Not that he did it deliberately or even consciously. He brought it not because it had appealed to his fancy, or because it had seemed a pleasing acquisition to display to his countrymen, but because it had become a veritable part of himself. He sang it even as Salis and Uhland had done, because his new soul had had in Germany its birth and its beginning. It was romanticism, but it was far removed from that of the first wild Frederick Schlegel type, that worshiped the moon, loved its neighbor's wife, and joined the Catholic Church; it was of the later school—dreamy and meditative, full of delicious sadness and longing, of subdued medievalism, of vagueness and hazy outline, of "old forgotten, far-off things and battles long ago"—in a word, the romanticism of Uhland.

It was inevitable that the poet sooner or later should have essayed the ballad, that literary form so peculiarly the province of romanticism. He had read Arnim and Brentano with eagerness. "The boy's 'Wonder-Horn,'" he exclaimed in "Hyperion," "I know the book almost by heart. Of all your German books, it is the one which produces upon my imagination the most wild and magic influence. I have a passion for ballads. . . . They are the gypsy children of song, born under green hedge-rows, in the leafy lanes and by-paths of literature—in the genial summertime."

Ballads, indeed, had been almost his first thought when he looked about him for poetic material during that first period at Cambridge. "The Wreck of the Hesperus" was the fifth poem that he wrote. "I have been looking at the old northern sagas," he confides to his journal in 1838, "and thinking of a series of ballads or a romantic poem on the deeds of the first bold Viking who crossed to this western world, with storm spirits and devil machinery under water." He proposed to Hawthorne that they collaborate in Arnim-Brentano style for the production of a collection of marvelous fairy tales and ballads for boys.

The proposal to Hawthorne was evidently an impulse. Soon after we find Hawthorne writing him, "You refuse to let me blow a blast upon the 'Wonder Horn.' Assuredly you have a right to make all the music on your own instrument; but I should serve you right were I to set up an opposition —for instance, with a cornstalk fiddle or a pumpkin-vine trumpet." Hawthorne's threatened trumpet gave out at length the well-known "Wonder Book," and Longfellow's blast was the "Ballads and other Poems" of 1841.

The horn rang at frequent intervals during all the rest of the poet's life. "The Norman Baron," "Walter von der Vogelweid," "The Phantom Ship," "The Emperor's Bird's Nest," "Oliver Basselin,"

"Victor Galbraith," "A Ballad of the Dutch Fleet" —they all have the true ballad ring; they might be translations from Uhland. Their charm lies in their simplicity, their haunting melody, their human interest, their dreamy indistinctiveness, their echoes of the dim past. They are romantic in their every line; they have nothing American about them. "The Wreck of the Hesperus" might have happened in the North Sea, and Paul Revere's ride with a change of names might have been an episode of the German wars.

What Longfellow was after the publication of this second volume of poems he remained. His third residence in Germany in 1842 deepened his romanticism, but it did not modify it. He had discovered his vocation. The sudden and widespread popularity of his poetry had first astonished and then sobered him. The voice of the people was unmistakable, and it was like a call from on high. No more prose; life was poesy. "I have been giving as much time as possible to the young poets," he writes from Mariensberg. He had found Freiligrath and had spent many delicious days with him in his romantic home on the Rhine. Young Germany attracted him not at all; he was of Uhland and the Rhine, not of Heine.

He came home to write "The Belfry of Bruges" and "Nuremberg," poems breathing romanticism

from every line. The very choice of Nuremberg
as the subject of a poem is enough to classify the
poet, for was not that dreamy old city, "that pearl
of the middle ages," the very apotheosis of romanticism? When Tieck and Wackenroder traveled
together over Germany, they had entered the old
town in a sort of dream. "In a species of æsthetic
intoxication," says Brandes, "the friends wandered
around the churches and the graveyards; they stood
by the grave of Albert Dürer and Hans Sachs; a
vanished world arose before their eyes, and the
life of ancient Nuremberg became to them the
romance of art." It became in a way the capital
city of the romantic movement, and all that it was
to those early dreamers Longfellow has caught in
his poem:

Quaint old town of toil and traffic, quaint old town of
    art and song,
Memories haunt thy pointed gables, like the rooks that
    round them throng:

Memories of the Middle Ages, when the emperors,
    rough and bold,
Had their dwelling in thy castle, time-defying, cen-
    turies old.

.   .   .   .

Vanished is the ancient splendor, and before my
    dreamy eye

Wave those mingled shapes and figures, like a faded
    tapestry.

Not thy councils, not thy Kaisers, win for thee the
    world's regard;
But thy painter, Albrecht Dürer, and Hans Sachs, thy
    cobbler bard.

This yearning for the ideal, this turning away
from the commonplace present to the vague medieval world where fancy and the imagination may
foot it free, is the very life of romanticism. But
the later German school softened its pictures of
the Middle Ages. It delighted in sentimental musings amid the ruins, in pathetic legend, in dreamy
pictures of monks and harpers and knights and
radiant maidens with soft blue eyes. Heine, the
harshest critic of the school, declared that in Uhland's writings "the naïve, rude, powerful tones of
the Middle Ages are not reproduced with idealized
fidelity, but rather they are dissolved into a sickly,
sentimental melancholy." Nearly half of Longfellow's poems are medieval in background, and it
is the medievalism of Uhland. In work like "The
Golden Legend," an adaption of "Der Arme Heinrich," he is at his best. Its atmosphere from
beginning to end is that which plays over all of
his most characteristic work; soft melancholy, vague
yearnings, feeling above everything. To G. P. R.

James the poem resembled "an old ruin with the ivy and the rich blue mold upon it." It is rather the dream of a monk over his rubrics.

It is but natural that the Romish Church with its traditions and its impressive ceremonials and institutions should appeal strongly to the poet, as it did to all of his school. He drew upon it constantly for his imagery and his epithets: "the owl is a grave bird, a monk, who chants midnight mass in the great temple of nature"; the old clock on the stairs is also "a monk, who crosses himself and sighs, Alas."

> The winds like anthems roll;
> They are chanting solemn masses,
>   Singing, "Pray for this poor soul,
>   Pray, pray!"
>
> And the hooded clouds, like friars,
>   Tell their beads in drops of rain,
> And patter their doleful prayers;
>   But their prayers are all in vain,
>   All in vain!

Indeed to read the poet is like entering some ancient Gothic cathedral with its subdued light, its half-crumbled monuments of crusaders, its softly murmuring organ, its shuddery vaults with the bones of maidens, its slow procession of chanting monks, its coolness and its mystery.

Touch Longfellow where you will and you will find German romance. It shows itself in his devotion to Dante, that mystic of mystics, that "spokesman of the Middle Ages."

I enter and I see thee in the gloom
    Of the long aisles, O poet Saturnine!
    And strive to make my steps keep pace with thine.
The air is filled with some unknown perfume,
The congregation of the dead make room
    For thee to pass; the votive tapers shine;
    Like rooks that haunt Ravenna's groves of pine
The hovering echoes fly from tomb to tomb.
From the confessionals I hear arise
    Rehearsals of forgotten tragedies
    And lamentations from the crypts below;
And then a voice celestial that begins
With the pathetic words, "Although your sins
    As scarlet be," and ends with "as the snow."

It shows itself in his Fichte-drawn message of consolation: be resigned, all is Providence. It shows itself in his choice of material.

"The romantic school," says Beers, "sought to reinforce its native stock of materials by *motifs* drawn from foreign literatures, and particularly from Norse mythology and from Spanish romance." In his passion for Northern myth Longfellow surpassed even Schlegel and Uhland. His translations and adaptations and above all his "Hiawatha," that "Indian edda" as he called it, that poem which gives not only the meter but the very atmosphere and soul of the Finnish "Kalevala," attest this. For his fondness for Spanish romance one has only to read his earliest drama.

Romanticism is only another name for youth and aspiration. With the middle years of life the colors fade; the vague melancholy which somehow is inseparable from young manhood is forgotten; experience disciplines the imagination; life takes on more restrained and sober moods. Uhland ceased to sing long before middle life; Heine was a romanticist only during his early years. Longfellow's distinctively romantic period was over before 1849. It was then that he began to think of the larger art, and to plan a "tower of song with lofty parapet."

But it is not the work of this latter period, tinged with romanticism even as it is, that stands to-day in the popular mind as Longfellow. It is the little handful of lyrics written near the year 1840 that the world at large now associates with his name. The dramas, the later lyrics, the "Christus," even the "Tales of a Wayside Inn," are unknown to the man in the street, but he knows "The Psalm of Life" and "The Bridge." A college class of two hundred men, asked recently to write without preparation each a list of the poems of Longfellow, handed in altogether only thirty titles, and these in the order of frequency of mention were: "Evangeline," "Hiawatha," "Miles Standish," "The Village Blacksmith," "The Psalm of Life," "The Children's Hour," "Paul Revere's Ride," "The Building of the Ship," "The Day is Done," "The Bridge," "The Skeleton in Armor," "The Wreck of the Hesperus," "The Old Clock on the Stairs," "The Rainy Day," "Excelsior," "The Reaper and the Flowers," "The Footsteps of Angels," "The Arrow and the Song," "Resignation," "The Arsenal at Springfield," and "Maidenhood." The rest were scattering. Of this list only "Hiawatha," "Miles Standish," "The Children's Hour," and "Paul Revere's Ride" were written after 1849. The list is suggestive. This is Longfellow as the people know him, but this is also the Longfellow of the Heidelberg vision—the Longfellow of unchecked German romance. It was this element that gave him his popularity. The age was revolting against sentimentalism, but it caught eagerly at the new tone of soft melancholy, of melodious pathos, of idealized antiquity, of genre art, of mysticism subdued by Goethe; in a word, it caught eagerly at German romanticism for the first time whispering its haunting music in English ears.

Longfellow was distinctively a lyrist. Although half of all his original poetry is in dramatic form, he was as far from being a dramatist as was Uhland, who also wrote dramas. The drama requires action, plot, absolute definiteness: distinctness first of all. There must be evolution of character, cause and effect, a steady and irresistible march of events toward the final culmination. It must deal, too, with intensely individualized figures that stand out objectively against a background that does not dominate or distract. But Longfellow was first of all subjective; he saw through the lens of his own soul—shadowy ethereal beings; he could tell of his own emotions and aspirations and longings, but he was powerless, like all of the romantic poets, to view life objectively, to paint sharp outlines, to work step by step to an inevitable climax.

He came the nearest to the dramatic in "The Spanish Student," but even this is essentially lyric. It is a young man's dream, full of romantic sentiment, of effects without cause, of vague characterization; charming situations rather than dramatic development. To quote a criticism on Tieck, "all its author's care is lavished upon what he calls the climate of events, their atmosphere and fragrance, tone and color, the mood they inspired, the shadow they cast, the light in which they are seen, which is invariably that of the moon." Longfellow's poetic works fill nine volumes, yet if his lyrics were published alone they would fill scarce one, a remarkable fact when we consider that he was a lyrist only, a lyrist as preëminently as was Salis or Ronsard. He is at his best only in the poetry of moments, of moods, of the individual soul. And of all his lyrics the most spontaneous and genuine are his sonnets, the work almost wholly of his later years; and it is because they welled from his own heart and are not, like so much that he wrote, "poetry to the second power"—poetry about poetry.

Longfellow, then, was a lyrist of the German romantic school. Like Uhland, he felt rather than saw.

Hawthorne could not use the material for "Evangeline"; it was too vague and dispersive to grip his imagination. To Longfellow it was simply pathos; he could feel it and that was enough. He never visited the Grand Pré region, or the Mississippi, or the Falls of Minnehaha; there was no need of it. Hölderlin had never visited Greece before he wrote his "Hyperion" with chapter after chapter of description. To have made the visit might have spoiled the picture. Realism, truth to actual externals, even to the historical facts in the case, amounted to little in Longfellow's scheme. It was the atmosphere and the feeling that counted. He cared only to call up the *märchenwelt* with the golden mist over it, with its delicious sadness, and its pathetic human figure dimly seen, and the result is a book that has been wept over by two generations of schoolgirls. The heroine, *Evangeline,* is a mere abstraction impossible to visualize. Heine declared that "the women in Uhland's poems are only beautiful shadows, embodied moonshine." "French romanticism," says Brandes, "produces clearly defined figures; the ideal of German romanticism is not a figure but a melody, not definite form but indefinite aspiration." Evangeline is a feminine Heinrich von Ofterdingen, seeking the world over for the blue flower, and losing it in the end just when it seemed in her grasp.

And it is so of "Hiawatha." It is romantic through and through, unreal even to ghostliness, touching the actual world only here and there. Its atmosphere and its melody are everything: moon-light, starlight, romantic love, the days that are forgotten, and over all sentiment and pathos. The Indians are in reality monks and medieval knights and first cousins to the gods of Northern mythology.

> Downward through the evening twilight
> In the days that are forgotten,
> In the unremembered ages,
> From the full moon fell Nokomis,
> Fell the beautiful Nokomis,
> She a wife, but not a mother.
>
> Downward through the evening twilight
> On the Muskoday, the meadow,

On the prairie full of blossoms.
"See! a star falls!" said the people.
From the sky a star is falling.

There among the ferns and mosses
There among the prairie lilies
On the Muskoday, the meadow,
In the moonlight and the starlight
Fair Nokomis bore a daughter,
And she called her name Wenonah,
As the first-born of her daughters.
And the daughter of Nokomis
Grew up like the prairie lilies,
Grew a tall and slender maiden,
With the beauty of the moonlight
With the beauty of the starlight.

A vague dream it is of fairy-land, of monsters and
marvels, the fancies of a childlike people; and its
main charm is "the moonlight and the starlight,"
the soft Indian summer that envelops it like a haze.
But as Ibsen said of Schiller's "Jungfrau," "there
is no experience in it. It is not the result of powerful personal impressions, but is a composition."

And this brings us to the main criticism that must
be made of all the romantic school: their work is the
result of conscious intention. The *Sturm und
Drang* of a literature is expulsive, creative, unconscious. The poet like Bürger and Burns and Whittier sings because he must, but the romancers, as

Goethe has well expressed it, live "in a period of forced talent." All but a few of Longfellow's early "psalms," and sonnets, were written with books face-down about his writing-pad. He prized translation since it acted as a stimulant. "It stirs up germs of thought." Imagine Burns or Bürger or Keats saying this. As a result his work "induces," as Emerson expressed it, "a serene mood." Seldom do we feel the heart beat faster and suddenly hold our breaths as we catch glimpses of new worlds. All is melodious and serene, in an atmosphere of delicious twilight, and the atmosphere and the melody are everything.

His poetry is really American only in its themes. He cared little for the prosaic, bustling life of his native land; his heart was elsewhere. None of our writers traveled so little in their own country; aside from one trip to Washington he never got further west than New York. He looked eastward rather than westward; the study in the old Craigie House had only eastern windows. The burning problems, the fiery struggle of the forties and fifties really bored him at times. "Dined with Agassiz to meet Emerson and others," he writes in his journal in that tumultuous year 1856. "I was amused and annoyed to see how soon the conversation drifted off into politics. It was not till after dinner in the library, that we got upon anything really interesting." It is like Dumas's turning from the subject of tailors' bills and rents and the cost of living to that of romance with the remark, "Let us now turn to real life." With Sumner, that flame of fire, for his bosom friend, it was impossible for the poet to be wholly indifferent to passing events; he could even write a few graceful and colorless lyrics on slavery that are to Whittier's as water to aqua regia, yet he seems never to have caught the full thrill and meaning of the land and the age in which his life had been cast. He remained to the last the gentle, lovable monkish scholar, content with his friends and his dreams of olden times, oblivious of the fact that a mighty epic was enacting at his very door.

He is our Jean Paul, "the beloved," with his cheery optimism, his belief in the worth of the individual, his *genre* pictures, his soft dreamy idyls, his Fichte message of resignation, and he is our Uhland with his half-lights, his softened mysticism, his medieval atmosphere, his serene level of excellence. Whether or not his great influence upon the common people at the moment when they were at their most receptive stage was altogether good, is open to question. When America like a schoolgirl was hungry for culture and for poetry, Longfellow gave German romance and he gave little else. He came at the only moment in our history when he could have had a full hearing, or at least at the only moment when he could have been given the leading place to the exclusion of all others. His enormous popularity, his contagious sentimentalism, his breath of the Old World at this moment when America was peculiarly susceptible—all this, coming at the moment when a new group of poets was gathering, cast a shadow over a whole period of our poetic history. To Longfellow more than to any other cause may be traced the general lack of stamina in American poetry during two generations of poets.

But it is vain to criticize; whatever we may say, Longfellow's place is secure. He will be our beloved poet, just as Uhland and Jean Paul are beloved. His lyrics of consolation will still console the feminine heart though they contain only Fichte set to melody and moonlight. But his influence upon the future cannot be a large one. America and the world have outgrown German romanticism. Lowell wrote young Howells: "You must sweat the Heine out of you as men do mercury"; the young poet of the new century must sweat out Longfellow. We demand to-day not vagueness but sharpness of out-- line. Whitman is our prophet of to-day, and his influence is spreading and deepening. Full and clear comes the demand: Show us life; tell us the truth of life in the concrete, in words that bite and burn. The office of the poet no longer is merely to please, or to induce a serene mood. Mere fancy and prettiness, mere conceits and melody, mere atmosphere, mere traditions soft with the years, and longings and dreamings no longer satisfy. The poet is the seer: it is for him to look beyond the day and the year; to voice the truth of our own times, of our own selves, of our native land, and of the years that are yet to be.

THE MODERNNESS OF PHILIP
FRENEAU

-

It is food for thought that the late war, by all confessed the most perfect masterpiece of Mars, must pass into record as the war that produced no poetry. A few sporadic lyrics here and there, but how many poems may one mention from memory without consulting the collections of war verse? And yet the lives of empires, the greatest and oldest in Europe, trembled for years in the balance, armies with their backs to the last wall fought for the very life of their country, and deeds of heroism were done by millions. Never has there been such need for "Marseillaise" rouses, for soul-kindling battle-hymns, for blood-stirring hero ballads, for threnodies and laments at the open graves of martyrs of freedom, for interpretations of the souls of nations, for psalms of comfort, or of faith, or of exultation.

Especially has this been true of America. Is democracy worth giving one's life for if it cannot be sung? Is the American ideal worth holding

up for the world if it is not so tremendous a thing
that only poetry can voice it? We were silent, and
yet no nation ever had theme more poetic; no nation
ever entered war on higher grounds and no nation
ever had its imagination stirred by a tradition more
romantic. When America sent her young men to
France she sent them on a crusade. Every one of
them as his feet pressed the soil on which perhaps
he was to shed his blood could say in his heart,
"Lafayette, we are here." We need not expand the
thought. No poet ever had a more stirring theme.

But who is the laureate of "France allied"? He
is still Philip Freneau, dead ninety years; with Walt
Whitman, the single American voice of 1871—"O
Star of France"—in the second place. Whom will
one name as the third? We are inclined to speak
apologetically of Freneau if we ever speak of him
at all. He wrote too much, he mingled with a little
undoubted poetry a dreary mass of trash; it is
easy to dismiss him with faint praise: he lived in
the twilight of our poetry, and he wrote as best
he could without readers, or adequate criticism,
without poetic companions and without reward.
And yet for our richest output in many areas of our
poetry we still must return to him. Would that
he had been alive and at the height of his powers
when the German armies in 1914 swept through
Belgium and down into France! His songs of

"France allied" should have been gathered at the opening of the war and sent broadcast over America.

It was the conviction of Freneau that the French Revolution, that struggle that ended in 1918 with the fall of the kaiser and the czar, began in the free forests of America. He voiced it again and again. In 1791 this was his exulting cry:

From the spark that we kindled, a flame has gone forth
To astonish the world and enlighten mankind:
With a code of new doctrines the universe rings,
And Paine is addressing strange sermons to kings.

Had he lived in August, 1914, this, from his "On the Fourteenth of July, 1792," would have been the type of his war-cry, his challenge to the Hun, his exultant toast:

> By traitors driven to ruin's brink
> Fair Freedom dreads united knaves.
> The world must fall if she must bleed;
> And yet, by heaven! I'm proud to think
> The world was ne'er subdued by slaves—
> Nor shall the hireling herd succeed.

> Boy! fill the generous goblet high;
> Success to France shall be the toast:
> The fall of kings the fates foredoom,
> The crown decays, its splendours die.

In December we find him pouring forth his fiery

"On the Demolition of the French Monarchy." It has a singularly modern ring. Thus might he have described the first Battle of the Marne:

> The Gaul, enrag'd as they retire,
> Hurls at their heads his blaze of fire—
> What hosts of Frederick's reeking crew;
> Dying, have bid the world adieu,
> To dogs their flesh been thrown!
> Escap'd from death, a mangled train
> In scatter'd bands retreat:
> Where, bounding on Silesia's plain,
> The Despot holds his seat;
> With feeble step, I see them go
> The heavy news to tell
> Where Oder's lazy waters flow,
> Or glides the swift Moselle.

In a foot-note Freneau explained that "the Despot" was "the Monarch of Prussia." And the poem closes with what is half a prophecy:

> O France! the world to thee must owe
> A debt they ne'er can pay:
> The Rights of Man you bid them know,
> And kindle Reason's day!
> Columbia, in your friendship blest,
> Your gallant deeds shall hail—
> On the same ground our fortunes rest,
> Must flourish, or must fail:
> But—should all Europe's slaves combine

> Against a cause so fair as thine,
> And Asia aid a league so base—
> Defeat would all their aims disgrace,
> And Liberty prevail!

And with true bardic rapture he peers into the future, even to our own day, perhaps; this is what he sees:

> I see them spurn old laws,
> Indignant, burst the Austrian yoke,
> And clip the Eagle's claws:
> From shore to shore, from sea to sea
> They join, to set the wretched free,
> And, driving from the servile court
> Each titled slave—they help support
> The Democratic Cause!

Again in a foot-note Freneau explains: by "the Eagle," he says, he means "the imperial standard of Germany."

Again and again as the war progresses he cries out in exultation, or urges on the battling hosts of freedom, as in "On the Portraits of Louis and Antoinette in the Senate Chamber," in the ringing lines of "On the French Republicans":

Americans! when in your country's cause
You march'd, and dar'd the English lion's jaws,
Crush'd Hessian slaves, and made their hosts retreat,
Say, were you not Republican—complete?

Friends to Republics, cross the Atlantic brine,
Low in the dust see regal splendour laid:
Hopeless forever sleeps the Bourbon line.

In "To a Republican with Mr. Paine's Rights of
Man," he sketches the duty of the American republic:

Be ours the task the ambitious to restrain,
And this great lesson teach—that kings are vain;
That warring realms to certain ruin haste,
That kings subsist by war, and wars are waste:
So shall our nation, form'd on Virtue's plan,
Remain the guardian of the Rights of Man,
A vast Republic, fam'd through every clime,
Without a king, to see the end of time.

At the civic feast given Citizen Genêt in Philadelphia, May 18, 1793, Freneau was ordered to
translate Citizen Pichon's impassioned "Ode à
la Liberté," and after the seventh toast there was
sung "with great effect," according to Bache's "Aurora," Freneau's "Ode," though Conway, in his
life of Paine, mentions that it had been sung in 1791
at the November festival of the London Revolutionary Society. The ode unquestionably is Freneau's,
since he included it in the 1795 edition of his poems.
It should be included in every collection of our national hymns:

God save the Rights of Man!
Give us a heart to scan

Blessings so dear;
Let them be spread around
Wherever man is found,
And with the welcome sound
Ravish his ear.

Let us with France agree,
And bid the world be free,
While tyrants fall!
Let the rude savage host
Of their vast numbers boast—
Freedom's almighty trust
Laughs at them all!

Though hosts of slaves conspire
To quench fair Gallia's fire,
Still shall they fail:
Though traitors round her rise,
Leagu'd with her enemies,
To war each patriot flies,
And will prevail.

No more is valor's flame
Devoted to a name,
Taught to adore—
Soldiers of Liberty
Disdain to bow the knee,
But teach Equality
To every shore.

The world at last will join
To aid thy grand design,

Dear Liberty!
To Russia's frozen lands
The generous flame expands:
On Afric's burning sands
Shall man be free!

In this our western world
Be Freedom's flag unfurl'd
Through all its shores!
May no destructive blast
Our heaven of joy o'ercast,
May Freedom's fabric last
While time endures.

If e'er her cause require!—
Should tyrants e'er aspire
To aim their stroke,
May no proud despot daunt—
Should he his standard plant,
Freedom will never want
Her hearts of oak!

Certainly had Freneau been alive in 1914 he would have joined with all his powers those heroic souls like Roosevelt who demanded that America at once take her part in the struggle. In July, 1793, "On the Anniversary of the Storming of the Bastile," he raised his voice in no uncertain note urging his countrymen to fly to the aid of the nation that had aided them in their extremity.

Ye sons of this degenerate clime,
Haste, arm the barque, expand the sail;
Assist to speed that golden time
When Freedom rules, and monarchs fail;
　　All left to France—new powers may join,
　　And help to crush the cause divine.

Ah! while I write, dear France Allied,
My ardent wish I scarce restrain,
To throw these Sybil leaves aside,
And fly to join you on the main:
　　Unfurl the topsail for the chace
　　And help to crush the tyrant race!

And his lyric of 1795, "The Republican Genius of
Europe," might well be taken as a summing up of
the lessons of the great war from 1914 to 1918:

Emperors and kings! in vain you strive
　　Your torments to conceal—
The age is come that shakes your thrones,
Tramples in dust despotic crowns,
　　And bids the sceptre fail.

In western worlds the flame began:
　　From thence to France it flew—
Through Europe now, it takes its way,
Beams an insufferable day,
　　And lays all tyrants low.

Genius of France! pursue the chace
　　Till Reason's laws restore

Man to be Man, in every clime;—
That Being, active, great, sublime
Debas'd in dust no more.

Even the war of the flying-machines would not
much have surprised Philip Freneau. As early as
1784, in his poem, "The Progress of Balloons," he
had prophesied aërial warfare:

If Britain should ever disturb us again,
(As they threaten to do in the next George's reign)
No doubt they will play us a set of new tunes,
And pepper us well from their fighting balloons.

Freight, he prophesied, would be carried whole-
sale through the skies, post-riders would "travel
like ghosts on the wings of the air, and stages
would all spurn the ground in disdain":

The stagemen, whose gallopers scarce have the power
Through the dirt to convey you ten miles in an hour,
When advanc'd to balloons shall so furiously drive
You'll hardly know whether you're dead or alive.
The man who in Boston sets out with the sun,
If the wind should be fair, may be with us at one,
At Gunpowder Ferry drink whiskey at three,
And at six be at Edentown ready for tea.
(The machine shall be order'd, we hardly need say,
To travel in darkness as well as by day.)
At Charleston by ten he for sleep shall prepare
And by twelve the next day be the devil knows where.

Few of our American poets have deserved more than Philip Freneau the ancient title of "seer," the one who sees the hidden meanings of things and who may look with revealing eye into the secrets of the years that are to be.

II

The work of Freneau during the French Revolution period of the 1790's was but an incident in his poetic career. From the first he was the poet of Revolution. He had thrown his soul into the war between the colonies and the mother country and had voiced with passion every phase of the struggle, and he had been a pioneer in the romantic revolt a quarter of a century before Wordsworth.

His poetic career had begun in college, where Madison, later to be President, was his room-mate. He had excelled in Latin and Greek, and he had dreamed of poetry over the volumes of the English poets, especially those of Pope and Gray. Before he was out of his teens he had written an epic. Poetry he determined should be his life-work. He surrendered himself to it with all the abandon of the adolescent. He thought poetry, he lived it, he dreamed of nothing else. And to his credit, though he faced all his life those conditions that drove the poetic completely out of Madison and all the other of his contemporaries, he remained to the end of his life, as best he could, unfalteringly true to the dream of his youth. Inferior as much of his poetic product is, we must remember always that he gave his generation at every crisis the poetry that generation best could understand.

He was born into an age and an environment almost utterly unpoetic. Early America had no time for the muses. He who sows the wilderness and hopes to reap the fruits of his toil can have no avocation; culture and the world of art forever must be to him a far-away dream. If in addition to this' the sower has, as part of his religious creed, a contempt for the bright and the beautiful, there will be at least no written poetry. For two centuries America wrote her poetry in deeds. She was without artistic taste, without centers or standards of culture, and, if we except the devotees of the sermon and the almanac, without a reading class. In the North the muses were the drudges of religious dogmatism; in the South they had been cast out by the practical goddess of affairs. The mother land furnished no inspiration; seldom in the history of poetry had the fire burned so low. Freneau in his apprentice days realized the difficulty. He wrote:

There are few writers of books in this new world, and amongst them very few that deal in works of imagination. In a country which two hundred years ago was peopled only by savages and where the government has ever in effect been no other than republican, it is really wonderful that there should be any polite original authors at all in any line, especially when it is considered that according to the common course of things any particular nation or people must have arrived to or rather passed their meridian of opulence and refinement before they consider the possession of the fine arts in any other light than a nuisance to the community.

America before the Revolution was destitute of even the germs of an original literature, and yet Freneau, with his optimism and fervid republicanism dreamed of an independent American literature. He saw it, however, only in a very distant future. Even after the Revolution we find him confessing that "they [English writers] are excusable in treating the American authors as inferiors, a political and a literary independence of a nation being two very different things. The former was accomplished in about seven years and the latter will not be completely effected, perhaps, in as many centuries." Before there could be an original American literature there must be some great primal impulse that should stir mightily the whole people, that should shake from their hands the old books and the old models, that should arouse them to a true realization of themselves, and that should clear the atmosphere for a new and broader view of human life. Such.

cataclysms are always needed, but they are often centuries apart.

Fortunately for America such an upheaval was at hand. It came with appalling suddenness. The colonists had had no gradual preparation for the idea of separation from England. As late as 1775 Franklin declared before the House of Commons that in all his journeyings up and down the colonies he had not heard expressed one single wish for independence. Even after Concord and Bunker Hill Freneau, the radical, could write:

> Long may Britannia rule our hearts again,
> Rule as she ruled in George the Second's reign.

The idea of independence came all in a moment, but once it had come it went with leaps and bounds to extremes. Never in all history has a whole people been lifted by such rapid stages into a region of such vast outlook. We can trace the growth of the new spirit, not decade by decade, but month by month: Justice, Freedom, Independence, and then the radiant vision of perfect Liberty and the Rights of Man, and then, like a torrent, the sense of boundless possibilities and glorious destiny:

> No pent-up Utica contracts our powers,
> But the whole boundless continent is ours.

The soul of man, stirred by such ideals and successful in realizing them beyond his dreams, struggled for utterance. It is such upheavals in human society that make poets and bring outbursts of song and periods in the history of literature. But there was no burst of song in America; instead there followed one of the most pathetic spectacles in literary history—a people with a vision that transported them into the clouds, yet powerless through environment and early education to voice that vision in song. The South, thrilled by the new spirit, turned it at once into action, and took the leadership in war and statesmanship. New England lifted up her voice, but she could speak only through the medium of old spiritual conceptions and worn-out poetic forms. A young Connecticut parson, thrilled through and through, poured his enthusiasm into a heroic epic of the wars of Joshua; a brilliant Boston lad would sing of "War and Washington," but he must set it to the tune of Dryden; and a gifted Connecticut satirist, overflowing with the poetic spirit, was content simply to add new American cantos to "Hudibras." With all her rimers and all her inspiration New England gave forth not a single original note. It was a repeating of the old spectacle of a heavenly anthem sung unto shepherds, unto those unable to give it utterance.

We see them, however, struggling heroically with the burden. From 1774, when Dwight completed his "Conquest of Canaan," "the first piece of this kind ever attempted in this country," until 1808, which ends the period with Barlow's "Columbiad," the "Polyolbion" of American poetry, the years are strewn thick with the wrecks of epics. Every poet of the era felt his soul burn with epic fire. Charles Brockden Brown when only sixteen had started no less than three of these Homeric efforts; one on the discovery of America and one each on the conquests of Mexico and Peru. It was our heroic era, but it yielded almost nothing of value.

It was in 1772, at the opening of this age of epics, that Freneau, just graduating from Princeton, found his first poetic opportunity. Already over his Vergil he had dreamed of Columbus as a greater Æneas who had sailed into the pathless West to discover a world and to plant therein seeds of a mightier than Rome, but his work, like all schoolboy epics, had resulted only in fragments which were to strew his earlier volumes. But now commencement was at hand. Here was a chance indeed; here was a theme commensurate with the occasion. Like Milton, he would essay "things unattempted yet in prose or rhyme":

Now shall the adventurous Muse attempt a theme
More new, more noble, and more flush of fame
Than all that went before.

Never were graduation exercises based on broader foundations. The two young graduates, for he worked in conjunction with his classmate Brackenridge, bewail at every step their limitations of space. The plan they suggest is the plan of a "Columbiad." They would begin with *all* the tale of Columbus; they would rehearse the story of Cortés and Pizarro; they would discuss at learned length the origin and the characteristics of the Indians; they would tell the story of the early colonies; and would trace the course of settlement and review the progress and the promise of agriculture and commerce; they would peer into the future and mark the time

when we shall spread
Dominion from the North and South and West,
Far from the Atlantic to Pacific shores
And shackle half the convex of the main.

But, alas, the time! An epic cannot be condensed into a graduation poem. Suddenly Freneau (and we must not read the poem from later reprints where the author frankly admits that he has added new lines for "a supposed prophetical anticipation of subsequent events") bursts into true prophetic rapture. Remember this was in 1775, when the wild

Western frontier was almost within sound of the
Atlantic:

> I see, I see,
> A thousand kingdoms raised; cities and men
> Numerous as sand upon the ocean shore.
> The Ohio soon shall glide by many a town
> Of note; and where the Mississippi stream,
> By forest shaded, now runs weeping on,
> Nations shall grow, and estates not less in fame
> Than Greece and Rome of old. We too shall boast
> Our Alexanders, Pompeys, Heroes, Kings,
> That in the womb of time yet dormant lie,
> Waiting the joyful hour of life and light,—
> O snatch me hence, ye muses, to those days
> When through the vail of dark antiquity
> Our sons shall hear of us as things remote,
> That blossomed in the morn of days.

It is not a great poem if we measure it by absolute standards; but it is a very great poem if we
view it in connection with the conditions that produced it. Full as it is of Latin influence and com-
mencement-day zeal, it is the first real poem that
America ever made; the first poem that was impelled hot from a man's soul. It is more than this:
it is the first fruit of a new influence in the world
of letters—the first literary product of that mighty
force that set in motion the American and the
French Revolutions with all that they mean in human

history. The poem at times reaches the heights. "Alas!" cries the young singer with a ring in his voice unknown in English poetry since the "spacious days,"

Alas!

How could I weep that we were born so soon
Just in the dawning of these mighty times
Whose scenes are painting for eternity.

Here at last is an inspired and original singer in the wilderness of the New World; here at last is a poet who can voice for humanity the new message from free-aired America.

III

It is significant that this earliest poet should have come from the middle colonies. He was neither Puritan nor Cavalier. He had inherited with his Huguenot blood an intense love for liberty, religious as well as civil, a taste for the bright and beautiful, a vivacious imagination, a sensitive, excitable nature that longed for variety and found delight in movement, and a sturdy self-reliance and independence that made him unwilling long to follow the lead of another. "If fortune," he writes in his young manhood, "or the ill taste of the public compell you ever to turn shallopman on the Delaware, let it be your first care to have command of the boat."

There was nothing in the boy's early environment and training to repress this fearless, beauty-loving spirit. New York, where he was born in January, 1752, was to a degree neutral territory between the extremes of the North and the South. The father, a wine-merchant in easy circumstances, had filled his home with books and refinement, and had looked carefully to the education of his children. At fifteen Freneau was so well prepared for Princeton that the president sent to his parents a special letter of congratulation.

The young student's instincts were refined and scholarly. There are evidences that he read while in college nearly all the English poets. When he first began to write verses for himself we do not know. It was certainly early; when we catch our first certain glimpses of the youth, poetry has become with him a passion and almost a vocation. As early as 1768 we find him making a poetic paraphrase of the book of Jonah, in the orthodox manner and measure of Pope, to be sure, but remarkably sustained and finished for the work of a freshman. A little later he tried his hand at a more original task, a piece of characterization and local color, "The Village Merchant," a poem so good that twenty-six years later he deemed it worthy of separate publication. As his college course progressed his themes became more ambitious. He made in blank verse a poem on "The Pyramids of Egypt"; charmed with "L'Allegro" and "Il Penseroso," he repeated their sweet music in "The Ode to Fancy" and "The Citizen's Resolve," the most fanciful and genuinely poetic lyrics that up to the time had sprung from American soil. Then as he read in his Seneca the prophetic words which he has translated in his "Columbus and Ferdinand":

The time shall come when numerous years are past,
The ocean shall dissolve the hand of things
And an extended region rise at last;

And Typhis shall disclose the mighty land
Far, far away where none have roved before,
Nor shall the world's remotest region be
Gibraltar's rock or Thule's savage shore,

he napped out an epic of the New World. "Columbus to Ferdinand," "The Antiquity of America," "Discovery," "Pictures of Columbus," and, last of all, the brilliant "Rising Glory of America," that epic prelude, are but the scattered and distorted wreckage of this glorious vision. Thus did the poet serve his apprenticeship; thus singing did he go from college into the world.

So far Freneau had seen life only at a distance, through the medium of his books. His next period was one of disillusion. Unable at once to study

a profession he became a private tutor, but after
an experience of thirteen days he made his escape,
and late in 1772 went to Somerset County, Maryland, to assist his classmate Brackenridge with his
little academy. From this exile he writes Madison:
"I have printed a poem in New York called 'The
American Village,' containing about four hundred
lines, also a few short pieces . . . as to the main
poem, it is damned by all good and judicious judges.
My name is in the title page." He is full of poetical plans; poetry is his real vocation. "I am
now reading physic at my leisure hours, that is when
I am neither sleeping, hearing classes or writing
poetry, for these three take up all my time." Everything but poesy is distasteful; teaching he abomi-
nates. "It worries me to death and by no means
suits my 'giddy wandering brain.' . . . We have
about thirty students in this academy who prey
upon me like leaches. When shall I leave this
whimpering pack and hide my head in Acomack?"

The book "damned by all good and judicious
judges" has been "lost," as Freneau expressed it, "in
the lumber of forgotten things." Only a single
mutilated copy survives to testify that it was the
honest work of a true poet, one who was not
ashamed to put his name on the title-page. Its
freshness and originality were doubtless its doom.
The age, as Wordsworth was to learn twenty years

later, was unaccustomed to pictures of homely things made with the eye upon the object. Gradually the young poet awoke to the realization of his situation: America was unprepared for her prophet; she would not listen to him. The discovery shocked and embittered him. "Barbers cannot possibly exist as such," he writes, "among a people who have neither hair nor beards. How then can a poet hope for success in a city where there are not three persons possessed of elegant ideas?" Again in his clever tale of the sick author, who recounts in what we to-day recognize as the true Stocktonian manner the various transmigrations of his soul during the centuries, he writes:

I remember I wrote poetry as long ago as in the reign of Ezra-bel-haraden, one of the most ancient kings of Persia. . . . I have been a drayman's horse, a Jamaica's field negro, a sailor in an English man-of-war, and last of all, to complete my misery, am now doing penance as an American poet. What will become of me next I cannot yet tell. Certain, I am, however, that be the change what it may, it cannot be very much for the worse.

He ever dreamed of seeking more congenial regions:

Long I have sat on this disastrous shore
And sighing, sought to gain a passage o'er
To Europe's towers, where, as our travellers say,
Poets may flourish, or, perhaps they may.

For a year or more Freneau's pen was dipped in vinegar. His intense hatred of oppression, his anger at the insolence of the British at Boston, his bitterness of soul, all combined to fill him with a kind of berserker rage. During the autumn of 1775 sarcasm and satire fairly rolled from his pen. The patriots were delighted; here was something they could appreciate. To this day Freneau is remembered chiefly on account of this work. In August and September he wrote no less than six long poems, four or five of which were issued at short intervals as pamphlets. It is worthy of note, however, that to none of these hasty outpourings did the poet affix his name.

IV

This first period of satire was cut short late in 1775 by a business venture which took the poet to the West Indies. "Mac Swiggen," his valedictory to the public and to his critics, is worthy of the pen that in later years produced "English Bards and Scotch Reviewers." There is real pathos in its closing lines:

I to the sea with weary steps descend,
Quit the mean conquest that such swine must yield
And leave Mac Swiggen to enjoy the field.

In distant isles some happier scene I'll choose
And court in softer shades the unwilling Muse.

The change was a salutary one. Amid the novel scenery and dreamy beauty of the tropics, Freneau forgot his rage, forgot the narrow carping of his critics, and the bitterness of his soul. During the next year and more he did his strongest and most enduring work. "The Beauties of Santa Cruz," "The House of Night," and "The Jamaica Funeral," all written during this auspicious interval, give us the true measure of Freneau's power.

In "Santa Cruz" he pours out his first rapture over the tropic isles. The teeming vegetation, the novel plant forms—the mangrove, the palmetto, the tamarind—the luscious fruit and brilliant flowers, the sudden and fierce hurricanes, the sensuous beauty of the southern night when

The drowsy pelican wings home his way
The misty eve sits heavy on the sea,

thrilled him and stirred within him all that was poetic. "Surely," he cries, "such were the isles that happy Flaccus sung," and again,

O grant me, gods, if yet condemned to stray,
At least to spend life's sober evening here.

The summer isles "betwixt old Cancer and the midway line" have never had a more inspired laureate;

to this day "Santa Cruz" is the noblest song ever called forth by the West Indies.

Freneau now entered the region of pure invention. With his "House of Night" he became one of the earliest pioneers in that dimly-lighted region which was soon to be exploited by Coleridge and Poe. The poem is the first distinctly romantic note heard in America. Moreover, one may search in vain in the English poetry of the early romantic movement for anything that can equal it in strength of conception and in sustained mastery over the vaguely terrible. It is a "vision of the midnight hour," in which the poet is led to a mysterious "dome" where he becomes, despite himself, a witness of the death of the grim monster Death himself. The atmosphere of the poem is vague and awful. The page that recounts the poet's departure from the house of night quaking with fear—

Beneath my feet substantial darkness lay
And screams were heard from the distempered ground,

his timid look behind him to find the windows of the infernal dome a "flaming hell-red," the fearful shrieks of the dying monster within the walls, the "hell-red wandering light" that led to the graves, the sudden boom of the sexton's bell above him, and then the troop of specters galloping fiercely on Death's horses, while "their busy eyes shot terror to my soul"—all this shows the power of the man and what he might have been had he lived in a literary atmosphere with competent criticism to guide him. As a product of pure imagination the poem is most remarkable, especially when we view it in connection with the English literature of its day. In its weird supernaturalism it anticipated Scott, and in its early atmosphere of unrelieved horror it clearly anticipated Coleridge.

In "The Jamaica Funeral" Freneau outlines his early philosophy of life. The poet is growing in power and is fast breaking from the influence of Gray, his early master. It is a Gallic philosophy that he outlines; he is becoming infected with Deism; he is a true bacchanalian. Is there not a ring of the "Rubaiyat" in a stanza like this:

Count all the trees that crown Jamaica's hills,
Count all the stars that through the heavens you see,
Count every drop that the wide ocean fills—
Then count the pleasures Bacchus yields to me.

V

Freneau's second period of satire began after his confinement in the British prison-ships during the summer of 1780. The experience aroused within him a fury of indignation which he poured out with hot pen. In a bitter, passionate fury he bade farewell to the muse of his choice and turned to the sterner muse of satire who alone could "suit the taste." During the next three years he wrote the greater number of those satires and songs which have earned for him the title of "Poet of the Revolution." Every movement of "the insolent foe" called out a scathing criticism; every heroic deed of the struggling patriots called out a lyric. His poems of this period are in themselves a history of the last years of the war. His heart was in his work; the prison-ship had blotted for a time all memories of the old bitterness, his early dreams, everything save the one thought of his "injured country's woe." He lampooned without mercy Cornwallis, Clinton, Carleton, and the Royalist printers, Rivington and Gaine. He sang tender lyrics of the patriot dead at Eutaw Springs who

> saw their injured Country's woe;
> The flaming town, the wasted field;
> Then rushed to meet the insulting foe;
> They took the spear—but left the shield.

He celebrated the naval victories of Barney and of Jones, and he called down maledictions on the ship that bore the "worthless Arnold" from American shores. It is interesting in these days after our war with Germany to find Freneau's opinion of the Teutonic troops that fought against the patriots during the Revolution. He was unsparing in his denunciation. They are "the slaves of kings," "brutish," "stupid," "smit with the love of countries not their own." They are drunkards "drinking from German sculls old Odin's beer." They are worse than this. For troops with which to conquer republican America the despot George

> His phrenzy rampant with the right divine,
> Explored the ancient world, to chain the new,
> And tired, the despot searched each dark recess
> And ransacked hell, to find the hireling Hesse.

Freneau had personal experience of German *Kultur*. When a prisoner on the *Hunter* hospital ship he was attended by a Hessian surgeon, who was the only medical man the hundreds of sick prisoners were allowed.

> Fair science never called the wretch her son,
> And art disdained the stupid man to own.

This doctor's treatment was heroic. "Nostrums from hell" he poured out in indiscriminating profusion.

> On those refusing he bestowed a kick,
> Or menaced vengeance with his walking-stick;
> Here uncontrolled he exercised his trade,
> And grew experienced by the deaths he made;
> By frequent blows we from his cane endured
> He killed at least as many as he cured.

In his prose narrative of his life on the prison ship Freneau is still more specific. One night three of the prisoners made their escape in the ship's boat.

This occasioned new trouble. The doctor refused to come on board, and as he rowed past us next morning to see somebody in the *Jersey*, which lay near us, some of the sick calling to him for blisters, he told them to put tar on their backs, which would serve as well as anything, and so rowed away. However, after two or three days his wrath was appeased, and he deigned to come on board again.

And he the sole doctor for a hospital full of patients, the most of them critically ill.

These are more than the fleeting voices of a newspaper muse. Scott declared that "Eutaw Springs" was "as fine a thing as there is of the kind in the language." "The Memorable Victory of Paul Jones," written when America was full of the first news of the battle, is one of the glories of American literature. Longfellow or Whittier never wrote a more stirring ballad. It moves with leaps and bounds; it is full of the very spirit of the battle.

> She felt the fury of her ball,
> Down, prostrate down, the Britons fall.
> The decks are strew'd with slain,
> Jones to the foe his vessel lashed
> And while the black artillery flashed
> Loud thunders shook the main.

It is not impertinent to observe that Thomas Campbell was but four years of age when this appeared.

This stirring lyric, with half a dozen more equally spirited, makes Freneau not only the earliest but in many respects the strongest of American naval lyrists. In dash and fire, in ability to catch and reproduce the odors and the atmosphere of the ocean, in enthusiasm and excitement that is contagious and that plunges the reader at once into the heart of the action, and in glowing patriotism that makes the poems national hymns, no American poet has excelled this earliest singer of the American ocean. Campbell in later years excelled Freneau as a poet of battle on the sea, but it was the elder singer who furnished him his inspiration and taught him the possibilities of the ocean as domain for poetry. Freneau was the pioneer. That Campbell read many of his poems we know, and that he even took from them at least one whole line, without acknowledging the theft, is all too evident.

It is to be regretted that these stirring naval lyrics have been so long lost and forgotten. No true American can read without a thrill of pride and of patriotism such songs as "Captain Jones' Invitation" and "The Death of Captain Biddle," the intrepid seaman who from the *Randolph* poured death into the British ship—

> Tremendous flash! and hark, the ball
> Drives through old Yarmouth, flames and all,

and then at the moment of victory was blown up
by his own magazine; or again "Stanzas on the
New Frigate Alliance," the gallant ship "who walks
the ocean like its queen" and "Guards her native
shore," and "Barney's Victory over the General
Monk," that rollicking song of battle and of triumph, and best of all, perhaps, "The Sailor's Invitation," which is full of the very salt and vigor
of the western seas. It was not Scott or Cooper
that added the domain of the ocean to literature; it
was Freneau. His books are full of the roar and
the sweep of the ocean, which he knew as the
farmer knows his ancestral acres. There is no more
true and vigorous picture of an ocean voyage and a
naval combat than that contained in Canto I of "The
British Prison Ship." The episode of the boat-
swain's fiery prayer just before the conflict is
unique in literature.

VI

The Revolution over, Freneau, after following
with stinging invective the departing foe and after
showering with ridicule and scorn Rivington and

Gaine and the discomfited Royalists, found his occupation gone. The impetuous tide of his hate
and his outraged sense of justice and of freedom
had made him for a time forget his early dreams.
He had realized keenly that no poet can build a
permanent fame upon satire, and yet to serve his
injured country he would wield no other pen.
The enemy vanquished, there was no more need for
satire. But his countrymen, delighting in the bit-
ing sarcasm and the hard blows which they could
fully appreciate and enjoy, demanded more. .Fre-
neau turned upon them with bitterness: "For men
I keep a pen," he cried, "for dogs a cane!" He
would use the cane no more. But who would listen
to aught but rant and ridicule; who had ears to
appreciate anything else? Fate had thrown him into "a bard-baiting clime." A wave of the old bitterness swept over him:

Expect not in these times of rude renown
That verse like yours will have the chance to please:
No taste for plaintive elegy is known
Nor lyric ode—none care for things like these.

He would leave, even as he left in 1776, so
cheerless an environment. Business again called
him from his country; he became the captain of a
coasting vessel plying between New York and

Southern ports. There is in his second farewell to the muse a note of real pathos:

> Then, Sylvius, come—let you and I
> On Ocean's aid once more rely,
> Perhaps the Muse may still impart
> Her balm to ease the aching heart.
> Though cold may chill and storms dismay
> Yet Zoilus will be far away.

Thereupon he became our poet of the sea. For years he was a captain on the Atlantic, wrecked time and again during voyages to the Southern ports and the West Indies. No poems written in America are so full of the very presence and soul of the ocean. When one reads his "The Hurricane," for instance, first published with the title "Verses made at Sea in a Heavy Gale," knowing from the footnote that "Captain Freneau's ship survived the violent hurricane off Jamaica, July 30, 1784, when no more than eight out of 150 sail of vessels in the ports of Kingston and Port Royal were saved," the poem becomes a living thing.

The poem "Hatteras" opens with the realistic line:

> In fathoms five, the anchor gone.

And there is the very roll of the ocean in its broken stanzas:

The dangerous shoal, that breaks the wave
In columns to the sky;
The tempests black, that hourly rave,
Portend all danger nigh:
Sad are my dreams on ocean's verge!
The Atlantic round me flows,
Upon whose ancient angry surge
No traveller finds repose.

There is vagabond flavor to his very titles, "Stanzas Written at the Foot of Monte Souffriere, near the Town of Basseterre, Guadaloupe," "Stanzas written at the Island of Maderia," "On the Peak of Teneriffe," "Stanzas written in Blackbeard's Castle," "Lines written at Sea," the last with its opening stanza:

No pleasure on earth can afford such delights
As the heavenly view of these tropical nights:
The glow of the stars, and the breeze of the sea,
Are heaven—if heaven on ocean can be.

And is there not an epigrammatic quality about this nautical summing up of the Bermuda Islands:

When verging to the height of thirty-two,
And east or west you guide the dashy prow;
Then fear by night the dangers of this shore,
Nature's wild garden, placed in sixty-four.
Here many a merchant his lost freight bemoans,
And many a gallant ship has laid her bones.

VII

Here was a man equipped by nature for a true poet, a man with a message, yet dwarfed and silenced by his environment. America was not ready for her singer. It took half a century more to make way in the wilderness for the new message that had been whispered to Freneau in his young manhood. Had he been a great world poet he would have been heard despite all difficulties, he would have trampled down the barriers about him and compelled his age to listen, but the task was beyond him. America to this day has produced no poet who single-handed and alone could have performed such a labor of Hercules. Freneau turned deliberately to the world of affairs and suffered his early dream to fade gradually away.

In June, 1786, the very year that witnessed the Kilmarnock edition of Burns, there appeared from the press of Francis Bailey of Philadelphia the first collected edition of Freneau's poems. It was published with hesitation; its author was at sea; for more than a year the manuscript had been in the hands of the printer. From his advertisement it appears that his only hope for the success of the volume lay in its satire and songs of the Revolution, which, as they had appeared "in newspapers and other periodicals in the different states of America during the late war," had been read with "avidity and pleasure."

This volume to this day has never received the consideration which it deserves. It was the first collection of poems deserving of the name ever made by an American poet. But it is far more than a mere bibliographical curiosity; it contained the first germs of true original poetry that America produced. It was, moreover, the work of a man who was not content merely to follow, but who left his contemporaries behind and pushed vigorously, though crudely, it must be confessed, into untrodden regions and blazed pathways in the wilderness. Had he like the later Longfellow been allowed to seek the European sources of culture and to live easily in poetic environment, who may tell what would have been the result?

Had this early volume been an English book, it long ago would have figured largely in the histories of the romantic and naturalistic movement which resulted in the outburst of song that has marked our present century. That Freneau was a pioneer in the dim, romantic world that was to be explored by Coleridge and Poe no one may doubt who reads his "House of Night"; that he was a pioneer in the movement that succeeded in throwing off the chain forged by Pope is evident from even a cursory examination of his editions. "The Wild Honeysuckle," for instance, which was written in 1786, twelve years before the appearance of the "Lyrical Ballads," is as spontaneous and as free from Pope as anything by Wordsworth. It is a nature lyric written with the eye upon the object, without recollection of other poetry, and it draws from the humble flower a lesson for humanity in the true Wordsworthian manner. Before Freneau, American poetry had been full of the eglantine, the yew, and the Babylonian willow, the nightingale, the lark—the flora and the fauna of Hebrew and British bards. Classic English poetry had looked away from the actual landscape and had been about as British in background as the "Eclogues" of Vergil. In Freneau we find for the first time the actual life of the American forest—the wild pink, the elm, the wild honeysuckle, the pumpkin, the blackbird, the squirrel, the "loquacious whip-poor-will"—and in addition to this the varied life of the American tropic islands. We find for the first time examples of that true poetic spirit that could find poetry in humble and even vulgar things; that furthermore, like Burns, could draw from the phenomena of lowly nature deep lessons for human life. He sees the reflection of the stars in the bosom of the river:

> But when the tide had ebbed away
> The scene fantastic with it fled.
> A bank of mud around me lay,
> And sea-weed on the river's bed.

And from this he draws the obvious moral. Consider what Pope would have said of mud. Indeed, to appreciate Freneau, one must habituate one's self to the atmosphere of the classic age and view things from the classic point of view. Whether Freneau influenced the school of poets who in England broke away from the eighteenth century methods it is useless to ask. We may observe, however, that Freneau's poems were known and read freely in England at the dawn of the critical period in British poetry, and that even Scott could "lift" without comment a whole line from one of them.

In his use of his native land and his familiar surroundings as a background for art Freneau discovered the poetical side of the Indian, and thus became the literary father of Brockden Brown, Cooper, and the little school of poetry which in the early years of the century fondly believed that the aboriginal American was to be the central figure in the poetry of the New World. To the little real poetry that there is in the Indian, Freneau did full justice. He went, however, to no such absurd lengths as did Cooper and Eastburn and Whittier. His "Indian Death Song"—if the poem indeed be his—which is full of the wild, stoical heroism of the brave who is dying beneath the torture of his enemies, makes all that is possible of the theme. There has been no more true and poetic rendering of this distinctly American phase of human character. In "The Indian Student" he has done justice to the Indian's love for the forest and to the untamable wildness of his nature. "The Dying Indian" and "The Indian Burying Ground" sum up all that is poetic in Indian legend and all that is pathetic in the fate of the vanishing race. Poetry, if it is to confine itself to the truth, can do little more for the Indian.

VIII

Such was Philip Freneau, a man in every respect worthy to bear the title "father of American poetry." He was the first true poet born upon our our continent; he realized in his early youth his true vocation; he gave himself with vigor and enthusiasm to his calling; he fitted himself with wide reading and classic culture; he received the full inspiration of a great movement in human society; he lifted up his voice to sing, but he was smothered and silenced by his contemporaries. He was all alone; he had about him no circle of "Pleiades" to encourage and assist; he had no traditions behind him that would compel silence. He was out of step with the theology of his generation; he was out of tune with the music of his day; he was beating time half a century ahead of the chorus about him. The people have to be educated to revolution, and America had not yet learned to take the initiative in things intellectual and esthetic. She must follow the literary fashions beyond the sea. Freneau was for breaking violently from England and for setting up a new standard of culture and literary art on this side of the water.

> Can we never be thought
> To have learning or grace,
> Unless it be brought
> From that damnable place?

But he reckoned without his countrymen. Not until Emerson's day did it dawn upon Amercia that it was possible for her to think for herself and make poetry that did not echo the bards of England. Thus did America reject her earliest poet; thus did she stop her ears and compel him to lay aside his seven-stringed lyre for the horn and the bagpipes. Freneau lived to see his discarded harp in full tune in other hands, first in England and then in his own land. There is something pathetic in the

figure of the old minstrel who had realized almost
nothing of his early dream and yet who had been
told by the great Jeffries that the time would surely
come when his poems would command a com-
mentator like Gray, who had been extravagantly
praised by such masters as Scott and Campbell, who
had written to Madison as late as 1815, "my
publisher tells me the town will have them [his
verses] and of course have them they will"—it is
pathetic to see this poet in his hoary old age, for
he lived until 1832, realizing that he had been utterly forgotten, witnessing the triumph of the very
songs that had haunted his youth, and seeing those
who had not half his own native ability crowned
by those who had rejected and forgotten him.

America has been unjust to Freneau. For a
century she left his poems in their first editions,
which are now rare and costly; she scattered his
letters and papers to the winds; she garbled and
distorted his life in every book of reference and
left untold the true story of his career. The present
generation knows him only as "the poet of the Revolution," and they dismiss him unread with the flippant criticism that he was a hasty and slipshod
maker of newspaper verse nearly all of which has
reached a deserved oblivion. That this is unjust
and unfounded every one who has read Freneau can
bear witness. He was a scholar of real attain-

ments; he was a critic with discernment; he was a conscientious workman. That he labored upon his lines with care can be proved by following the thoughtful changes in his different editions; that he followed poetry with all the passion of a Poe there is abundant proof; that he regarded his satires and his jingles as a poetic avocation is written all over his literary remains; and that he was forced to abandon the muse of his choice we have attempted to show. There are few sadder spectacles in our literary history than the old poet deliberately abandoning the dream of his youth, and cutting from his later volumes the greater part of such lyrics as "The House of Night" and "The Jamaica Funeral" because a crude public would not understand and tolerate. But time works slowly with her verdicts; true merit in the end is sure to receive its deserts, and Freneau may even yet be given the place that is his.

THE CENTENARY OF BRYANT'S POETRY

THE publication of Bryant's first significant book, "Poems by William Cullen Bryant," Cambridge, Massachusetts, 1821, a thin little volume of forty-eight pages, containing "The Ages," "To a Waterfowl," "Translation of a Fragment of Simonides," "Inscription for the Entrance to a Wood," "The Yellow Violet," "Song," "Green River," and "Thanatopsis," marks the beginning of classic American poetry. So often has this been repeated in the text-books, and so continually has it been iterated in the schools, that it has become for all of us an axiom to be accepted without question. But with the present year has come a new sensation. The book is now entering upon its second century. The first undisputed American classic has outlasted three generations: American poetry is now of age.

The American short story, if we count "Rip Van Winkle" as the earliest specimen, celebrated its centennial in 1919; the American novel, if we count "The Spy" as the beginning, became of age in 1921, but somehow Bryant seems farther away from us than Irving though Irving died in 1859, and farther away than Cooper though he died in 1851. Bryant is our oldest classic American writer in a peculiar sense. It is now over forty years since he died, the measure of a generation, but at the time of his death he had lived for half a century beyond the period of his really distinctive work. As a poet he sprang into fame as early as 1817, and from that point on there was not a time when he was not rated among the greatest of American poets. Our grandfathers and great-grandfathers settled it that he was a classic. During the lifetime of us all he has been a half-mythical figure, a patriarchal engraving on the walls of schoolhouses. The poems we associate with his name seem the appropriate work of such a bard: contemplations of death, peerings into the abysmal gulfs of time, Druidic meditations amid the ancient forests. He has been our bardic figure, the hoary-bearded gleeman of our period of origins, our half-mythical Homer. It has seemed to throw back the beginnings of our poetry into a region primeval; it has given it an atmosphere more mellow than we could have deemed possible.

With a century of perspective we may begin to speak now with confidence. The contemporary jealousies, ambitions, friendships, have been forgotten; the claques of the Percivals, the Hallecks, the

Pierponts, the Danas have passed completely into oblivion; the extravagant overpraisings of the early editors like Stoddard have been reduced to real 'value—one may now see over the underbrush. What of William Cullen Bryant after a century of his work?

II

Criticism of Bryant must begin always with the statement that he was a New Englander. In his poetic product—and in none other is he distinctive —he is no more to be classed as a Knickerbocker than is Whittier. He was a descendant of Puritans in unbroken lines, the best blood of New England— the Aldens, Bryants, Howards, Ameses, Harrises, Haywards, Kieths, Mitchells, Packards, Snells, Washburns—English with a mixture of Calvinistic Scotch. The family early had moved from the Massachusetts Bay environment westward into the mountains. When Bryant was born, it was at Cummington in the Berkshires on a farm more remote from city influences than even Whittier's. It was a Puritan home of the older type, a survival. Puritanism we know died first at the large centers; it persisted in all its primitive sternness and austerity for a generation or two more in the remoter valleys and quieter villages; lingered indeed far down into the last century when it faded out. Bryant was the last conspicuous example of it: the last of the Puritans.

To understand him at all one must study the home in which he was reared, the household of his grandfather Snell in which were passed those impressionable years that molded him. Here an atmosphere sternly Calvinistic: the Bible read aloud in solemn tones; prayers morning and evening ringing always with the fervid poetic diction and the resonant doom notes of Hebrew prophets. One solemn petition, reiterated daily, filled the childish imagination with something like terror: "Let not our feet stumble on the dark mountains of eternal death." He was nurtured upon Watts's psalms and hymns, repeating with unction at three "with his book in my hand and with such gestures as were prescribed for me" such tremendous stanzas as

Spare us, O Lord! aloud we pray;
　Nor let our sun go down at noon;
Thy years are one eternal day,
　And must thy children die so soon?

The boy pleased the grim Puritan grandfather. At ten he received from him a ninepenny piece for a rimed version of the first chapter of Job. Rewarded thus, he proceeded to paraphrase the one hundred and fourth Psalm. Storm and stress of soul came before his teens. "The prayer of the publican in the New Testament was often in my mouth, and I heard every variety of prayer at the Sunday evening services conducted by laymen in private houses." Before him always was the iron grandfather: "I can hardly find words to express the awe in which I stood of him."

But there was another influence in the home. The version of Job, rewarded by the grandfather because of its piety, was condemned by the father because of its poetic crudity. The father had tastes which one would hardly expect to find in that austere environment. He had been at Harvard for a time, he had received medical instruction from the famous French exile Laprilète, he had been surgeon of a merchant vessel, had been detained a year among the French of the West Indies, had sailed to the East Indies and rounded the Cape of Good Hope where he had suffered shipwreck—stormy petrel, indeed, in the remote Berkshire village. He brought a whiff of the world—French, which he read and spoke with fluency, polished manners, fastidiousness in dress, religious broadness that went even to Unitarianism, and, most important of all as we see it to-day, a taste for the refinements of art and literature that manifested itself in new books added to the primitive Watts and Milton and Bunyan of the family store: Pope's "Iliad," Thomson, Goldsmith, Cowper—indeed "volumes of most of the eminent English poets." "He wrote verses himself," his son goes on, "mostly humorous and satirical. He was not unskilled in Latin poetry, in which the odes of Horace were his favorites. He was fond of music, played on the violin, and I remember hearing him say that he once made a bass viol."

The young Bryant was fragile, precocious, over-intellectual, predisposed to consumption, the grim specter of which haunted him even into manhood like a foreboding of death. His little sister faded and died during that home period of his life when every emotion stamps the soul. Everything—his puritanical environment, his frail hold upon the physical, his reading in the elegiac school of poets: Young, Gray, Parnell, Blair—all inclined him to meditation, melancholy, poetic thought.

He appears never to have had a boyhood. Never in his recollection was there a time when he was not pointed out as the writer of remarkable poetry. As a child he declaimed original verse as a school exercise; at thirteen he was the author of a book so successful—sad stuff now—that a second and enlarged edition was printed, at fourteen he was preparing for college under the tutelage of his grandfather's brother, another grim Puritan, who drove the boy mercilessly, allowing not a moment for play, through interminable Latin: in eight months through the "Colloquies" of Corderius, all of Vergil, the "Orations" of Cicero, and the New Testament in Latin. Then came the Greek under another inflexible divine: the Rev. Mr. Hallack.

I was early at my task in the morning, and kept on till bedtime; at night I dreamed of Greek, and my first thought in the morning was of my lesson for the day. At the end of two calendar months I knew the Greek New Testament from end to end almost as if it had been English.

At fifteen he entered the sophomore class at Williams, and after two terms he left, dissatisfied with the intellectual standards of the college. Such was the boy Bryant.

His hopes of attending Yale disappointed by financial conditions at home, he spent the autumn unsettled. Now it was that his father brought him from Boston Southey's "Remains of Henry Kirke White"—red-letter day for the young poet. Here was a kindred soul, a genius stricken with consumption before life had fairly opened, and crying out in agony of spirit. "I read the poems with great eagerness and so often that I committed several of them to memory, particularly the ode to the Rosemary." Strange choice it would seem now. Here is the opening stanza:

Sweet scented flower! who art wont to bloom
   On January's front severe,
   And o'er the wintery desert drear
To waft thy waste perfume!
Come, thou shalt form my nosegay now,
And I will bind thee round my brow;
   And as I twine the mournful wreath,
I 'll weave a melancholy song;
And sweet the strain shall be, and long,
   The melody of death.

Kirke White as we read him to-day has little save his sentimental melancholy and his echoes of earlier music—Milton, Cowley, Thomson, Young —but to the young Berkshire Puritan who had been reared in daily contemplation of death and who felt that he too was early for the tomb, he was a twin soul. His declamatory, "Thanatopsis"-like poem "Time," his lyric "To an Early Primrose" suggestive of "The Yellow Violet" to come, his titles "Thanatos" and "Athanatos," all had their effect upon the maturing poet.

There were other influences. "I remember reading, at that time, that remarkable poem, Blair's 'Grave,' and dwelling with pleasure upon its finer passages. I had the opportunity of comparing it with a poem on a kindred subject, also in blank verse, that of Bishop Porteus on 'Death' "—strange field of study for youth of sixteen. Other books he found: "a thin volume of the miscellaneous poems of Southey," and Cowper, whom he studied anew. "I now passed from his shorter poems, which are generally mere rhymed prose, to his 'Task,' the finer passages of which supplied a form of blank verse that captivated my admiration."

The autobiography ends here, but enough is given to explain the early Bryant: his Puritan soul with its brooding sense of death; the melancholy pathos of Kirke White; the resonant funereal declamation of Blair, notably in such passages as that beginning,

What is this world?
What but a spacious burial field unwalled?

and, finally, the easy naturalness of Cowper's blank verse. That the young student, aware as he must have been of his own powers, should be trying his pen as he pored over his masters, was inevitable. At some time during the period he made an attempt of his own, an exercise we may call it—several attempts indeed—and stowed them away in his desk uncompleted to be elaborated some time perchance into finished wholes.

III

The time had come to leave Latin and Greek and poetry. Literature as a profession was impossible in America. "Some men of taste and learning amongst us," to quote his words in 1818, "might occasionally amuse their leisure with poetical trifles," but with Bryant there could be no divided allegiance. The crisis of his life was upon him. What struggles he passed through we do not know: there are no self-revealing letters as in Longfellow's case. We know only that he chose the law and that he gave himself to it with all the Puritan earnestness that formerly he had given to his college preparation. His poem "To a Friend on His Marriage," published in "The North American Review" in 1818 and manifestly written during the period of his legal studies, indicates that he deliberately abandoned the muses. He turned to his "harp, neglected long," only to celebrate a friend's marriage:

Such be thy days.—O'er Coke's black letter page,
Trimming the lamp at eve, 't is mine to pore;
Well pleased to see the venerable sage,
Unlock his treasur'd wealth of legal lore;
And I, that lov'd to trace the woods before,
And climb the hill a play mate of the breeze
Have vow'd to tune the rural lay no more,
Have bid my useless classicks sleep at ease,
And left the race of bards to scribble, starve and
   freeze.

Farewell.—When mildly through the naked wood,
The clear warm sun effus'd a mellow ray;
And livelier health propell'd the vital flood,

Loitering at large, I pour'd the incondite lay,
Forgot the cares and business of the day,
Forgot the quirks of Lyttleton and Coke,
Forgot the public storms, and party fray;
And, as the inspiring flame across me broke,
To thee the lowly harp, neglected long, I woke.

When "Thanatopsis" appeared in "The North American Review," he had completed his four years of legal study, had been admitted to the bar, and had practised law for two years. He was twenty-three years of age and had settled down into his profession with no thought of change. To get the impression that he was toying half-heartedly with the law and that he was scribbling poetry when he should have been studying legal cases, one must neglect all that we know of him. He was grandson of that grim Puritan who had put him in front of him at the hay-raking to rap his heels if he fell behind. Through his whole life he applied himself unreservedly to the duty at hand.

Literary fame came suddenly and by accident. The story that his father found in his desk fragments of his earlier poetical exercises and took them to the editors of "The North American Review" bears all the marks of truth. A glance at the poems in their earlier form is convincing. Never would author present his material in such form: the four riming quatrains, boyishly inferior, printed as if they were a part of the blank verse fragment, the abrupt beginning and the sudden ending of the main piece as if it were a part wrenched out of a whole, and the second piece without even a title. This latter fragment, afterward to be expanded under the title, "Inscription for the Entrance of a Wood," surely must have been written after reading Southey's collection of "Inscriptions," perhaps after that entitled "For a Tablet on the Banks of a Stream." It reads like the blank verse of the later Bryant:

Stranger! a while upon this mossy bank
Recline thee. If the Sun rides high, the breeze
That loves to ripple o'er the rivulet
Will play around thy brow, and the cool sound
Of running waters soothe thee. Mark how clear
They sparkle o'er the shallows; and behold,
Where o'er their surface wheels with restless speed
Yon glossy insect, on the sand below
How its swift shadow flits. In solitude
The rivulet is pure, and trees and herbs
Bend o'er its salutary course refreshed;
But, passing on amid the haunts of men,
It finds pollution there, and rolls from thence
A tainted stream. Seek'st thou for Happiness?
Go, Stranger, sojourn in the woodland cot
Of Innocence, and thou shalt find her there.

But exercises though they are, unfinished fragments, musings of a young student over his books, they have within them nevertheless the breath of life. As one comes upon them amid the general feebleness of verse in "The North American Review," the interminable translations of Boileau's satires into labored heroics, the hackneyed translations from Horace, the effusions like "Hope and Memory" and "The Cyprian Queen," and the pompous ode in schoolboy Latin, it is like coming upon a cold spring in the illimitable desert. One who approaches them, however, in this setting will learn a secret—secret at least to the authors of textbooks: the poems as we have them to-day have suffered change until they are almost new creations.

To call "Thanatopsis" an example of precocity is foolishness. The original piece is a fragment echoing the spirit of Kirke White's "Time"; but the later "Thanatopsis" is a vital unit. Its soul was not given it until 1821 when the poet was twenty-seven. When called upon to print his poems after his Harvard rendition of "The Ages," he molded the fragment into a whole, expanding the original forty-seven lines into eighty-one—among the additions the well-known opening and closing parts, the original having opened with the lines

> Yet a few days, and thee
> The all-beholding sun shall see no more

and closed with the line

And make their bed with thee,

changing the point of view completely, and adding everywhere touches of distinction.

He had discovered a new master. To Richard H. Dana he once remarked that "upon opening Wordsworth, a thousand springs seemed to gush up at once in his heart, and the face of nature, of a sudden to change into a strange freshness and life." The nature of the change one may see in the additions and the emendations to the original draft of "Thanatopsis." The reflections upon the universality of death become no more sentimental and puritanic, as in the case of Kirke White; they become a part of the great voice of nature. Nature has become a teacher, a comforter, and a religion.

The emendations everywhere are significant. In the original, for instance, the lines ran:

> Then venerable woods—rivers that move
> In majesty, and the complaining brooks
> That wind among the meads and make them green.

In the final version this was expanded to——

> Then venerable woods—rivers that move
> In majesty, and the complaining brooks
> That make the meadows green; and, poured round all,
> Old Ocean's gray and melancholy waste.

In the orginal this:

That veil Oregan, where he hears no sound,

was changed to the well-known

Where rolls the Oregon, and hears no sound.

In the original this:

> Thousands more
> Will share thy destiny.—The tittering world
> Dance on to the grave. The busy brood of care
> Plod on, and each one chases as before
> His favorite phantom.

In the final version significant changes in almost every line:

> All that breathe
> Will share thy destiny. The gay will laugh
> When thou art gone, the solemn brood of care
> Plod on, and each one as before will chase
> His favorite phantom.

The full influence of Wordsworth came later—best seen, perhaps, in "A Winter Piece," a poem that without the slightest trace of plagiarism could not have been written by one who had not read Wordsworth's "Lines Composed a Few Miles Above Tintern Abbey." The heart of Wordsworth's poem is this:

> How oft
> In darkness, and amid the many shapes
> Of joyless daylight; when the fretful stir
> Unprofitable, and the fever of the world,

Have hung upon the beatings of my heart,
How oft, in spirit, have I turned to thee,
O sylvan Wye! Thou wanderer through the woods,
How often has my spirit turned to thee!

And of Bryant's it is this:

And when the ills of life
Had chafed my spirit—when the unsteady pulse
Beat with strange flutterings—I would wander forth
And seek the woods. Then sunshine on my path
Was to me as a friend. . . .
. . . Then the chant
Of birds, and chime of brooks, and soft caress
Of the fresh sylvian air, made me forget
The thoughts that broke my peace.

Nature was to both the healer, the pastor, the
soothing presence that brought again sanity and
joyousness. Bryant never proceeded beyond this
conception of nature, but Wordsworth, as we shall
see, passed on into larger conceptions and so became a poet immeasurably larger and immeasurably
more prophet-like.

No man ever achieved poetic fame with less of
striving than did Bryant. The fragments of poetry
anonymously published in a scholarly literary review
could bring no immediate popularity, but they could
do what was better for the poet: they could draw
the attention of the Boston circle which had in its

hands the best that America could offer. The
praises of the editors—Dana the leading spirit—
led the young barrister to empty his first portfolio.
"Translation of a Fragment of Simonides," "To a
Waterfowl," and "To a Friend on His Marriage"
appeared in the March, 1818, number. For the
July number he was asked to review the Rev. Soly-
man Brown's "An Essay on American Poetry," and
his response was that careful essay which deserves
to be printed as the general introduction to the history of nineteenth century American poetry. Until
this day there has been no better study of the literary
conditions of the early years of the American republic:

English in our origin, and owing to the character
of our birthplace, almost all that we have cause to be
proud of in our natures; speaking her language, and
reading her literature with the same commonness as
if it were our own; boasting of her works of genius
in the entire forgetfulness that they are not ours; and
defending them with the same earnestness of partiality
as if our own reputation were at stake; we seem to
have been unmindful that it was possible for us to
have a literary character at home and writers of our
own to read and admire. We look to England for
almost all our learning and entertainment; our met-
aphysicks and morals are drawn from her; and for
poetry, the common reading of all countries, we enter

into the assembly of her bards alone. This continued dependence upon England has not only turned us away from the observation of what is well done here, but has begotten a distrust of our own judgment and taste. We hesitate at pronouncing an opinion on what has not received judgment there; and dare not confess where we have been offended or pleased, lest her tribunals of criticism should, by and by, come down upon us and tell us we are wrong.

Warning his countrymen against all extravagant claims and all extravagant hopes of equaling the great literatures of the older nations, he nevertheless strikes up boldly for an independent native product.

National gratitude—national pride—every high and generous feeling that attaches us to the land of our birth, or that exalts our characters as individuals, ask us that we should foster the infant literature of our country. . . . The poetry of the United States, though it has not yet reached that perfection to which some other countries have carried theirs, is yet even better than we could have been expected to produce, considering that our nation has scarcely seen two centuries since the first of its founders erected ·their cabins on its soil, that our literary institutions are yet in their infancy, and that our citizens are just beginning to find leisure to attend to intellectual refinement and indulge in intellectual luxury, and the means of rewarding intellectual excellence.

The flattering attentions of the leading American review laid again upon the young man the old bewitching spell. He was like the boy who has renounced forever the object of his early infatuation and who suddenly finds himself smiled upon by her whom he was supposed to have forgotten. That he had given up the study and enjoyment of poetry is not for a moment to be supposed. His essay "On the Use of Trisyllabic Feet in Iambic Verse" in the September, 1819, "Review" he called a "little retrospect which I have taken of the usage of our poets who have written in blank verse," and he speaks as one who has read comparatively all of Shakspere and the older dramatists, Milton, Dryden, Young, Thomson, Dyer, Glover, Cumberland, Akenside, Armstrong, and Cowper.

In 1821 Richard H. Dana had begun his "The Idle Man," a distinctive little periodical written wholly by its editor save for the poems by Bryant: "Green River" in the second issue, "A Walk at Sunset" in the third issue, and "Winter Scenes" in the fourth. And the same year Boston again pushed him into publicity in a way decidedly surprising: he was asked to deliver the annual poem before the Phi Beta Kappa of Harvard College—an unprecedented request: he of the two terms in the meager inland college addressing the most critical and academic body in America. The theme that possessed him was the same that had come to the young Freneau whose "The Rising Glory of America" had rendered distinctive the Princeton graduation of 1771, and to Barlow who dreamed his life long over that tremendous conception which he called at first "The Vision of Columbus." It was a peculiarly American theme: the long roll of the ages culminating in the establishment in the New World of the hope of all lands.

> Here the free spirit of mankind, at length,
> Throws its last fetters off; and who shall place
> A limit to the giant's unchained strength,
> Or curb his swiftness in the forward race?

His effort was successful to the degree that a printed edition was called for, and in response the young poet put forth the significant volume of 1821.

The first book of poems it was that America without apology might offer to the world; a production that any nation might be proud to add to its treasures. It contained the best of all that Bryant was destined to offer; all the qualities that we associate with his poetry were in it. Had he died in 1821, America to-day would be mourning the loss of a poet as commanding as Wordsworth.

The rest is told quickly. Like many another, he who had been "well pleased" with Coke and the theory of the law had become disgusted with the actual practice of it; "the dregs of men" it forced upon him, and all the barbarous janglings of litigation. His swift, unlooked-for rise to literary prominence added to his unrest. The break came in 1825: the abandoning of the law and the assumption in New York of the editorship of a struggling literary magazine. The venture proved to be a losing one: the magazine failed, leaving him in the somber mood described in his poem "The Journey of Life." Then came temporary employment upon the New York "Evening Post," and finally in 1829 the promotion to the chief editorship. During the next half-century he lived in the maelstrom of a great city daily. Thus. swiftly the life of Bryant.

IV

All of the poet that is distinctive came before the end of his first year in New York. The publication in 1826 of the poem "I Cannot Forget with What Fervid Devotion," whatever may have been its date of composition, marks the end. Rarely has the poet so disclosed his whole heart.

I cannot forget with what fervid devotion
    I worshipped the visions of verse and of fame;
Each gaze at the glories of earth, sky, and ocean,
    To my kindled emotions, was wind over flame.

And deep were my musings in life's early blossom,
   Mid the twilight of mountain-groves wandering
      long;
How thrilled my young veins, and how throbbed my
      full bosom
   When o'er me descended the spirit of song!

'Mong the deep-cloven fells that for ages had listened
   To the rush of the pebble-paved river between,
Where the kingfisher screamed and gray precipice
      glistened,
   All breathless with awe have I gazed on the scene.

Till I felt the dark power o'er my reveries stealing,
   From the gloom of the thickets that over me hung,
And the thoughts that awoke, in the rapture of feeling,
   Were formed into verse as they rose to my tongue.

Bright visions! I mixed with the world, and ye
      faded,
   No longer your pure rural worshipper now;
In the haunts your continual presence pervaded,
   Ye shrink from the signet of care on my brow.

In the old mossy groves on the breast of the mountain,
   In deep lonely glens where the waters complain,
By the shade of the rock, by the gush of the fountain,
   I seek your loved footsteps, but seek them in vain.

Oh, leave not forlorn and forever forsaken,
   Your pupil and victim to life and its tears!

But sometimes return, and in mercy awaken
The glories ye showed to his earlier years.

It was a period of struggle, of abandoning poetry
and returning to it like a child that runs away, but
at times is filled with irresistible longings to return.
For the 1826 "Atlantic Souvenir," the first of the
annuals, he sent a poem which he called "Nature,"
a poem he later put into his collected edition without
a title and without the last stanza. It is another
document in the period of struggle, another cry
from the depths of his soul.

NATURE

I

I broke the charm that held me long,
The dear, dear witchery of song:
I said the poet's idle lore
Should waste my prime of years no more;
For poetry, though heavenly born,
Consorts with poverty and scorn.

II

I broke the charm, nor deemed its power
Could fetter me another hour;
Ah, thoughtless! how could I forget,
Its causes were around me yet;
For wheresoe'er I looked, the while,
Was nature's everlasting smile.

III

Still came, and lingered on my sight
Of flowers and streams the bloom and light,
The story of the stars and sun,
And these and poetry are one:
They, ere the world had fixed me long,
Recalled me to the love of song.

IV

Thus where the cliff, abrupt and steep,
Looks down upon the sullen deep,
Far from his mother's side, the child
Sat playing on the verge, and smiled:—
She laid her bosom bare, and won
From the dread brink her truant son.

Before finally surrendering himself to the business that was to engulf him he tried earnestly the door by which Irving had escaped. He had come to New York to enter the literary life, to become a professional man of letters, a creator of literature and only literature. There was no money in poetry and he turned to prose. Between 1827 and 1832 he wrote no less than thirteen short stories. For "The Talisman," which he edited, he contributed "An Adventure in the East Indies," "The Cascade of Melsingak," "Recollections of the South of Spain," "A Story of the Island of Cuba," "The Indian Spring," "The Whirlwind," "Phanette des

Gauldmes," and "The Marriage Blunder." For "Tales of Glauber Spa" he wrote "The Skeleton's Cave" and "Medfield," and for various periodicals he wrote others.

That one who had written poetry that is undeniably of classic quality could write tales so devoid of art and all that fiction demands is one of the unexplainable things. His "The Marriage Blunder," for instance, begins with a dissertation upon marriage, tells at length of a journey the author once made into the Red River country, describes with minuteness a man he met there, and then proceeds with a story told him by this stranger. The story proper begins on the twelfth page, after one third of the total number of words has been used. In his tale "The Whirlwind," instead of saying that a Baptist minister was on his way to Lexington to baptize some converts, he explains that he was going "to perform beside the translucent streams and under the venerable trees of that fine region, those picturesque solemnities of his sect, to which they love to point as a maniform emblem of purification from moral pollution, and of the resurrection from the death of sin and the sleep of the grave."

The poet Bryant died at length in the city newspaper office. The poems that insure him room among the poets are those few desultory moments before he had lost his early vision, and the world had crowded in and robbed him. They are only a handful; they bulk not much larger than Poe's anthology. We may venture to name them: "Thanatopsis," "The Yellow Violet," "Inscription for the Entrance to a Wood," "To a Waterfowl," "Green River," "A Winter Piece," "A Walk at Sunset," "Hymn to Death," "November," "A Forest Hymn," "The Death of the Flowers," and "I Cannot Forget with What Fervid Devotion." One more we may add, perhaps, "The Prairies," inspired by his entrance for a moment into a new and fresh world, and there are many who would plead for "To a Fringed Gentian" and "The Journey of Life." The rest do not greatly matter.

Fragmentary—that is the first impression. Genius repressed, deliberately smothered out, a series of farewells to the muse, and brief returns as to stolen pleasure, then silence or worse than silence—the voice of a poet abandoned of the inspiring presence and unconscious of his loss. Bryant's poems are a miscellany of glorious fragments with here and there a supreme lyric. The bits of blank verse, "A Forest Hymn," "Hymn to Death," "A Winter Piece," and the like, impress one as fragments from a larger whole, wonderfully finished columns for a temple never completed, never even planned. What might have been if, like Wordsworth, he could have given his life entirely to poetry, we may not ask.

As it is, he was the scant blossom of New England puritanism before it was touched by the transcendental fertilizer, the single yellow violet of a cold spring:

> Of all her train, the hands of Spring
>   First plant thee in the watery mould,
> And I have seen thee blossoming
>   Beside the snow-bank's edges cold.

It was no native wild flower: an Old World species rather, grown stately, prim, pale by transplanting into new soil, old-fashioned, simple—no doubling and fringing, no flashy colorings to stir the passions. Puritanism breathed from its every petal, an eighteenth century puritanism totally unaffected by Wesleyanism despite all the influences of Cowper.

Only half-heartedly was the young poet a child of the nineteenth century. He was of the classicists, law-bound as by iron, self-contained, reticent. Such a one, with such an ancestry and such a schooling, will not let himself go, he will do nothing in passion, he will not bare his soul nor cry aloud. No "native wood notes wild" for him: he will form himself upon the tradition of the elders. Listen to him as at twenty-four he instructs his fellow-bards: "We speak not of a disposition to emulate whatever is beautiful and excellent in their [the English poets] writings, still less would we be understood as intending to censure that sort of imitation which, exploring all the treasures of English poetry, culls from all a diction, that shall form a natural and becoming dress for the conceptions of the writer—this is a course of preparation which every one ought to go through before he appears before the public."

Anything like self-revelation he shrank from. He would not republish from "The North American Review" his really beautiful "Lines to a Friend on his Marriage," but he could cherish as if it were gold the undistinctive translation from Simonides which had appeared in the same number. He aimed at the intellect of his reader, and he leaves him cold. Like all other New Englanders, he preached constantly, but it was with the calm, contemplative voice of Watts rather than with the passion of Wesley.

But cold though he was, we may not say that the emotional within him was atrophied. It is only because it was not that he lives to-day. We make a list of the few poems where for a moment he forgot his eighteenth century manners and cried from his heart, and as we study them we wake to the realization that we have duplicated the little list upon which his fame must depend. "The Waterfowl" is a cry from a soul deeply stirred, and so are "Green River" and "I Cannot Forget," and the "Death of the Flowers." "The Hymn to Death," 1821, contains a bit of unconscious self-revealing that throws a flood of light upon the poet. The first two thirds of it is in the stately Bryant manner, a contemplative treatise upon Death, as detached and as brilliantly conventional as Pope's "Essay on Man," a cold argument just as one argues upon politics, but before the poet had finished, his father died and the poem turned suddenly into a cry from a man's soul.

> Alas! I little thought that the stern power
> Whose fearful praise I sang, would try me thus
> Before the strain was ended. It must cease—
> For he is in his grave who taught my youth
> The art of verse, and in the bud of life
> Offered me to the muses. Oh, cut off
> Untimely!

In his treatment of nature he was influenced by Wordsworth, but not fundamentally. In spirit he was of the eighteenth century even here. There is little in him of the democratic and the social. His is the soul of a Wharton and a Logan who would retire to the woods for their own pleasure and profit. His ideal is the Puritan one of self-realization, self-improvement, self-salvation. He would retire from the "haunts of men" as often as possible to repurify himself, to forget amid the beauties of nature the misery of the crowd, to revive the visions of his boyhood spent amid the solitudes, and to get nearer to God whom, in the jostling crowd, he could not feel. His are the poems of a solitary soul intent upon contemplation of the deeper problems, a soul that escapes now and then into the silences for itself alone.

Really he was not of the nineteenth century at all. Wordsworth underwent the same experience but quickly he passed on into the larger outlook of the new century. To him nature grew to have a social import. He looked upon it

> Hearing oftentimes ..
> The still, sad music of humanity.

Unlike Bryant he could romanticize it, fill it with transcendental idealism, and even pantheistic attributes. To Wordsworth it became at length but a natural step from nature as perceived by the senses to Nature as revealed by the kindled poetic imagination, and peopled with the creations of the primitive poets :

             Great God! I 'd rather be
A pagan suckled in a creed outworn;
So might I, standing on this pleasant lea,
Have glimpses that would make me less forlorn,
Have sight of Proteus rising from the sea;
Or hear old Triton blow his wreathed horn.

In other words, Wordsworth was a romanticist, a transcendentalist, a poet of the new century, while Bryant was an eighteenth century Puritan who went into the solemn forest and mused alone upon life and death and God.

His real contribution to American poetry came from his personality rather than from his message; that majestic, solemn individuality that wrought itself without effort into all that he did during the brief period of his inspiration. There is a bardic ring to his song that one finds in no other modern poet. Print his lines without their verse form and often they might be mistaken for passages from Ossian. This for instance from "A Walk at Sunset":

Oh, sun! That o'er the western mountains now goest down in glory! ever beautiful and blessed in thy radiance, whether thou colourest the eastern heaven and night mist cool, till the bright day-star vanish, or on high climbest and streamest thy white splendours from mid-sky.

Or this from the lyric "Lines on Revisiting the Country":

Ay, flame thy fiercest, sun! thou canst not wake, in this pure air, the plague that walks unseen. The maize leaf and the maple bough but take, from thy strong heat, a deeper, glossier green. The mountain wind, that faints not in thy ray, sweeps the blue streams of pestilence away.

One feels that the stanza would have been more Bryant-like could he have put it into unrimed chant-measure and ended it with

Sweeps away the blue streams of pestilence.

His blank verse, solemn and resonant, like the reverberations of organ tones down the aisles of a cathedral, is one of the glories of American literature. He did but little, but that little is permanent. American poetry began as the American nation began, with a tremendous note of seriousness, with a broadness of view commensurate with the continent, with the voice of primeval forests and boundless prairies, yea, even with "The Song of the Stars" and "The Firmament."

And though he learned his art of eighteenth century England he is nevertheless our own; last voice of our earlier traditions, first voice of our larger visions as a new nation under the sun. He used the materials of the western world; the native waterfowl, the yellow violet, the primitive forests. Not wholly in his turns of phrase is he free of Pope and his century—he can call fishes "the scaly herds" and he can advise Dana to change his "The Dying Crow" to "The Dying Raven"—yet most marvelously is he American if one reads him in comparison with his contemporaries. He draws his figures and illustrations from the life about him. Even in his essay on "Trisyllabic Feet," in which he remarks that Young imitated Pope to his own disadvantage, he will use a native comparison: "It was like setting the Mississippi to spout little *jets d'eau* and turn children's waterwheels."

And it was no narrowly localized America that he sang; no little provincial area glorified, no New England insulated and made a *new* England. The freshness and broadness of the western world are in his song. The first unquestioned poet in America was the first all-*American* poet. Our literature opens with a note that is a worthy prelude to all that may be in the centuries to come.

The influence of Bryant upon the New England group that arose in the thirties was peculiar. His success as a poet and the chaste beauty of his nature lyrics stimulated nearly all of them to their first efforts, but his distinctive note was echoed by few of them. He led them undoubtedly to native themes, but he imparted to none his classic soul.

The influx of transcendentalism and of romanticism quickly overcame his influence and swallowed him up. Wordsworth, Byron, Shelley, Keats, Tennyson, and the German romanticists ruled the mid-years of the century until the early pioneer classicist was forgotten. His "Thanatopsis" and his solemn contemplations of death may for a time have prolonged our period of sadness and sentiment, that adolescent growing period in America; but not enough to be worth our study.

He is a lone, cold peak on the horizon of our poetry, grand and solemn in the morning twilight of American song. He did but little, but that little is unlike anything else in the range of our literature. He is the poetic monument of our early Puritan origins, the mark upon the border-line between the old passing order and the new world that was to be.

POE'S "ULALUME"

POE was preëminently a lyrist. With a soul abnormally sensitive, with nerves that every harsh note jangled, endowed with an intense longing for human sympathy, yet with a nature that was fated by its very elements to be misunderstood at every point, with a pride that forbade explanations, that curled the lip and suffered in silence, Poe early became self-centered and introspective. If a man needed sympathy and help it was he, yet he received none. With his sensitive physical nature an indulgence that in another man would have been but a slight misstep was with him a fall, yet the world made no distinctions. Misunderstood, out of touch with normal humanity, he became bitter. He found no companionship save his own soul, no food save his own heart, and this rendered morbid his thoughts, distorted his perspective, and made abnormal all his standards of measure. Like Byron, he projected himself into all that he did. At length it became impossible for him to look at life objectively. He must be the hero of his stories; he must use no scenery, no atmosphere save that found in his own soul. If he sang, it must be a bitter song about his own bitter life. Even his dramatic fragments are lyrics. To him any poetry save the short impassioned lyric, which owing to its very intensity must be brief, was impossible. In his "Poetic Principle," he contended that even "Paradise Lost" was but "a series of lyrics."

With this conception of the nature of poetry, Poe, who, whatever else he might have been, was a consistent artist, took up the lyre only in moments of passion; and that these moments came but seldom is shown by the scantiness of his lyrical product. Few poets have won commanding place with so small a margin of actual accomplishment. Poe's whole poetic product makes but a thin volume, and if from it we remove those poems which almost alone establish his fame, we shall reduce it to a dozen pages. Poe walks among the great lyrists of the world by virtue of not more than ten lyrics. Roughly in the order of their production these lyrics are "The Sleeper," "The City in the Sea," "Israfel," "The Haunted Palace," "The Conqueror Worm," "The Raven," "Ulalume," "The Bells," "For Annie," and "Annabel Lee." But even with a list as small as this Poe is secure in his fame. There is an atmosphere about these lyrics that is wholly undefinable; a weird music that is half unearthly; a mysterious force that is all but irresistible. They seize upon the imagination of the reader and bear it into the regions that only the imagination may tread, through strange lands with names from the realms beyond Xanadu, they harrow him with exotic cadences, they chill him with a fear of he knows not what, and everywhere they follow him with that low, wild music that suggests the accompaniments of Eastern necromancy.

The most spontaneous of all his lyrics, the one that flashes its light into the greatest number of chambers in the poet's soul, is "Ulalume," perhaps the least understood of all Poe's writings. The average reader gets from it very little save a strange melancholy music and a sense of the terrible that he finds difficult to explain. To some it has seemed humorous. Willis, its first critic, classed it as "a curiosity in philologic flavor." To him it was simply a "skilful exercise of rarity and niceness of language." To some critics it has seemed but the wild vagaries of an insane master poet, to others a fanciful elegy for an idolized wife, to others it has been inexplicable. Not long ago a university lecturer, after dwelling upon the nameless atmosphere and the unearthly music of the poem, declared as his opinion that no one would ever be able to discover what the poet had really meant. He doubted if Poe had known himself what he meant. It is very sure that without the life of the poet as a commentary "Ulalume" is a hopeless enigma. Read after a careful study of the circumstances that created it, however, it becomes clear, and, what is more, it throws light upon the poet's inner life. "Ulalume" is not an elegy; it is not a threnody for a lost wife or an etherealized Lenore; it is not a display of mere verbal dexterity; it is not the incoherence of an insane master—it is an honest lyric that leads us to a man's heart; it is a cry of utter despair from a man's inmost soul.

Poe wrote this poem in the autumn of 1847, at the lowest ebb of his career. One year earlier, in the autumn of 1846, he had found the limit of his physical powers. Constant overwork and unrelieved mental strain had combined with dissipation to reduce him to a state bordering upon collapse. His brain refused to obey him; it became impossible for him to work, and upon him depended the support of a sick wife and her mother. During the late autumn and early winter of 1846–47 this little family suffered all the extremes of poverty. Unable to furnish sufficient fire, or covering, or food, Poe saw his wife, who needed the most delicate care, in want of the bare necessities of life, and sinking daily lower and lower. The well-known description of this home, written by Mrs. Gove, who late in January happened to discover the perishing family, is one of the most pathetic in our literary annals:

There was no clothing on the bed, which was only straw. . . . The weather was cold and the sick lady had, the dreadful chills that accompany the hectic fever of consumption. She lay on the straw bed, wrapped in her husband's greatcoat with a large tortoiseshell cat in her bosom. . . . The coat and the cat were the sufferer's only means of warmth except as her husband held her hands and her mother her feet.

The end came January 30, and Poe, after following on foot the coffin to the grave, sank in almost total collapse. "I did not feel much hope," writes Mrs. Shew, his nurse, who was also a physician, "that he could be raised up from brain fever, brought on by extreme suffering of mind and body —actual want and hunger and cold having been borne by this heroic husband in order to supply food, medicine, and comforts to his dying wife, until exhaustion and lifelessness were so near at every reaction of the fever that even sedatives had to be administered with extreme caution."

Poe rallied from this first fever only to suffer in March a relapse which for weeks threatened his life. The summer and autumn of 1847 were a period of slow convalescence. He had been near to death, and near to insanity. The extremely sensitive organism had been so rudely shaken that never again was it to be in adjustment. At first a great horror, a darkness, and utter despair had settled over him, but little by little he began to lay hold on the threads of life. At length he could even hope for brighter days. Though shattered in body and nerve and mind, he began to plan a great prose poem, "Eureka," which was to be the crowning effort of his life. The sympathy and help of Mrs. Shew, who with his mother had snatched him from death, began to arouse in him the pale, uncertain vision of a new life of love and hope. But such dreams were only for intervals. His old past, with its horrors, confronted him at every step. It ruled him like a demon and drove him powerless into despair. Poe lived two and a half years after the death of his wife, and during it all his life was an alternation between brief and feverish intervals of hope, and long periods of half-insane delirium, of blackness, and despair. He yearned with all the power of his nature for sympathy. "Unless some true and tender and pure womanly love saves me," he wrote to Mrs. Shew only a year before the final tragedy at Baltimore, "I shall hardly last a year longer alive." All those half-insane love-episodes of this period of Poe's life were but results of this eager longing for some one who could understand, some one who could rescue him from his past that was hurrying him on.

With this chapter of Poe's life understood, "Ulalume" becomes at once clear. It was written at the close of Poe's year of horrors—the October of his "most immemorial year"—immemorial since it seemed to drag its horrible length back to the utmost bounds of his memory, and since it lay as a vague, half-forgotten dream. The poem, like "The Raven," "The Haunted Palace," and others, is an allegory, though not all of its imagery is symbolic. The poet no longer lives in the old familiar world. He has entered a "misty mid region" that is not life, that is not death—a ghoul-haunted forest of cypress, a region of unrelieved horror and blackness. His heart is hot and volcanic; it is like a sulphurous current of lava hissing and groaning through an Arctic waste of death. He is alone; he has no companion, no confidant, save his own soul; he is driven to commune with himself. But his active brain has become sluggish and palsied, and at times he forgets his awful surroundings. It even seems at times as if there was to be a morning; to his palsied consciousness there appears a hint of dawn. A pale nebulous light appears in the east. It is like the rising of a new hope; it is a goddess who has seen his tears and has understood the torment, the never-dying worm in his soul, who, despite the horror which surrounds him, has dared to come to him, and to look upon him "with love in her luminous eyes," who will lead him by the hand from the horrors in which he is powerless into the path to the skies. The lines quiver and throb with passion. Oh, the ecstasy of being at last understood, of being in contact with one who could know and sympathize!

Was it Mrs. Shew who first gave Poe this vision of a new hope? If one reads the poem "To L. M. S.——," the first recorded word of Poe after his escape from death, and "To——," "Not long ago the writer of these lines"—written to Mrs. Shew just after "Ulalume"—and then reads the despairing letter of June, 1848, he will find it hard to believe it otherwise. In "To——" he clearly asserts that it is Mrs. Shew whom he sees at the end of the cypress vista:

> Alas, I cannot feel; for 't is not feeling,
> This standing motionless upon the golden
> Threshold of the wide-open gate of dreams,
> Gazing entranced adown the gorgeous vista,
> And thrilling as I see, upon the right,
> Upon the left, and all the way along,
> Amid empurpled vapors, far away,
> To where the prospect terminates—*thee only.*

But the world of despair rushes quickly back upon his soul. A moment of ecstasy and then his sluggish brain remembers. This pale star, too pale to be real, is sent but to increase his torment. It is the work of ghouls, a thing of horror, to shudder at and to fear. In an agony of revulsion of feeling his soul sinks into the dust. But his wavering, palsied brain cannot long be constant either to hope or despair. Again the vision beckons him upward; hope and joy and beauty seem about to bloom once more in his blackened life. Eagerly he follows the pale star which is so full of hope and beauty and which "flickers up to heaven through the night," but he is "stopped by the door of a tomb." The star is but a phantom, the work of a demon who knows how to make his hell complete; after every struggle he is thrown back helpless upon his own blasted soul. Mrs. Shew respected him, pitied him, admired him, but she did not love him. Her answer was final. There is no escape. Fate has taken every precaution "to bar up the way and to ban it"; he is alone with his dead in the ghoul-haunted cypress, and all visions of hope are but to mock and torment him.

This, then, is the meaning of "Ulalume." It is a sob from the depths of blank despair; it is the most pathetic poem in American literature. Everything about it attests its genuineness. It is not finished; it is a spontaneous outpouring of feeling, unpolished, unrevised. Such work was uncommon with Poe, who labored over his lyrics sometimes for years. I am inclined to believe that the account of the composition of "The Raven" is largely true.

The more spontaneous the song the nearer we get to the heart of the singer. From the mechanical point of view "Ulalume" is the most unfinished of the poet's productions. Its monotony of expression; its snail pace; its frequent discords; its cockney rimes; its abundance of pleonasm are positive blemishes, and yet they increase the value of the poem as a human document. Perhaps the most notable peculiarity, not to say defect, of "Ulalume" is its repetition. Yet this is significant. It shows that the poet's mind was almost in a state of collapse. It worked feebly. An idea, when it came, was hovered over and repeated with slight change until another idea came to reinforce it.

That the poem is the work of an abnormal mind is stamped everywhere upon it. For the poet to imagine two personalities within himself, which held converse with each other, which strenghtened and fortified each other, is in itself a symptom of insanity. It is this strange separation of the poet into two personalities that is the chief source of ambiguity in the poem. At every point the poem seems remote from ordinary human experience. Its geography is not of this world; its proper names, "Auber" and "Yaanek," belong to another planet: its atmosphere is that of ghoul-land, of the "misty mid region" that no man has ever actually known. Its haunting music comes from its abundant alliteration and rime, but more from its abnormal repetend, which we have shown to be a symptom of intellectual disease.

It was Poe's fate to be misunderstood. His own generation looked only at his external life. He was marvelously gifted, they said, but he was an unholy thing, a demoniac from the tombs, who tore himself upon the rocks and whom no man might bind, a victim of vices and passions. They made no excuse for him, they tried to cover none of his defects, they sought for none of the hidden fountains of his life. The present judges him more kindly, but even now it is not fully understood what manner of man he really was. No one can study to its heart a lyric like "Ulalume" and not feel the pathos that lay in its creator's soul. The fatal gift of genius separated him from his fellow-men, deprived him of human sympathy, and drove him for companionship to live a hermit with his own soul. What wonder that his perspective became distorted, that he became morbid and unnatural, the companion of strange fancies? What utter pathos in his bitter cry for help: "For months I have known that you were deserting me, not willingly, but none the less surely—my destiny—

Disaster, following fast and following faster, till his
    song one burden bore—

Till the dirges of his Hope that melancholy burden
  bore—
      Of 'Never—nevermore.'"

"Ulalume" is the epitome of Poe's last years. It
is the picture of a soul hovering between hope and
inevitable despair, a soul longing passionately for
a sympathy which it can never have, a soul struggling toward the light yet beaten back at every
point, a soul that realized as few other souls ever
have the supernal beauty which is possible in human
life, yet condemned like Tantalus never to share
its joys.

ULALUME

The skies they were ashen and sober;
  The leaves they were crispèd and sere.—
  The leaves they were withering and sere:
It was night in the lonesome October
  Of my most immemorial year:
It was hard by the dim lake of Auber,
  In the misty mid region of Weir
It was down by the dank tarn of Auber,
  In the ghoul-haunted woodland of Weir.

Here once, through an alley Titanic,
  Of cypress, I roamed with my Soul—
  Of cypress, with Psyche, my Soul.
These were days when my heart was volcanic
  As the scoriac rivers that roll—

As the lavas that restlessly roll—
　Their sulphurous currents down Yaanek
　In the ultimate climes of the pole—·
That groan as they roll down Mount
　　　Yaanek
　In the realms of the Boreal Pole.

Our talk had been serious and sober,
　But our thoughts they were palsied and
　　　sere—
　Our memories were treacherous and sere—
For we knew not the month was October,
　And we marked not the night of the year.
　(Ah, night of all nights in the year!)
We noted not the dim lake of Auber
　(Though once we had journeyed down
　　　here)—
Remembered not the dank tarn of Auber,
　Nor the ghoul-haunted woodland of Weir.

And now, as the night was senescent
　And star-dials pointed to morn—
　As the star-dials hinted of morn—
At the end of our path a liquescent
　And nebulous luster was born,
Out of which a miraculous crescent
　Arose, with a duplicate horn—
Astarte's bediamonded crescent
　Distinct with its duplicate horn.

And I said: "She is warmer than Dian;
　She rolls through an ether of sighs—

She revels in a region of sighs.
She has seen that the tears are not dry on
These cheeks, where the worm never dies,
And has come past the stars of the Lion,
    To point us the path to the skies—
    To the Lethean peace of the skies—
Come up, in despite of the Lion,
    To shine on us with her bright eyes:
Come up through the lair of the Lion,
    With love in her luminous eyes."

But Psyche, uplifting her finger,
    Said: *h* "Sadly this star I mistrust—
    Her pallor I strangely mistrust:
Ah, hasten!—ah, let us not linger!
    Ah, fly!—let us fly!—for we must."
In terror she spoke, letting sink her
    Wings until they trailed in the dust.—
In agony sobbed, letting sink her
    Plumes till they trailed in the dust—
    Till they sorrowfully trailed in the dust.

I replied: *II* "This is nothing but dreaming:
    Let us on by this tremulous light!
    Let us bathe in this crystalline light!
Its Sibyllic splendor is beaming
    With hope and in Beauty to-night:—
    See!—it flickers up the sky through the
        night!
Ah, we safely may trust to its gleaming,
    And be sure it will lead us aright—

We safely may trust to a gleaming,
  That cannot but guide us aright,
  Since it flickers up to Heaven through
    the night."

Thus I pacified Psyche and kissed her,
  And tempted her out of her gloom—
  And conquered her scruples and gloom;
And we passed to the end of the vista,
  But were stopped by the door of a tomb—
  By the door of a legended tomb;
And I said: "What is written, sweet sister,
  On the door of this legended tomb?"
  She replied: "Ulalume—Ulalume!—
  'T is the vault of thy lost Ulalume!"

Then my heart it grew ashen and sober
  As the leaves that were crispèd and sere—
  As the leaves that were withering and sere;
And I cried: "It was surely October
  On *this* very night of last year
  That I journeyed—I journeyed down here—
  That I brought a dread burden down here,—
  On this night of all nights in the year,
  Ah, what demon hath tempted me here?
Well I know, now, this dim lake of Auber—
  This misty mid region of Weir:
Well I know, now, this dank tarn of Auber,
  This ghoul-haunted woodland of Weir."

Said we, then—the two, then: "Ah, can it
  Have been that the woodlandish ghouls—

The pitiful, the merciful ghouls—
To bar up our way and to ban it
From the secret that lies in these wolds—
From the thing that lies hidden in these
wolds—
Have drawn up the spector of a planet
From the limbo of lunary souls—
This sinfully scintillant planet
From the Hell of the planetary souls?"

Lightning Source UK Ltd.
Milton Keynes UK
UKHW011845210119
335961UK00014B/949/P